NEW RESEARCH ON PARENTING PROGRAMS FOR LOW-INCOME FATHERS

This book presents state-of-the-art findings of research on fatherhood programs, funded by the Fatherhood Research and Practice Network (FRPN), which advance knowledge and practice in the fathering field.

New Research on Parenting Programs for Low-Income Fathers includes research on how to engage mothers to support father–child contact and to successfully employ social media and online technology for practice. It offers findings on how to increase paternal engagement and parenting skills and to include fathers in policies and programs for children and families. It discusses the importance of providing staff training and resources to practitioners who work directly with fathers. Chapters also provide summaries of key implications for evidence-based practice and future directions for research that encourage effective fatherhood practice.

This book is an excellent resource for therapists, social workers, fatherhood educators, fatherhood practitioners, researchers, and policy makers on how to inspire positive father engagement with children and healthy coparenting relationships.

Jay Fagan is Professor in the School of Social Work at Temple University and Co-Director of the Fatherhood Research and Practice Network, USA.

Jessica Pearson is Co-Director of the national Fatherhood Research and Practice Network and Founder and Director of the Center for Policy Research in Denver, Colorado, USA.

NEW RESEARCH ON PARENTING PROGRAMS FOR LOW-INCOME FATHERS

Edited by Jay Fagan and Jessica Pearson

Routledge
Taylor & Francis Group
NEW YORK AND LONDON

First published 2021
by Routledge
605 Third Avenue, New York, NY 10158

and by Routledge
2 Park Square, Milton Park, Abingdon, Oxon, OX14 4RN

Routledge is an imprint of the Taylor & Francis Group, an informa business.

© 2021 selection and editorial matter, Jay Fagan and Jessica Pearson; individual chapters, the contributors.

The right of Jay Fagan and Jessica Pearson to be identified as the authors of the editorial material, and of the authors for their individual chapters, has been asserted in accordance with sections 77 and 78 of the Copyright, Designs and Patents Act 1988.

All rights reserved. No part of this book may be reprinted or reproduced or utilized in any form or by any electronic, mechanical, or other means, now known or hereafter invented, including photocopying and recording, or in any information storage or retrieval system, without permission in writing from the publishers.

Trademark notice: Product or corporate names may be trademarks or registered trademarks, and are used only for identification and explanation without intent to infringe.

Library of Congress Cataloging-in-Publication Data
A catalog record for this title has been requested

ISBN: 978-0-367-36343-7 (hbk)
ISBN: 978-0-367-36342-0 (pbk)
ISBN: 978-0-367-36344-4 (ebk)

Typeset in Bembo
by MPS Limited, Dehradun

Jay dedicates this book to his wife, Jo; two daughters, Anna Fried and Lisa Fagan; his son-in-law, Eric Fried; and his grandson, Jordan Fried.

Jessica dedicates this book to her grandchildren: Zeke, Jude, Ezra, and Nomi Lev; Ronin and June Bucy; and Asher Pearson.

CONTENTS

About the Authors   *x*
Foreword   *xxiii*
Acknowledgments   *xxvii*

1 Introduction   1
   Jay Fagan and Jessica Pearson

2 The Effectiveness of Responsible Fatherhood Programs Targeting Low-Income and Nonresident Fathers: A Qualitative Meta-Synthesis   12
   Erin Kramer Holmes, Clare R. Thomas, Braquel R. Egginton, Virginia K. Leiter, and Alan J. Hawkins

3 Does Curriculum Matter? A Randomized Control Study of the "Developing All Dads for Manhood and Parenting Program (DAD MAP)" Curriculum   29
   Bright Sarfo and Vernon Wallace

4 Factors Associated With Fatherhood Program Effectiveness: A Randomized Controlled Trial of TYRO Dads   44
   Young-Il Kim, Sung Joon Jang, and Brenda J. Oyer

5   Engaging Fathers in Perinatal Home Visiting: Early
    Lessons From a Randomized Controlled Study of Dads
    Matter-HV   58
    *Jennifer L. Bellamy, Justin S. Harty, Aaron Banman, and Neil
    B. Guterman*

6   A Mixed-Methods Evaluation of *Key to Kane*, a
    Text-Messaging Intervention for Fathers in Hawaii   74
    *Selva Lewin-Bizan, David "Kawika" Mattos, and Edeluisa
    "Edel" Baguio-Larena*

7   Challenges and Opportunities for Engaging Unmarried
    Parents in Court-Ordered, Online Parenting Programs   90
    *Claire S. Tomlinson, Brittany N. Rudd, Amy G. Applegate,
    and Amy Holtzworth-Munroe*

8   A Mixed-Methods Study of a Mother-Only Program to
    Enhance Coparenting Relationships   105
    Jay Fagan, Jessica Pearson, and Abigail Henson

9   Fatherhood and Coparenting: A Study of Engaging
    Mothers in Paternal Involvement Interventions   118
    *Armon R. Perry, Aaron C. Rollins Jr., Ebony O'Rea, and
    Abby, F. Perez*

10 Engaging Mothers in Coparenting Services With the
    Nonresident Fathers of Their Children via Fatherhood
    Programs: Insights Into Barriers and Solutions   133
    Kimberly Gentry Sperber and Sarah W. Whitton

11 "You Gotta Make Them *Feel*": A Study of Evidence-
    Informed Strategies for Addressing Domestic Violence in
    Fatherhood Programs   148
    Kristie A. Thomas and Fernando Mederos

12 Journey of a Policy Change to Include Fathers in
    Homeless Shelters   168
    Karin M. Eyrich-Garg and Karen M. Hudson

13 Estimating the Monetary Value of Fatherhood Programs   183
    Richard A. Chase

14 Developing Father Inclusion Policy at the State Level: A
    Qualitative Assessment of Enablers and Barriers   198
    Jessica Pearson

15 What Have We Learned and Where Do We Go
    From Here?   215
    Jessica Pearson and Jay Fagan

Index   *235*

ABOUT THE AUTHORS

Amy G. Applegate, Clinical Professor of Law and Ralph F. Fuchs Faculty Fellow, and Director of the Viola J. Taliaferro Family and Children Mediation Clinic, joined the faculty at the Indiana University Maurer School of Law in 2001. Ms. Applegate currently teaches mediation theory and practice in the clinical law program that she developed at the Law School. Through this program, law students provide mediation services to indigent and low-income litigants in disputed custody, parenting-time, and other family law cases. Ms. Applegate has received teaching, research, and service awards for her work. She has been a leader in clinical legal education on the national level, and actively and significantly involved in state and local bar activities, with a special emphasis in the areas of delivery of pro bono services, training mediators, and mediation ethics. Ms. Applegate and colleagues have conducted research on family law issues, focusing on families experiencing parental divorce or separation. She and her colleagues have developed and tested the best methods of screening for a history of intimate partner violence (IPV) in cases seeking family mediation. They also conduct randomized controlled trials testing the effectiveness of family law interventions, including different mediation approaches (for both families with and without histories of IPV) and online parent education programs. Ms. Applegate has co-authored many publications in her research areas. Additionally, she has presented individually, as well as with her collaborators, in presentations at state, national, and international conferences about her research and practice areas.

Edeluisa "Edel" Baguio-Larena is the Chief Executive Officer of Maui Family Support Services, Inc. (MFSS), a private nonprofit agency providing 40 years of continuous services to the children and families of Maui County.

Through multiple programs that include Early Head Start–Center base and Homebased, Early Identification and Community Resources, Healthy Families America, Youth Services, and more, the mission of MFSS is to promote healthy family functioning by providing supportive services that build on family strengths. She joined MFSS in 2001 and served in various leadership positions within the agency until she became the CEO in 2014. Her interests include community and family engagement, early childhood education, participatory leadership, and management. Ms. Baguio-Larena holds a bachelor of science in social work and a master's in international and intercultural management. Most importantly, Ms. Baguio-Larena and her husband, who live in Maui, HI, are the proud parents of boy and girl twins who are turning 15 soon. Every day, they inspire Ms. Baguio-Larena to invest her time and energy in supporting families and children to thrive.

Aaron Banman, PhD, LCSW, is an Assistant Professor, at Grace Abbott School of Social Work at the University of Nebraska at Omaha (UNO) and a Faculty Fellow at the Support and Training for the Evaluation of Programs (STEPs) at UNO. He earned his PhD at the University of Chicago, School of Social Service Administration, where he was a recipient of a Doris Duke Fellowship for the Promotion of Child Well-Being. He received his master's of social work from Columbia University School of Social Work, and a BA in social work from St. Olaf College. Dr. Banman's research interests include fathers and fathering; prevention of child maltreatment; child welfare; intervention development and adaptation; evidence-based practice; and implementation of evidence-based practice within human services organizations. He has worked on the Dads Matter project since its inception.

Jennifer L. Bellamy, PhD, is the Associate Dean for Research and Faculty Development and Professor at the Graduate School of Social Work (GSSW) at the University of Denver. She received her master's of science in social work from The University of Texas at Austin in 2000. Before earning her PhD, she worked as a Crisis Counselor and a Project Coordinator for a multisite demonstration project serving young, unmarried, low-income fathers. Dr. Bellamy completed her PhD at the Columbia University School of Social Work in 2006 and postdoctoral training at the George Warren Brown School of Social Work at Washington University in Saint Louis in 2008. Her current research and scholarship focus on the engagement of fathers in child and family services, child welfare, and evidence-based practice. She is currently engaged in the development and testing of strategies and interventions to better serve fathers in child welfare as Principal Investigator on the Fathers and Continuous Learning in Child Welfare Project in Partnership with Mathematica Policy Research. Dr. Bellamy is also the Co-Developer of an intervention designed to better engage fathers in home visiting services to prevent child maltreatment called Dads

Matter-HV. She serves as Board Member-At-Large for the Society for Social Work and Research and Co-Chairs the Council on Social Work Education Evidence-Based Practice Track.

Richard Chase, Senior Research Manager at Wilder Research, for 37 years worked with diverse community-based groups, foundations, and government agencies to design and carry out useful studies focused on equity, outcomes, and improvement. Now retired, Richard led Wilder's economic studies unit, which conducts cost–benefit and return on investment studies of educational and social programs. Richard studied early childhood policies, services, and indicators and evaluated the effectiveness of school readiness, prevention, and capacity-building programs for children, youth, and families. He also co-developed tools for measuring and promoting family and community knowledge and engagement through an asset-based approach (https://www.wilder.org/wilder-research/research-library/center-family-and-community-data-knowledge-and-well-being-0). Richard holds a doctorate in American Studies from the University of Minnesota.

Braquel R. Egginton, received her MS in marriage, family, and human development from Brigham Young University and is currently working toward a PhD in human environmental science at the University of Missouri. The focus of her research is to explore the diversity of the stepfamily experience to identify factors that promote positive family interactions and resilience for these families. This includes an exploration of the nonresidential parent–child relationships in addition to children's relationships with their resident biological and step-parents. Recent work has also included an exploration of stepcouple relationships, and the positive impact couple relationship education programs can have for these couples.

Karin M. Eyrich-Garg, LCSW, is an Associate Professor and MSW Program Director at Temple University School of Social Work. Her training is in social work and psychiatric epidemiology. Dr. Eyrich-Garg's research focuses on vulnerable populations, with special attention to people experiencing homelessness. She has examined the strength and resilience as well as challenges these populations encounter. Her research has included the topics of substance use, mental health, technology use, engagement in treatment, faith/spirituality, and volunteerism. Dr. Eyrich-Garg is also a Licensed Clinical Social Worker. She has practice experience with women experiencing homelessness and co-occurring substance use and mental health problems; families who have a child with a behavioral health disorder; and youth in the foster care system.

Jay Fagan, PhD, is Professor in the School of Social Work at Temple University and Co-Director of the Fatherhood Research and Practice Network, funded between 2013 and 2019 by the Administration for Children and Families (Grant

#90PR0006, OPRE). His research has focused on father–child relationships and coparenting in nonresidential and low-income families; responsible fatherhood programs; coparenting interventions for low-income, nonresidential fathers; fathers with children in Head Start and child welfare; adolescent fathers; family structure effects on young children; fathers and early childhood programs; fathering in the context of family processes; and the relationship between childcare and work–family balance among low-income women. He is currently conducting studies on the association between early paternal and maternal risk and child social-emotional development in middle childhood. He published the textbook, *Fathers and Early Childhood Programs* (Delmar Publishing, 2004), with Dr. Glen Palm, and *Clinical and Educational Interventions with Fathers* (Haworth Press, 2001), with Dr. Alan J. Hawkins. Dr. Fagan has published 88 peer-reviewed research papers, mostly on fathers. He was the founding editor of the journal, *Fathering*. He has taught human behavior and social environment courses at Temple University since 1990.

Neil B. Guterman, PhD, serves as Dean and Paulette Goddard Professor at the NYU Silver School of Social Work. Dr. Guterman holds scholarly interests in services targeting children and violence, with special interest in child abuse and neglect prevention. He has published numerous peer-reviewed articles on these topics and is the author of *Stopping Child Maltreatment Before it Starts: Emerging Horizons in Early Home Visitation Services* (Sage, 2001). His expertise has been sought by the U.S. Surgeon General's Office, the Centers for Disease Control and Prevention, the International Society for Prevention of Child Abuse and Neglect, Prevent Child Abuse America, Children's Trust Funds, and the National Conference of State Legislatures. He consults as an editor to a number of professional journals, including *Child Abuse and Neglect*, *Social Work*, and the *American Journal of Public Health*, and serves on the editorial board of *Child Maltreatment*. Dr. Guterman is a Fellow of the American Academy of Social Work and Social Welfare and previously served as Dean, the Moses and Sylvia Firestone Professor, and Director of the Beatrice Cummings Mayer Program in Violence Prevention at the University of Chicago School of Social Service Administration. From 1993 to 2006, he served on the faculty of the Columbia University School of Social Work and was a Lady Davis Postdoctoral Fellow at the Hebrew University in Jerusalem. Dr. Guterman holds a PhD in Social Work and Psychology, and an MSW from the University of Michigan. He earned his BA in psychology with highest honors from the University of California, Santa Cruz.

Justin S. Harty, MSW, LCSW, is a doctoral candidate at the University of Chicago School of Social Service Administration. He earned bachelor's degrees in both sociology and philosophy from the University of Illinois at Urbana-Champaign in 2011. He received his master's of social work, with a concentration in children and families from the Jane Addams College of Social

Work at the University of Illinois at Chicago in 2013. After earning a master's degree, Mr. Harty worked for three years as a foster care worker in Chicago. He is a licensed clinical social worker serving child welfare–involved fathers and provides father-focused trainings to child welfare, foster care, and family-strengthening agencies around father involvement and engagement. Mr. Harty's research interests include the outcomes and preparedness of young fathers aging out of the foster care system, father engagement in child welfare services, and father-related social services in the history of the social work profession. His current research examines ways to better serve fathers in home visiting, child welfare, and foster care settings. He is currently conducting his dissertation research on the experiences and needs of young Black fathers in foster care as they leave state care and transition to independent adulthood and early fatherhood. He is a Research Assistant on the Dads Matter-HV study testing a father-focused enhancement to home visiting services. He is also the Project Coordinator and Research Assistant on the California Youth Transitions to Adulthood Study (CalYOUTH), examining the impact of extended foster care among transition-age foster youth in California.

Alan J. Hawkins, PhD, is a Professor and Director of the School of Family Life at Brigham University in Provo, Utah. He earned a PhD in Human Development and Family Studies at Pennsylvania State University in 1990. Dr. Hawkins' scholarship and outreach efforts focus on educational interventions and policies to help couples form and sustain healthy marriages and relationships and to help fathers be deeply involved in the lives of their children. He is widely cited for his work that examines the overall effectiveness of marriage and relationship education, as well as fatherhood education, including nearly 10 peer-reviewed meta-analytic studies of the overall effectiveness of these educational programs. He has been intricately involved in state and federal policy efforts to strengthen families. In 2002–2003, he was a visiting scholar with the Office of Planning, Research, and Evaluation (OPRE), Administration for Children and Families, working on the Federal Healthy Marriage and Responsible Fatherhood Initiative. He was the Research Director for the original National Healthy Marriage Resource Center from 2004 to 2006. He is the past-Chair of the Utah Marriage Commission. He has served on the Research Advisory Group for the Oklahoma Marriage Initiative since 2010.

Abigail Henson, PhD, is an Assistant Professor in the School of Criminology and Criminal Justice at Arizona State University. Her research interests include policy and program evaluation and the impact of corrections and policing on identity, families, and communities. Her work strives to shift narratives and eliminate stigmas by both engaging in strengths-based, human-centered frameworks and applying a critical gaze toward systemic injustices.

Erin Kramer Holmes, PhD, is the Marjorie Pay Hinckley Associate Professor in the Brigham Young University School of Family Life. She earned her PhD at The University of Texas at Austin. Dr. Holmes' research focuses on fathering, mothering, and the work–family interface. For her research in these areas, Dr. Holmes won the National Council on Family Relations Award for Best Research Article by a New Professional, and was a finalist for the international Rosabeth Moss Kanter Award for Excellence in Work-Family Research (placing her article in the top seven of 2,500 articles published on work and family in 2012). She has received various departmental, college, and university awards for her research, teaching, mentoring, and service. She currently serves on the editorial boards of *Journal of Marriage and Family*, *Family Relations*, and *Journal of Family Theory and Review*.

Amy Holtzworth-Munroe, PhD, is a Professor in Indiana University's (IU) Department of Psychological and Brain Sciences. She has a PhD, in clinical psychology, from the University of Washington. She has conducted research on intimate partner violence (IPV) since the mid-1980s. Her research initially compared the social information processing skills of violent and nonviolent husbands and the communication behaviors of violent and nonviolent couples. Her team then developed and tested a typology of male batterers, highlighting dimensions that differentiate various types of IPV. Since 2006, in collaboration with others, Dr. Holtzworth-Munroe has conducted research on family law issues, focusing on families experiencing parental divorce or separation. The research team has developed and tested IPV screening measures for cases seeking family mediation. They also conduct randomized controlled trials testing the effectiveness of family law interventions, including online parent education programs, mediation approaches designed to help parents focus on their children's needs, and mediation approaches designed to be safer for parties reporting high levels of IPV. Dr. Holtzworth-Munroe has co-authored numerous research publications, encyclopedia entries, and book chapters on IPV and family law. She has served as a grant reviewer and on journal editorial boards. She was a member of Association of Family and Conciliation Court (AFCC) national taskforces writing policy on family law issues, such as new AFCC guidelines for child custody evaluators to use when assessing IPV. Dr. Holtzworth-Munroe is a Fellow in the Association for Psychological Science, and a recipient of the Stanley Cohen Distinguished Research Award from the AFCC.

Karen M. Hudson, PhD, LSW, Children's Hospital of Philadelphia and University of Pennsylvania. Her practice interests converge at the intersection of health caredelivery, advocacy, health education, the training of health care professionals, and family homelessness. Her practice efforts involve improving the health and wellness of children and families experiencing homeless and reducing health disparities that could negatively impact this goal. Her research interests have focused on both the exclusion and inclusion of fathers from family homeless shelters and efforts to understand the barriers to their involvement and contributions to the health and wellness of their children living in shelters.

Sung Joon Jang is Research Professor of Criminology and Co-Director of the Program on Prosocial Behavior at the Institute for Studies of Religion at Baylor University. His research focuses on the effects of strain and religion on criminal offending and desistance and has appeared in various journals of criminology and criminal justice. Mr. Jang is currently conducting a series of studies on the rehabilitative effects of faith-based programs on prisoners in Colombia and South Africa as well as in the United States.

Young-Il Kim is Department Chair and Assistant Professor of Sociology at George Fox University. Prior to joining George Fox, he worked as a Postdoctoral Scholar and a Research Assistant Professor at the Baylor Institute for Studies of Religion, where he embarked on a research project that spawned a chapter in this edited book. His research interests revolve around family, voluntary associations, and prosocial behavior. He has published articles on these topics in *The Sociological Quarterly*, *Social Science Research*, *Nonprofit and Voluntary Sector Quarterly*, *Sociological Perspectives*, and *Review of Religious Research*.

Virginia K. Leiter is a graduate student in the Brigham Young University School of Family Life. Her research interests include fathering, mothering, poverty, and immigration, with a focus on intersectionality between these factors.

Selva Lewin-Bizan, PhD, is a teaching faculty at the Lynch School of Education and Human Development at Boston College, and was previously a faculty member at the University of Hawaii at Manoa. She teaches developmental and methodology courses and guides students in independent research. Dr. Lewin-Bizan's practice and research interest and experience lie in the area of fatherhood, ranging from direct work with parents to basic research on the father–child relationship to evaluation research of programs that aim to support men's parenting. She has collaborated with practitioners and state-level government on studying and responding to central issues of concern for fathers and fathering. Dr. Lewin-Bizan earned a PhD in developmental psychology from the Lynch School at Boston College, a Master's degree from the School of Social Service Administration at the University of Chicago, and a Bachelor's degree from the Bob Shapell School of Social Work at the Tel-Aviv University.

David "Kawika" Mattos is the Program Supervisor and Lead Facilitator at Kāne Connections, the men's support team at Maui Family Support Services, Inc. (MFSS), a private nonprofit agency providing 40 years of continuous services to the children and families of Maui County. The mission of MFSS is to promote healthy family functioning by providing supportive services that build on family strengths. Mr. Mattos also provides life skills classes to men and women at the Aloha House Residential Treatment Center and is the current Chairman of the Hawaii State Commission on Fatherhood. Self-development and always learning something new have been Mr. Mattos's quest, even after dropping out of college after getting married and starting a family. He has learned psychology through many various ways, which has enhanced his own personal self-growth. Mr. Mattos lives in Maui, HI, and has been married to his wife for 33 years, is the father of four sons—two of them adopted biological brothers—and one daughter, ages 22–33, and the grandfather of four grandsons and two granddaughters, ages 2–13. Over the years he and his wife have also fostered more than 30 teenagers that were deemed high risk in the community. To be able to help, educate, and support others is truly a great blessing to him.

Fernando Mederos, Ed.D., is a practitioner and collaborator in studies focused on low-income men, domestic violence, and fatherhood. He is interested in approaches that build on men's strengths and core values to help them move toward self-care, responsibility, and safe and nurturing relationships with partners and children. In 2016, as adjunct faculty at Simmons College Graduate School of Social Work, he began collaborating with Dr. Kristie Thomas on research on fatherhood groups and low-income fathers. Before joining Simmons, he was Director of Fatherhood Engagement at the Massachusetts Department of Children and Families (DCF) for nine years (2006–2015). At DCF, he stressed the importance of identifying and working with all fathers and male caretakers (including stepfathers and boyfriends, for example) in the appropriate way, depending upon the men's strengths and risks. This strength- and responsibility-based approach built on strengths such as the desire to be a good father and responsible nurturing, but it also privileged the safety of all family members, and was proactive on mental health, substance abuse, and domestic violence.

Ebony O'Rea is the Founder of Making Changes Together, LLC, and is a Consultant for local and national organizations focused on building stronger communities and creating lasting impact. As a social worker, Ms. O'Rea has dedicated years to strengthening social networks, sharing opportunities, resources, and developing organizational strategies through facilitating conversations and trainings focused on education, leadership development, and community organizing. She cultivates relationships that deliver value, respect, accountability, and reciprocity. Ms. O'Rea earned her master's from the University of Louisville Kent School of Social Work, where her studies concentrated on policy change for social justice issues with a heavy emphasis on fatherhood practices and policy.

Brenda J. Oyer currently serves as Research Development Officer for Bowling Green State University (BGSU) in Ohio, where she assists faculty in developing their skills in grant proposal development. She completed her doctorate in Leadership Studies at BGSU in 2011. As a BGSU Adjunct Assistant Professor, she has developed and taught a service learning course, *Strengthening Families Affected by Incarceration*, and has taught a master's-level online statistics course for K-12 educators. From April 2013 to September 2019, Dr. Oyer served as the Associate Director of Research and Data for The RIDGE Project, Inc., a role in which she oversaw outcome measurement processes. She has a passion for helping incarcerated and formerly incarcerated fathers chart a better course for themselves and their families.

Jessica Pearson, Ph.D., founded and directs the Center for Policy Research (CPR) in Denver, Colorado, a nonprofit that works with human service agencies to implement and evaluate new programs to improve the lives of low-income children and their families. She also co-directs the Fatherhood Research and Practice Network (FRPN), funded between 2013 and 2019 by the Administration for Children and Families (Grant #90PR0006, OPRE). She and her CPR colleagues conducted some of the earliest national studies of divorce and custody mediation. She also has led dozens of evaluations of single and multi-state demonstration projects to make the U.S. child support program more family focused. This has included studies on establishing paternity in hospitals, addressing parenting time for parents with child support orders, compromising child support debt, using behaviorally-informed messaging, and establishing effective work and parenting programs to improve payment and father engagement. Pearson was Principal Investigator for the evaluation of the OCSE Responsible Fatherhood Demonstration Projects in eight states. She is currently working with eleven states on initiatives to include nonresident fathers in programs and policies dealing with children and families. Her work can be found on www.centerforpolicyresearch.org, and in articles published in Family Court Review, Family Law Quarterly, Family Process and Families in Society. She holds a Ph.D. in Sociology from Princeton University and co-authored an oral history of a farm community, *No Time But Place: A Prairie Pastoral*.

Abby F. Perez is a graduate research assistant currently pursuing a PhD in Urban and Public Affairs at the University of Louisville. As an aspiring ethnographer, her research focuses on homelessness as a crisis, the criminalization of poverty in America, issues of social equity, and the politics of race. Her doctoral dissertation examines how "home" is conceptualized within the processes of homelessness, and what COVID-19 shows us about the weaknesses in our already insufficient social support infrastructure for the homeless (or those at risk).

Armon R. Perry, PhD, is Professor and Director of the BSW Program at the University of Louisville's Kent School of Social Work, where he teaches Introduction to Social Work. Dr. Perry's research interests include fathers' involvement in the lives of their children, leading him to co-edit *Fatherhood in America: Social Work Perspectives in a Changing Society*, a comprehensive edited volume addressing the micro and macro factors shaping paternal involvement. Currently, Dr. Perry serves as the Principal Investigator of the 4 Your Child Program, a federally funded multi-site project that aims to increase nonresidential fathers' capacity for paternal involvement. In addition to his teaching and research, Dr. Perry has professional experience in the area of child protective services and as a parent education curriculum facilitator.

Aaron C. Rollins Jr., PhD, is Associate Professor of Urban and Public Affairs at the University of Louisville. He directs the Master of Public Administration Program as well as the Peace, Justice and Conflict Transformation Program. His research focuses on contemporary urban issues that disproportionally affect historically marginalized populations as well as the implication of goal-oriented performance measures.

Brittany N. Rudd, PhD, is an Instructor of Psychology in the Department of Psychiatry and the Director of the Implementation Science and System-Involved Youth Research Program in the Institute for Juvenile Research at the University of Illinois at Chicago. Dr. Rudd completed her doctoral training in clinical science at Indiana University, predoctoral clinical internship at the Children's Hospital of Philadelphia, and her postdoctoral training at the Penn Center for Mental Health at the University of Pennsylvania. The central theme of Dr. Rudd's program of research is improving access to quality mental health care among vulnerable populations. Specifically, informed by a public mental health model, her interests include (1) collaborating with community stakeholders to learn the best methods to implement evidence-based practices and improve mental health service delivery, (2) mental health care task-shifting and task-sharing, and (3) digital mental health and implementation supports. Dr. Rudd founded the Implementation Science and System-Involved Youth Research Program to improve the implementation of evidence-based policies and practices within systems that serve vulnerable youth, including those in the juvenile justice, child welfare, and family court service settings. She is currently engaging in a line of research to increase the adoption and implementation of suicide prevention practices within the juvenile justice system. The long-term goal of her research program is to transform nontraditional behavioral health settings (e.g., courts, juvenile justice) into hubs of evidence-based prevention and intervention to improve outcomes for disadvantaged and vulnerable youth who may never access behavioral health services in traditional outpatient settings.

Bright Sarfo, PhD, MSW, has 15 years of experience in research, program evaluation, and data analysis. He has a strong background in implementation research, literature reviews, measurement design, quantitative and qualitative methods, and behavioral intervention development. Dr. Sarfo is currently a Research Associate at MEF associates, where he supports projects research in the areas of fatherhood and healthy relationships using rigorous research designs, process analysis, and capacity-building strategies. At MEF, Dr. Sarfo has worked on national evaluation projects for federal agencies, including the Department of Labor and the Administration for Children and Families. He has worked as a lead liaison for local organizations to conduct process studies and provide technical assistance in the form of training, evaluation planning, and site monitoring. Dr. Sarfo has held leadership positions on projects examining fatherhood interventions, child support enforcement practices, economic empowerment initiatives, ending hunger approaches, and workforce development programs. He has contributed to the development of dissemination products and activities including reports, practitioner briefs, and presentations at professional conferences. Before joining MEF, Sarfo began his career conducting research in the areas of substance abuse, HIV prevention, and criminal justice at the Columbia University School of Social Work, where he earned his MSW and PhD. He earned his BA in psychology from Stony Brook University.

Kimberly Gentry Sperber, PhD, is the Director of the Center for Health and Human Services Research (CHHSR) at Talbert House. Dr. Sperber has spent her entire research career embedded within a practice agency with responsibilities for conducting research, helping treatment and administrative staff to operationalize research findings into practice, and assisting practitioners in assessing and monitoring fidelity to evidence-based practices. In 2013, she helped Talbert House to launch the CHHSR to strengthen the practitioner voice in research and to systematically foster both science-based practice and practice-based science across Talbert House programs. Her research interests center on the effectiveness of behavioral health and social service interventions, treatment responsivity, implementation of evidence-based practices in real-world settings, and the intersection of public health and criminal justice.

Clare R. Thomas is a PhD student at the University of Georgia studying human development and family science. Her research areas include fathering, mental health, coparenting, maternal gatekeeping, the work–family interface, and suicide bereavement. Recent research has included focus on Black fathers in Georgia, USA. She was raised the child of an Army officer in the U.S. military, living throughout the East Coast, Midwest, and Southern states. After receiving a bachelor of science degree in psychology from Brigham Young University, she worked for a nonprofit organization as a Program Manager until returning to Brigham Young University and receiving a master of science degree in marriage, family, and human development. She is living happily in Athens, GA, with her husband and son.

Kristie A. Thomas, PhD, is an Associate Professor and the MSW Program Director at Simmons University School of Social Work. Dr. Thomas has extensive practice, teaching, and research expertise in the anti-violence field. Her work focuses on developing and enhancing community-informed programs for people affected by intimate partner violence (IPV)—particularly those who are economically and socially marginalized. She recently completed a study funded by the Fatherhood Research and Practice Network that explores the important role fatherhood programs can play in IPV prevention. Dr. Thomas co-founded the Massachusetts-based Domestic Violence Program Evaluation and Research Collaborative, an ongoing academic-community partnership launched in 2011, and she is currently conducting several stakeholder-driven evaluation projects aimed at improving services for homeless and unstably housed IPV survivors. In addition to a robust portfolio of peer-reviewed articles, Dr. Thomas has authored online trainings and toolkits on IPV that are used widely by researchers and practitioners across the country. Dr. Thomas teaches across the MSW and PhD programs; she was awarded the Provost Award for Student-Centeredness in Graduate Teaching at Simmons University and the Early Career Excellence in Teaching Award by the American Evaluation Association.

Claire S. Tomlinson is a fourth-year clinical science graduate student at Indiana University. She received a bachelor's degree in psychology at University of Arizona, where she began studying families in the legal system, including children in the child welfare system. At Indiana University, Ms. Tomlinson investigates the evaluation and implementation of evidence-based practice in the family law field, with a focus on divorcing and separating parents. She is interested in family law programs, often based in courts, that are designed to minimize the negative impact of parental separation on the children in the family. Her current projects include the evaluation of programs such as family mediation and online parent education for separating or divorcing parents.

Vernon Wallace graduated from Morgan State University with a bachelor of science degree in telecommunications in 2002. Later that year, he became employed with a nonprofit organization in Baltimore City as Director of two homeless shelters in which he helped change thousands of lives in the span of 5 years. In 2007, Mr. Wallace first got involved in the Responsible Fatherhood field. As Program Coordinator of the Young Fathers' Program in Anne Arundel County, MD, he developed a passion for helping dads in need. He established several partnerships with community stakeholders, church leaders, local high schools, and jails and other state and county organizations, which helped take the program to new heights. In August 2011, Mr. Wallace joined the Center for Urban Families (CFUF) as Program Manager of the Baltimore Responsible Fatherhood Project (BRFP). Married and a father of two daughters, his passion for assisting dads grew tremendously. He has developed a thriving partnership with the Baltimore City Public Schools in efforts to be more intentional about increasing fathers' presence in the schools in Baltimore. He has strengthened the partnership with Baltimore City Child Support and sat on the advisory board assisting with policy change and instrumental in developing a debt-leveraging initiative to assist fathers in BRFP who have state-owed child support arrears. In addition, he assisted the dads of the Baltimore Responsible Fatherhood Project in paying over $400,000 in child support over the past four years!

Sarah W. Whitton, PhD, is a Professor in the Department of Psychology at the University of Cincinnati and Director of the Today's Couples and Families Research Program. Dr. Whitton's work aims to better understand modern couples and families, and to help them build and maintain the types of strong, stable relationships that promote the health and well-being of adults and children. Towards that aim, she conducts research to clarify how couple and family relationships affect health and develops relationship-focused interventions to improve the health and well-being of family members. Her current research is primarily focused on marginalized groups, especially sexual and gender minorities and stepfamilies.

FOREWORD

Since the mid-1970s, the number of nonresident fathers unable to meet their child support obligations has been growing because of declines in wages, marriage, employment, and labor force participation among men lacking a four-year college degree. Paradoxically, the government's commitment and resources to require these fathers to meet their child support obligations has been growing in the United States over the same period. Sadly, however, neither the nation's commitment, nor the resources that would enable them to do so has kept pace. Instead, every five years or so since the mid-1990s, Congress passes another round of funding for fatherhood services. Human service agencies around the country vigorously compete for these limited funds. The recipients, and the think tanks that provide technical assistance to these efforts and assess their effects, go into execution, largely in private, and without providing much feedback about the programs, their activities, and their consequences for fathers and families. Fortunately, in a recent five-year round, Congress also funded a small operation called the Fatherhood Research and Practice Network, which made small grants to collaborations between researchers and programs to address critical questions in the field and communicate the results to the larger research, practice, and policy communities. Results of 13 of these collaborations appear in this book.

The chapters in the book explore some of the most important topics in the field of fatherhood. Using a variety of techniques, from random control trials to qualitative studies, most chapters assess how parents react to the service they receive. The topics include the use of distance-learning technologies to serve fathers. This is a critical topic because many human service professionals, including those in fatherhood programs, hope that the emergency shift to digital learning during the COVID-19 pandemic produces long-term benefits. Coparenting is another critical topic the book explores. Practitioners realized early on that engaging mothers in support of fatherhood programs was critical. More recently, researchers have joined this call. The reason is obvious. If nonresident fathers are more than wallets, then we want fathers to engage with their children. Mothers are the most important asset or obstacle to this goal. Yet, opportunities to engage mothers in support of father–child interactions have for the most part been restricted to work with couples interested in marriage or with mothers and fathers whose children are in the child welfare system. Three chapters in this book make important contributions to our understanding of coparenting by examining efforts to engage mothers alongside fathers enrolled in responsible fatherhood programs.

The long-term challenge of fatherhood programs is financial sustainability, which is critical for reasons beyond operating costs. Since the field began to develop in the early 1990s, the federal government has been the primary funder of fatherhood programs. As a result, Congressional priorities, guided by dedicated professionals in the Department of Health and Human Services (DHHS), dominate the goals of fatherhood programs, as well as techniques practitioners use to achieve those goals. For example, in 2005, the Bush Administration required fatherhood programs to pursue the goal of healthy marriage, even though most fatherhood programs serve nonresident fathers who are no longer romantically involved with the mothers of their children. Despite their ongoing skepticism, fatherhood programs quickly adapted to this priority. More recently, trauma-informed care has been a priority required of fatherhood programs, since other fields of human service funded by DHHS, indicated that this practice was important in serving people from disadvantaged backgrounds. The dominance of federal funding means that the insights fatherhood practitioners develop about improving practice in their field are often less likely to be disseminated and tested throughout the field than are the priorities articulated in RFPs for federal funding. Developing a more diverse source of funding is therefore critical for the field. The book speaks directly to the issue of financial sustainability in two chapters that focus on encouraging state-based fatherhood initiatives.

What are some of the most critical insights gleaned from these new studies? First, chapters on the use of distance-learning technologies in fatherhood yield disappointing results. Online classes and material delivered over smartphones may help sustain programs during emergencies such as COVID-19. Such tools may also help fathers to retain and implement lessons they learn from in-person interactions with other fathers, facilitators, and case managers. However, on their own, these distance-learning technologies appear to have little impact on fathering behaviors. Thus, distance-learning technologies may improve the cost-benefit of fatherhood programs, which is an important finding that can guide the field moving forward.

The three studies of coparenting are more encouraging, even though results are mixed. Curiously, all three studies focused on programs that reach out to mothers through mother-only services, ignoring the potential for coparenting services targeting both parents during the first three years of a child's life, when many nonresident fathers maintain romantic relationships with the mothers of their children. One study found mothers distrustful of fatherhood programs and frustrated by fathers' behavior even though fathers were receiving services. The two other studies found mothers to be very receptive to fatherhood services and better able to coparent with the fathers of their children after participating in mother-only programs designed as adjuncts to fatherhood services. On balance, these results are encouraging because none involved extensive services to mothers and none required that mothers participate along with the fathers of the children. As a result, both the cost and logistical challenges associated with engaging mothers in fatherhood programs appear well within the reach of many fatherhood programs.

The studies focusing on sustainability also provide encouraging results, which may be beyond the purview of the programs themselves. One study shows that trusted intermediaries can serve as honest brokers between responsible fatherhood programs and state government stakeholders to leverage funds states usually devote to other children, youth, and family services in support of fatherhood programs. Another study provides helpful suggestions about how researchers can improve the sustainability and diversity of funding available for fatherhood programs, by monetizing a broad range of benefits and cost reductions of responsible fatherhood programs. Doing so would follow the example of the Head Start program, which when evaluated using long-term impacts on high school test scores and graduation, earnings, and criminal behavior is much more cost effective than when evaluated based upon immediate impacts on the preschool children that Head Start serves.

Where do we go from here? Besides filling important gaps in what we can glean from the large-scale, federally funded fatherhood demonstrations, which appear periodically, the book also provides concrete suggestions about needed policy and programmatic reforms. Readers could easily overlook the most important. Ongoing practitioner–researcher collaborations to strengthen every aspect of responsible fatherhood is critical. In an era of evidence-based and evidence-informed practice, fatherhood programs can no longer expect to receive public or even private support without demonstrating their effectiveness. This depends upon a healthy and respectful collaboration between practitioners, with insights and experience about their clients and their clients' families, and researchers, with expertise at measuring the outcomes of social interventions and testing their efficacy. If the researchers and practitioners involved in the included studies sustain their work and catalyze new efforts along these lines, facilitating such core collaborations could easily be one of the most important contributions of FPRN to the development of the field.

Second, the book's new systematic review of the impacts of fatherhood updates the findings of previous reviews showing that fatherhood programs provide positive outcomes, though with small effect sizes, on a range of outcomes, not including fathers' earnings or formal child support. This finding may frustrate the Congressional intent, but in the long run, it may be quite helpful. Federally funded fatherhood programs tend to focus on men from the most disadvantaged backgrounds—those with very low levels of education, criminal justice barriers, substance abuse, mental health problems, and so on. Fatherhood programs may be unable to have any substantial impact on the employment and earnings of such men or their abilities to provide financial support to their children. However, the studies in this book also show that fatherhood programs can positively engage these fathers in the lives of their children. Doing so, especially when children are young, may enable fathers to contribute to their children's language, reading and math skills, and socio-emotional development that will have much larger impacts on children's economic well-being than the small amounts of money these fathers could provide, even if they paid formal child support obligations in full. One study of a barbershop-based program to encourage fathers to read to their children, funded by FPRN, but not included in the volume, reports on a successful effort to engage fathers usually served by fatherhood programs, although impacts on children await further development. Moreover, many fathers who fail to meet their child support obligations in full are beyond the reach of federally funded fatherhood programs, because these fathers work regularly, though at wages too low to meet their basic expenses after paying their taxes and child support obligations. Reforming the Earned Income Tax Credit to provide the same tax relief and earnings incentives available to the mothers of their children and using fatherhood programs to increase the wages and work efforts of these fathers, would be a more effective way to increase the financial support available to millions of American children from nonresident fathers.

Finally, as the concluding chapter makes clear, "Making a change in key father outcomes is hard and takes intense and sustained interventions." Practitioners and researchers can hardly develop and provide such interventions at the level of funding currently available. The findings reported in this book underscore the importance of the researcher–practitioner collaborations and the role intermediaries can play in persuading states to allocate more children, youth, and family service funding in the direction of fatherhood services. These and other core insights included in the book make this book a must read for practitioners, policy makers, and researchers interested in the field.

Ronald B. Mincy, Maurice V. Russell Professor of Social Policy and Social Work Practice, Columbia University School of Social Work

ACKNOWLEDGMENTS

The editors of this volume wish to acknowledge the staff of the U.S. Department of Health and Human Services, Administration for Children and Families (Office of Planning, Research, and Evaluation [OPRE]) for their support and feedback on the individual research projects included in this volume. Funding for the Fatherhood Research and Practice Network (FRPN) and the studies included in this book was provided by OPRE, grant #90PR0006, 2013-2019. Without the support of OPRE, this collection of chapters would not have been possible. We also note that any opinions, findings, and conclusions or recommendations expressed in this material are those of the authors and editors and do not necessarily reflect the views of the U.S. Department of Health and Human Services, Administration for Children and Families, Office of Family Assistance, or OPRE. We also want to acknowledge the support and assistance of Rebecca Kaufman, Nancy Thoennes, Abigail Henson, Maggie Spain, Rachel Wildfeuer, and Maria Thomson. They were instrumental in the collection of data, assisting with the revision of chapters, editing, and carrying out the day-to-day activities of FRPN. We also want to acknowledge all of the members of the FRPN steering committee and work groups. These individuals are too numerous to list here, but their names can be found on our website (www.frpn.org).

1
INTRODUCTION

Jay Fagan and Jessica Pearson

Family life has changed dramatically in the United States and other industrialized nations during the past 50 years. Fewer adults marry; those who do frequently divorce. For every two marriages that took place in 2018, there was one divorce in the same year (Schweizer, 2019a), with remarriage rates for men declining by more than half between 1950 and 2017 (Schweizer, 2019b). Instead of marriage, more and more adults cohabit, with cohabitation accounting for 23% of all unions among women ages 19–44 (Manning, 2012) and 62% of births to never-married women (Lamidi, 2016). Cohabiting relationships frequently do not last long, with children born to cohabiting versus married parents facing over five times the risk of experiencing their parents' separation (Osborne et al., 2007). Finally, and perhaps most importantly, more and more children are being born to unmarried parents. Recent estimates show that about 40% of all births in the United States occur outside of marriage, up from 28% in 1990, with this being the case for 52% and 69% of all births to Hispanic and Black women, respectively (Wildsmith et al., 2018).

The net result of these trends is that about 21.9 million children had a parent who lived outside of their household in 2018, which represented more than one fourth (26.5%) of all children under 21 years of age (Grall, 2020). Necessarily, children must adapt to these changes. When parents divorce, or when unmarried parents separate, this typically means the children wind up sharing time with parents who reside in separate households. In many instances, children see the nonresident parent infrequently, especially when adults form new romantic unions. When the parent with whom the child resides remarries or forms a new cohabiting relationship, children must adapt to living with step-parents and possibly step-siblings. And although many unmarried fathers are usually involved and living with the family shortly after the child's birth, many transition to noncohabiting relationships within a few years and become gradually less involved (Amato & Rezac, 1995; Seltzer, 1991).

Another significant change in family life is the trend for women to participate in the labor force rather than stay at home to raise their children. In 1970, one half of all mothers were stay-at-home mothers (Cohn et al., 2014). This number fell to 29% of all mothers in 2012 (Cohn et al., 2014). Husbands and wives were employed in 48.8% of families in the United States in 2018 (U.S. Bureau of Labor Statistics, 2019). Only the husband was employed in 19.1% of married-couple families, and only the wife was employed in 6.8% of these families (no one was employed in 25.1% of married-couple families). In families maintained by women, 77.7% of women were employed in 2018 (U.S. Bureau of Labor Statistics, 2019). These trends have placed demands on fathers to become more involved in child care and to assume greater responsibility for raising children. In 2012, all fathers (i.e., co-resident and nonresident) between the ages of 25 and 59 spent an average of 20 minutes per day in physical child care tasks (e.g., putting child to sleep) and 12 minutes per day in developmental child care activities (e.g., reading to child) (Sayer, 2016). This amount of time is two to three times greater than the amount of time fathers spent in these activities in 1985.

Most fathers have managed to adapt to these family changes. In families experiencing divorce, fathers frequently assume joint custody of children. Recent data in one state (Wisconsin) revealed that between 1989 and 2010, shared custody increased from about 11% to 50% of all divorce cases (Meyer et al., 2017). In co-residing families, fathers have adjusted to mothers' involvement in the labor force by taking on child care responsibilities. Fathers and mothers are most likely to spend equal time with children when parents have comparable earnings. The total amount of time co-residing fathers spent with children was 73% that of mothers when mothers worked and their earnings were comparable to those of fathers (Raley et al., 2012).

This book focuses on a group for whom adaptation has been particularly challenging: low-income, nonresident fathers. Disproportionately comprised of minority men who face racist policies and practices, and long-term structural changes in the economy that penalize lower- and middle-skilled, less-educated male workers, these fathers experience a life shaped by low educational achievement, joblessness, and out-of-wedlock childbearing (Smeedling et al., 2011). Indeed, a portrait of 10,161 low-income, nonresident parents (90% of whom were fathers) who participated in the Child Support Noncustodial Parent Employment Demonstration (CSPED) project, which sought to improve employment and child support payments among noncustodial parents in the child support caseload in eight states, finds that 67% were Latino or African American, 25.7% did not complete high school or a GED, 43% had a high school diploma or GED and no further education, and 68% had been convicted of a crime. While slightly over half (55%) reported having a job in the past 30 days, those who did work for pay reported average monthly earnings of $769. On average, these men had 2.5 biological children, with an average of 1.8 partners, with whom only 13.6% were married while 52.4% and 25% were never married and divorced, respectively (Noyes et al., 2018).

Low-income, nonresident fathers often struggle to stay involved with their children. Unlike marital family law, which spells out the rights and responsibilities that divorcing parents have following their breakup, unmarried parents have no established guidelines specifying the father's visitation rights and no clear pathways to the legal proceedings that formalize issues such as custody and parenting time. As a result, unmarried, nonresident fathers routinely get a child support order without any mention of parenting time (Pearson, 2015), and between 2007 and 2015, the proportion of custodial mothers and nonresident fathers who failed to come to a formal or informal agreement specifying visitation rights and a child support order amount grew from 43% to 55% (Zill, 2019). Data from the 2006–2008 National Survey of Family Growth showed that 20% of fathers who live apart from their children visit their children more than once a week, 29% see their children at least once a month, 21% visit children several times a year, and 27% do not visit their children at all (Livingston & Parker, 2011).

Multiple factors contribute to fathers' lack of involvement with children, including tenuous and conflictual relationships with the child's mother, mothers and fathers forming new romantic relationships, unemployment and underemployment, inability to fulfill child support obligations, lack of education, history of incarceration, and having children with multiple partners (Edin & Nelson, 2013). Despite these challenges, many of these fathers are able to stay involved with their children, and when they are involved, children have better outcomes, including higher levels of academic achievement, fewer behavior problems, better peer relationships, and increased social-emotional competence (Adamsons & Johnson, 2013; Coates & Phares, 2019).

Children in single-parent households are a focus of public policy concern for several reasons. First, they are four times more likely to live in poverty and demonstrate negative outcomes, including doing poorly in schools, having emotional and behavioral problems, becoming teenage parents, and having poverty-level incomes as adults (McLanahan et al., 2013). They also have a dramatic impact on the public purse. An analysis of the annual expenditures made by the federal government in 13 major programs to help support father-absent homes resulted in the conclusion that they are conservatively at least $99.8 billion (Nock & Einolf, 2008).

U.S. Public Policy Response to Engage Low-Income, Nonresident Fathers

One major response to fathers' challenges with meeting their parenting responsibilities and the high cost of child poverty was the 1996 welfare reform law (P.L. 104–193). Welfare reform cut cash assistance and replaced it with time-limited, work-based welfare programs (TANF and the Earned Income Tax Credit) for low-income parents. Simultaneously, the law strengthened the formal child support system to underscore fathers' personal responsibility for their children and to reduce welfare benefit payments by reimbursing the state from child support paid by a nonresident parent (Cancian et al., 2008).

Another feature of P.L. 104–193 was to promote responsible fatherhood and motherhood with the goal of ending welfare dependence through employment and marriage, reducing out-of-wedlock pregnancies, and encouraging the formation and maintenance of two-parent families (Tollestrup, 2018). To that end, the 1996 legislation authorized $10 million per year of child support enforcement funds to States to establish and operate access and visitation programs; one target of these programs is nonresident fathers.

The passage of the Deficit Reduction Act of 2005 provided funding for a Healthy Marriage and Relationship Education (HMRE) and Responsible Fatherhood (HMRF) grants program that involved $50 million per year during 2006–2010 for awards to 90 organizations to operate fatherhood programs. Under the Claims Resolution Act of 2010, funding rose to $75 million per year for awards to 55 organizations. In 2015, a third round of grant funding of approximately $75 million per year was awarded to 39 organizations for five-year grants. And on June 30, 2020, grant applications were due for a fourth round of five-year competitive grants that is expected to provide financial support for 68 Responsible Fatherhood (RF) programs.

The U.S. government defines responsible fatherhood as "taking responsibility for a child's intellectual, emotional, and financial well-being" by choosing to be an actively engaged parent (U.S. White House, 2012, p.1). Whereas the HMRE programs provide classes on maintaining and forming positive partner relationships, RF programs offer classes on parenting and coparenting. Under federal law, RF programs are required to include activities in three key areas: 1) activities to promote marriage such as enhancing relationship skills and coparenting; 2) activities to promote responsible parenting such as teaching good parenting skills and practices; and 3) activities to foster economic stability, such as job training and employment service (Tollestrup, 2018). In 2015, these grants emphasized the importance of activities related to employment, economic stability, and workforce development (Administration for Children & Families, 2015).

TEXT BOX 1.1

Fatherhood program (FP) is the term used throughout this book to refer to services to fathers. Responsible Fatherhood Program (RFP) is used only to refer to programs funded by the Office of Family Assistance, Administration for Children and Families, U.S. Department of Health and Human Services.

Despite the substantial increase in programs for low-income fathers in the United States and the expenditure of an estimated $700 million by the Administration for Children and Families from 2006 to 2018 (Holmes et al., 2018), little is known about how these programs affect fathers and families. A relatively small number of rigorous evaluations of programs serving low-income fathers have been conducted. According to a virtually exhaustive catalogue of fatherhood programs (OPRE catalog of research on programs for fathers), there have been 150 studies of fatherhood programs since 1990, 90 of which included low-income fathers in their sample, and only 15 of which used well-designed and executed, rigorous evaluation methods (Avellar, 2011). Rigorous studies are those that include research designs or methods that provide unbiased estimates of the program's impact on fathers and families.

Since the OPRE catalog was published, there have only been a few additional rigorous evaluations of fatherhood initiatives (e.g., Rutgers University Economic Development Research Group, 2011). One such study was Parents and Children Together (PACT), which was a randomized controlled trial with 5,522 fathers conducted in four U.S. Responsible Fatherhood Programs. This impact evaluation demonstrated positive intervention effects on some outcomes (parenting, economic stability) but not others (relationship health, father well-being) (Avellar et al., 2018). Many more studies are based on less rigorous research designs, such as pretest/post-test studies that do not include control or comparison groups (e.g., Avellar et al., 2018; Robbers, 2011; Scourfield et al., 2012). With a few exceptions, the literature also yielded inconclusive results across all three programmatic activities (i.e., responsible fatherhood/effective parenting, economic security, and coparenting) as well as programs that address more than one of these programmatic activities.

In response to the small number of rigorous studies of fatherhood programs, the U.S. Department of Health and Human Services, Administration for Children and Families funded Temple University and the Center for Policy Research in Denver, Colorado, to develop a Responsible Fatherhood Network in 2013. The goals of the network were to (1) promote rigorous evaluation of fatherhood programs nationwide; (2) provide training to researchers and practitioners to conduct better quality evaluations; and (3) disseminate information that leads to effective fatherhood practice and research. Immediately after the Fatherhood Research and Practice Network (FRPN) was launched, the co-directors of this project (who are also the co-editors of this volume) solicited proposals from research-practitioner teams to conduct rigorous research that addresses gaps identified in the responsible research field. Over the course of six years (2013–2019), FRPN made awards ranging from $20,000 to $100,000 to teams comprised of researchers and practitioners, to conduct 21 studies of programs for low-income fathers and/or issues that affect the ability of low-income, primarily nonresident fathers to engage with their children and improve their parenting skills, provide economic support, and coparent with the mother of their children. In addition, FRPN made mini-awards of $10,000 to interagency teams in 11 states to initiate and/or strengthen father engagement in state programs and policies that affect children and families.

Overview of the Book

The current volume includes results of many of these studies. The aims of this book are to make findings from new research on fatherhood programs readily accessible to researchers and practitioners; provide practitioners with summaries of how each study has implications for evidence-based practice; and synthesize the findings of the studies and suggest future directions for research, practice, and policy. The studies in this book are grouped into six sections that address key questions in the fatherhood practice field.

Section One: The Status of Research on Fatherhood Programs

The first section examines the effectiveness of fatherhood programs targeting low-income and nonresident fathers. Erin Holmes and colleagues present a systematic review of 37 reports covering 47 independent studies. They focus on five desired outcomes for participants in fatherhood programs: positive father involvement, parenting, coparenting, employment/economic prospects, and child support payments. In addition to demonstrating the impacts of fatherhood programs on each of these outcomes, the chapter discusses factors that encourage program participation and retention.

Section Two: New Research on Elements of Effective Fatherhood Programs

These studies use rigorous techniques to consider some of the building blocks of effective fatherhood programs: the use of a structured curriculum versus a format that involves an unstructured peer support group, the impact of father attendance and program dosage on desired outcomes, and the effectiveness of conducting explicit staff training to enhance father engagement. All three studies in this section involve random assignment of fatherhood program participants to a group that received the experimental treatment versus a group that received no treatment or "business as usual" services. Thus, Bright Sarfo and Vernon Wallace examine outcomes at three and six months post program for 89 fathers randomly assigned to participate in the facilitated 16-session structured (DAD MAP) curriculum at the Center for Urban Families, and compare them to outcomes for 75 fathers assigned to participate in a facilitated 16-session unstructured support group. Young-Il Kim, Sung Joon Jang, and Brenda Oyer assess outcomes for 137 fathers randomly assigned to participate in TYRO Dads, a 20-hour group program delivered by trained facilitators in ten 2-hour sessions over five weeks, and compare them to outcomes for 115 fathers interested in taking the class who were randomly denied the opportunity. The outcomes assessed for both groups of fathers at the conclusion of the five-week program and three months later included parenting satisfaction, father–child interaction, and coparenting. Finally, Jennifer Bellamy and her team randomly assigned 85 home visitors to receive a manualized training program designed to encourage father participation in home visits and compared the experience of families served by staff that received this training with that of families served by 75 home visitors who did not receive training on father engagement. All three studies yield statistically significant findings pertaining to program effects and offer suggestions for practitioners and questions that remain to be answered in future research.

Section Three: New Research on the Use of Cell Phone and Online Technology to Engage Fathers and Message to Them About Parenting

The two studies in this section of the book explore the use of cell phones and online resources to engage fathers and try to teach them how to be effective parents. There is a lot of enthusiasm about the potential of new media with low-income, nonresident fathers, but its utility appears to be more nuanced when utilized in real-world settings. Selva Lewin-Bizan and colleagues examine father reactions to cell phone messages that aim to teach them to become more involved and effective parents. Amy Holtzworth-Munroe and her colleagues examine the reactions of unmarried mothers and fathers who received a court order to participate in an online parent education program aimed at improving their coparenting relationship.

Section Four: New Research on Mother Engagement and Coparenting

The strongest predictor of nonresident father engagement with his children is the quality of the relationship he has with the other parent (Fagan & Cherson, 2017). These studies examine the challenges associated with maternal engagement, how mothers may be engaged in interventions that aim to promote mother support for father involvement with their children, and the impact of mother participation in coparenting interventions on the attitudes and behaviors of both mothers and fathers. Armon Perry and his colleagues present the results of an experimental study that involved engaging a randomly selected group of 69 mothers in a one-time parent education workshop lasting approximately two hours and comparing their reports of father–child contact and their coparenting relationships with 84 randomly selected mothers who did not participate in the parenting workshop. All mothers in both study groups had fathers of their children who were enrolled in a fatherhood program known as *4 Your Child*. Jay Fagan, Jessica Pearson, and

Abbie Henson present the results of a pretest, post-test, and follow-up study of 127 mothers who attended at least one session of a six-session coparenting program known as *Understanding Dads*™. At all three stages of data collection, mothers were assessed on their attitudes and experiences with coparenting; qualitative interviews were conducted with mothers who participated and the fathers of their children, to find out whether coparenting, levels of conflict, and the ways in which disagreement was handled had changed following class participation. Kimberly Sperber and Sarah Whitten's chapter describes an effort to engage mothers in a coparenting intervention. Their semi-structured, qualitative interviews with 16 mothers and 30 fathers identify barriers to participation in coparenting services, factors that made participation more attractive or feasible, and the perceptions of the value and impact of coparenting services.

Section Five: New Research on Special Topics and Populations

The two studies in this section address practice and policy focusing on homelessness and domestic violence. Kristie Thomas and Fernando Mederos address how fatherhood programs might engage in effective domestic violence (DV) education and prevention. Their study includes a review of how widely used fatherhood curricula address DV. They conducted in-depth interviews about the issue with fatherhood field leaders ($n = 10$), facilitators ($n = 20$), and DV advocates ($n = 10$). The result is an evidence-informed framework that supports the needs and lived experiences of low-income fathers and includes recommended strategies for both program leaders and facilitators.

Based on interviews and focus groups with 127 individuals that included staff of a city oversight agency, staff at ten homeless shelters, and mothers and fathers residing in shelters, Karin Garg and Karen Hudson elucidate the process of making system-wide policy change to include fathers (with their families) in family homeless shelters in Philadelphia, Pennsylvania. The qualitative study highlights the process of adopting and implementing a new nondiscrimination policy requiring the inclusion of primarily African American fathers as residents in family emergency shelters, concerns regarding implementation, and factors that support compliance with the new policy.

Section Six: New Research on Fatherhood Policy and Program Sustainability

The fatherhood field struggles with limited funding, short-term grants, and cuts during tough economies. The disadvantaged men of color that they generally serve are frequently overlooked by administrators of family programs and the policy makers who generate them. The studies in this section of the book present approaches to making the economic case for fatherhood programs and to crafting multi-agency initiatives at the state level that are more inclusive of fathers.

Richard Chase shows how to monetize the economic returns and avoided costs associated with participation in fatherhood programs. He addresses more standard economic measures of outcomes including improved educational attainment, employment and wage rates, and compliance with child support payments, along with less conventional measures such as increased volunteerism, improved parenting, and lower criminal conviction rates. There is also a brief discussion of potential two-generation long-term child development and family well-being outcomes of father engagement. This includes possible savings associated with reduced special education, improved high school completion rates, and increased lifetime earnings for children.

Jessica Pearson's chapter describes a pilot project to help 11 states develop long-term plans to enhance father inclusion in state-level programs and policies through the award of mini-grants of $10,000 and the coordinated efforts of FRPN. Interviews with the planning teams and reviews of the planning materials they submitted at the conclusion of the one-year initiative revealed that their efforts were enhanced by piggybacking on existing initiatives, strengthening relationships with multiple state agencies and programs, securing high-level champions, and participating in the initiative which included structured meetings and cross-site learning communities. Major challenges were the difficulty of scheduling meetings with busy agency personnel and policy makers, changes in administration, the lack of data on father engagement at the state level, and the complexity and scale of the father engagement process.

Conclusions

The book concludes with a discussion of key lessons from the studies described in this volume for practitioners as well as potential areas of future research.

References

Adamson, K., & Johnson, S. K. (2013). An updated and expanded meta-analysis of nonresident fathering and child well-being. *Journal of Family Psychology, 27*(4), 589–599.

Administration for Children and Families. (2015). *Responsible fatherhood opportunities for reentry and mobility* (HHS-2015-ACF-OFA-FO-0992). https://ami.grantsolutions.gov/files/HHS-2015-ACF-OFA-FO-0992_0.htm.

Amato, P. R., & Rezac, S. J. (1995). Contact with nonresidential parents, interparental conflict, and children's behavior. *Journal of Family Issues, 15*(2), 191–207.

Avellar, S., Covington, R., Moore, Q., Patnaik, A., & Wu, A. (2018). *Parents and children together: Effects of four responsible fatherhood programs for low-income fathers* (OPRE Report #2018-50). U.S. Department of Health and Human Services, Administration for Children and Families, Office of Planning, Research and Evaluation. https://www.acf.hhs.gov/sites/default/files/opre/pact_rf_impacts_to_opre_508.pdf.

Avellar, S., Dion, M. R., Clarkwest, A., Zaveri, H., Asheer, S., Borradaile, K., & Zukiewicz, M. (2011). Catalog of research: Programs for low-income fathers.

Washington, DC: Office of Planning, Research, and Evaluation, Administration for Children.

Cancian, M., Meyer, D. R., & Caspar, E. (2008). Welfare and child support: Complements, not substitutes. *Journal of Policy Analysis and Management*, 27(2), 354–375.

Coates, E. E., & Phares, V. (2019). Pathways linking nonresident father involvement and child outcomes. *Journal of Child and Family Studies*, 28(6), 1681–1694.

Cohn, D., Livingston, G., & Wang, W. (2014). *After decades of decline, a rising share of stay-at-home mothers*. Pew Research Center. https://www.pewsocialtrends.org/2014/04/08/after-decades-of-decline-a-rise-in-stay-at-home-mothers/.

Edin, K., & Nelson, T. (2013). *Doing the best I can: Fatherhood in the inner city*. University of California Press.

Fagan, J., & Cherson, M. (2017). Maternal gatekeeping: The associations among facilitation, encouragement, and low-income fathers' engagement with young children. *Journal of Family Issues*, 38, 633–653.

Grall, T. (2020). *Custodial mothers and fathers and their child support: 2017* (Current Population Reports, P60-269). U.S. Census Bureau. https://www.census.gov/content/dam/Census/library/publications/2020/demo/p60-269.pdf.

Holmes, E. K., Hawkins, A. J., Egginton, B. M., Robbins, N., & Shafter, K. (2018). *Do responsible fatherhood programs work? A comprehensive meta-analytic study*. Fatherhood Research and Practice Network. https://www.frpn.org/asset/frpn-grantee-report-do-responsible-fatherhood-programs-work-comprehensive-meta-analytic-study.

Lamidi, E. (2016). *A quarter century change in nonmarital births* (Family Profiles, FP-16-03). National Center for Family & Marriage Research. https://www.bgsu.edu/content/dam/BGSU/college-of-arts-and-sciences/NCFMR/documents/FP/lamidi-nonmarital-births-fp-16-03.pdf.

Livingston, G., & Parker, K. (2011). *A tale of two fathers: More are active, but more are absent*. Pew Research Center. https://www.pewsocialtrends.org/2011/06/15/a-tale-of-two-fathers/.

Manning, W. (2012). *Trends in cohabitation: Over twenty years of change, 1987–2010* (Family Profiles, FP-13-12). National Center for Family & Marriage Research. https://www.bgsu.edu/content/dam/BGSU/college-of-arts-and-sciences/NCFMR/documents/FP/FP-13-12.pdf.

McLanahan, S., Tach, L., & Schneider, D. (2013). The causal effects of father absence. *Annual Review of Sociology*, 39, 399–427.

Meyer, D. R., Cancian, M., & Cook, S. T. (2017). The growth in shared custody in the United States: Patterns and implications. *Family Court Review*, 55, 500–512.

Nock, S. L., & Einolf, C. J. (2008). *The one billion dollar man: The annual public costs of father absence*. National Fatherhood Initiative. http://www.fatherhood.org/one-hundred-billion-dollar-man.

Noyes, J., Vogel, L. K., & Howard, L. (2018). *Final implementation findings from the Child Support Noncustodial Parent Employment Demonstration (CSPED) evaluation*. Institute for Research on Poverty, University of Wisconsin–Madison. https://www.irp.wisc.edu/wp/wp-content/uploads/2019/01/CSPED-Final-ImplementationReport-2019-Compliant.pdf.

Osborne, C., Manning, W. D., & Smock, P. J. (2007). Married and cohabiting parents' relationship stability: A focus on race and ethnicity. *Journal of Marriage and Family*, 69, 1345–1366.

Pearson, J. (2015). Establishing parenting time in child support cases: New opportunities and challenges. *Family Court Review*, *53*, 9–24.

Raley, S., Bianchi, S. M., Wang, W. (2012). When do fathers care? Mothers' economic contribute and fathers' involvement in child care. *American Journal of Sociology*, *117*, 1422–1459.

Robbers, M. L. (2011). Father involvement among young Hispanics. *Families in Society*, *92*(2), 169–175.

Sayer, L. C. (2016). Trends in women's and men's time use, 1965–2012: Back to the future? In S. M. McHale, V. King, J. van Hook, & A. Booth (Eds.), *Gender and couple relationships* (pp. 43–77). Springer.

Schweizer, V. (2019a). *Marriage to divorce ratio in the U.S.: Geographic variation, 2018* (Family Profile, FP-19-24). National Center for Family & Marriage Research. https://www.bgsu.edu/content/dam/BGSU/college-of-arts-and-sciences/NCFMR/documents/FP/fp-19-24-mar-div-ratio.pdf.

Schweizer, V. (2019b). *The retreat from remarriage, 1950–2017* (Family Profile, FP-19-17). National Center for Family & Marriage Research. https://www.bgsu.edu/content/dam/BGSU/college-of-arts-and-sciences/NCFMR/documents/FP/FP-19-17.pdf.

Scourfield, J., Tolman, R., Maxwell, N., Holland, S., Bullock, A., & Sloan, L. (2012). Results of a training course for social workers on engaging fathers in child protection. *Children and Youth Services Review*, *34*(8), 1425–1432.

Seltzer, J. A. (1991). Relationships between fathers and children who live apart: The father's role after separation. *Journal of Marriage and Family*, *53*(1), 79–101.

Smeedling, T.M., Garfinkel, I., & Mincy, R. (2011). Young disadvantaged men: Fathers, families, poverty, and policy. *The Annals of the American Academy of Political and Social Science*, *635*, 6–21.

Tollestrup, J. (2018). *Fatherhood initiatives: Connecting fathers to their children* (RL31035). Congressional Research Service. https://fas.org/sgp/crs/misc/RL31025.pdf.

U.S. Bureau of Labor Statistics. (2019, April 18). *Employment characteristics of families—2018* [News release]. https://www.bls.gov/news.release/archives/famee_04182019.pdf.

U.S. White House. (2012). *Promoting responsible fatherhood*. https://obamawhitehouse.archives.gov/sites/default/files/docs/fatherhood_report_6.13.12_final.pdf.

Wildsmith, E., Manlove, J. & Cook, E. (2018). *Dramatic increase in the proportion of births outside of marriage in the United States from 1990 to 2016*. Child Trends. https://www.childtrends.org/publications/dramatic-increase-in-percentage-of-births-outside-marriage-among-whites-hispanics-and-women-with-higher-education-levels.

Zill, N. (2019). *The new fatherhood is not benefiting children who need it most*. Institute for Family Studies. https://ifstudies.org/blog/the-new-fatherhood-is-not-benefiting-children-who-need-it-most.

2

THE EFFECTIVENESS OF RESPONSIBLE FATHERHOOD PROGRAMS TARGETING LOW-INCOME AND NONRESIDENT FATHERS

A Qualitative Meta-Synthesis

Erin Kramer Holmes, Clare R. Thomas, Braquel R. Egginton, Virginia K. Leiter, and Alan J. Hawkins

Rationale

Programs specifically targeting fathers have increased over time due to greater scholarly attention regarding the risk factors associated with family instability (Amato, 2005; Cherlin, 2010), increased federal funding for programs for unmarried or nonresident fathers, and rigorous evaluation studies of some programs (e.g., Fagan, 2008; Fagan et al., 2015; Fagan & Stevenson, 2002; Florsheim et al., 2012; Zaveri et al., 2015). Most notably, the Administration for Children and Families (ACF) responsible fatherhood initiative, which extended the work of nonprofit organizations, community, state, private secular, and faith-based efforts to strengthen fathers' connections to their children, has allocated $50–$75 million a year from 2006 to 2018 to support fatherhood programs for a total of about $725 million (for more details see Pearson & Fagan, 2019; Tollestrup, 2018).

Fatherhood programs explicitly focus on parenting behaviors that fall into three broad categories: economic support, father involvement/parenting skills and knowledge, and coparenting/healthy relationships (Fagan & Kaufman, 2015). Economic support programs typically involve teaching skills to gain employment or find a better job, to be more fiscally responsible, or to increase child support payments (Administration for Children and Families, 2009). Measurable outcomes include increases in employment rates, income, child support order establishment, and the payment of formal and informal child support (e.g., Pearson et al., 2003).

Father involvement and parenting programs teach men to be engaged and nurturing with their children, providing the parenting skills to do so. Outcomes in these programs are more diverse, including father reports of parent competence, parenting satisfaction, parenting stress, self-esteem, engagement with children, and father–child contact (Administration for Children and

Families, 2009). While one main objective of these programs is to increase the quality of the time men spend with their children (Amato & Gilbreth, 1999), programs targeting nonresident fathers are also facilitating increases in the quantity of father–child contact.

The nature of coparenting programs depends on the status of the father's relationship with his child's mother. Married or cohabiting fathers learn skills to strengthen their relationship, to take inventory of interpersonal strengths and weaknesses, how to communicate more effectively, and how to control aggressive behavior (Administration for Children and Families, 2009). Programs for nonresident fathers teach many of the same skills as resident programs, with the focus on improving the relationship with the mother. The coparenting relationship is the priority because it is among the largest predictors of nonresident fathers' involvement with their children (Carlson et al., 2008; Fagan & Palkovitz, 2011; McHale & Coates, 2014). Specific outcomes measured in these programs include relationship satisfaction, the strength of the coparenting relationship, communication, and social support (Fagan & Kaufman, 2015).

Meta-analysis is a systematic tool for reviewing a body of research by integrating findings from all quantitative studies on the same subject. Studies are coded on key variables, and results are standardized to allow for comparison. This analysis allows researchers to draw conclusions about the effectiveness of programs (Holmes et al., 2010). Our research team conducted a systematic, comprehensive meta-analysis of the effectiveness of fatherhood programs targeted primarily to unmarried, low-income, nonresident fathers based on evaluation studies that reported sufficient quantitative data to meet our criteria (Holmes et al., 2020). Ultimately, we focused on 30 independent studies that used experimental, quasi-experimental, and one-group/pre-post study designs that reported sufficient data for calculating effect sizes on targeted outcomes. Before running our analyses, we tested for potential differences in effects based on the study design (e.g., quasi-experimental vs. experimental design), and report type (e.g., journal article, public report, dissertation/thesis). In addition, we were concerned that results from one government-funded study—Parents and Children Together (PACT) with four independent sites totaling more than 5,000 fathers—would heavily weight the overall effect size. So, we tested whether the effects for these PACT sites were significantly different from the effect sizes for the rest of the studies. Similar to other meta-analyses, we discovered that the effect size for studies published in journals was significantly higher than for studies in public reports or dissertations/theses. We found no other differences in effects based on study design, or the PACT data.

We discovered that, on average, these programs produced small but statistically significant effects on father involvement, parenting, and coparenting; the strongest effect size was in coparenting. Unfortunately, these programs did not significantly impact father employment and economic well-being, nor did they significantly impact father payment of child support.

TEXT BOX 2.1 SUMMARY OF FINDINGS FROM FRPN META-ANALYSIS

With support from the Fatherhood Research and Practice Network (FRPN), and prepared under grant #90PR0006 from the U.S. Department of Health and Human Services, Office of Planning, Research, and Evaluation (OPRE) to Temple University and the Center for Policy Research, we conducted a systematic meta-analysis of evaluations of fatherhood programs targeting unmarried, never married, and low-income fathers (please see Holmes et al., 2020).

- We identified 25 published and unpublished reports with 30 independent studies. Of these, 21 employed a control/treatment design, and 9 employed a one-group/pre-post design.
- These programs produced small but statistically significant effects ($d = .099$, $p < .01$), resembling the effects of relationship education efforts in similar low-income, at-risk populations (Arnold & Beelmann, 2019).
- We explored five outcomes: father involvement, parenting, coparenting, employment and economic well-being, and payment of child support. We found the following:
  - Father involvement improved ($d = .114$, $p < .05$).
  - Parenting improved ($d = .110$, $p < .01$).
  - Coparenting improved ($d = .167$, $p < .05$). This was the strongest effect.
  - Unfortunately, father employment and economic well-being and payment of child support did not improve.
- We invited more evaluations of programs focused on unmarried, non-resident, low-income fathers.
- We also concluded that, in evaluations, we need reports of attrition, assessment of child outcomes, observational measures of outcomes, better statistical reporting to facilitate more meta-analyses, and better assessment of moderators such as father age, program location, child developmental stage, multi-partner fertility, and other barriers to father involvement. These reports will help evaluators and practitioners better understand what makes some programs more effective than others so we can all improve our efforts.

Brief Description of the Current Meta-Synthesis Study

In the process of searching for studies for our meta-analysis, we had to eliminate 77 of 107 possible reports because they did not provide the information necessary to code effects for the meta-analysis. The 77 eliminated reports were composed of 40 qualitative and 37 quantitative reports. While the rigors of such a careful systematic quantitative approach have many benefits, the boundaries are firm around what evaluations can be included in a meta-analysis. A meta-synthesis, on the other hand, allows researchers to integrate findings from multiple, related qualitative studies. It also allows researchers to code quantitative articles in a more qualitative way when those articles do not provide the information necessary to code effects for the quantitative meta-analysis. In our case, it allowed us to utilize many of the studies that were excluded from our previously conducted meta-analysis to gain valuable insight into why some fatherhood programs are more effective than others. Thus, the purpose of this chapter is to systematically synthesize the results of the previously excluded evaluations to continue answering the following questions: How effective are fatherhood programs at increasing unmarried, low-income, nonresident fathers' positive father involvement, parenting, coparenting behavior, employment, economic prospects, and child support payments? (See Holmes et al., 2020, for full details about the initial searching and coding process we used to locate the 77 articles we coded for this chapter.) In the next section of this chapter, we describe why we omitted 40 of the 77 reports from the meta-synthesis, yielding a final sample of 37 reports included in the current study.

Method

Our research team included five individuals: two PhD faculty, two graduate students, and one undergraduate student. We conducted our synthesis in three stages: 1) establishing inclusion criteria, 2) developing a codebook based upon our inclusion criteria, and 3) coding the reports and studies. When there were disagreements or concerns about the process, we consulted one another and came to an agreement to complete the coding of the study. Our codebook included codes for study methods, study design, publication type, participants (e.g., father only; father and coparent; father and child[ren]; father, coparent, and child[ren]; other), curriculum type, program length, geographic location, program location, recruitment procedures, retention rates, child outcomes (please note that none of the articles reported on child outcomes), our core outcomes as described throughout the chapter, other outcomes or main themes, the direction of effects as described below, and quotes from each qualitative report that best captured the outcomes studied. Below we present more detailed information about coding for study characteristics and outcomes.

Study Characteristics

To be included in this chapter, reports had to focus primarily on nonresident, low-income fathers. Per our prior meta-analysis, we kept reports if fewer than 35% of the sample were married (fathers could be cohabiting). We further note that in the programs we studied, nonresident fathers could still reside with some but not all of their children.

From the original 77 unusable articles in our meta-analysis, an additional 40 reports were excluded during coding for the following reasons: 18 were not evaluations, seven were based on samples with married fathers or in which residential status could not be determined, five did not focus specifically on fathering outcomes, three targeted divorced couples, six reported results from the same evaluations and sample that were already included in our meta-analysis, and we could not locate one of the reports from our original search. Thus, 37 reports remained for coding.

Some reports included multiple independent treatment groups; thus, from the 37 reports that remained, 47 independent studies were coded. Sixteen of these were qualitative, 26 quantitative, and five employed mixed methods. Sixteen of these quantitative studies used a pre-post design with no control group (four of these included a follow-up assessment), three employed a post-test only design without a control group, four used a quasi-experimental design (one of these included a follow-up assessment), and the remaining two used experimental designs (one of those included a follow-up assessment). Fourteen reports were coded from journal articles, four from dissertations, 26 from organizational reports, and three from books. These programs employed varying types of curricula. Seven programs were solely educational; 13 featured both education and support groups; five consisted of case management or employment services; five included both educational components and case management/employment services; 12 combined education, support groups, and case management/employment services; three used other methods; and two could not be classified. Program lengths also varied widely, with nine programs lasting between 4 and 8 weeks, eight lasting 11–16 weeks, four lasting about six months, and five lasting a year or more, while five had variable lengths or were reported only in number of program meetings or total hours and 15 had no length of time reported. Finally, 40 of these programs served fathers exclusively, while four served fathers and mothers who were not partners, and three served fathers and coparents.

Outcomes

Similar to our meta-analysis, we aggregated outcomes into five primary categories: father involvement (e.g., any interaction between fathers and their children), coparenting (e.g., father–mother relationship quality and cooperation with the mother), parenting (e.g., the development of positive parenting skills and parenting stress), employment and economic well-being (e.g., wages, employment status, number of work hours), and child support (e.g., formal and informal payments, administrative data of arears and payment of arears).

Coders tallied the outcomes across all qualitative and quantitative studies using a coding scheme to create a mean score for the direction of the effects across all coded studies (-1 = *negative effect*; 0 = *no effect*; 1 = *positive effect*). When statistical differences between groups were assessed quantitatively (e.g., calculating statistical differences between scores on a pretest and a post-test, or between a comparison group and a treatment group), our codes reflect significant difference. However, this was not the case for many of the studies we coded (i.e., qualitative studies). Thus, when no statistical differences between groups were assessed quantitatively, we based our codes on what the respondents reported. For example, if respondents consistently reported a positive effect, and the authors of the report concluded a positive effect, then the article was coded with a positive effect. The same was true for those reporting no effect or a negative effect. A mean score was then calculated to ascertain the average effect for each outcome. To create this mean score, we summed the scores for each outcome across the 47 different program reports that assessed that particular outcome, and then calculated a mean score. For example, 24 of the 47 program reports included an assessment of parenting, so our mean score is a reflection of the average code across those 24 reports. We acknowledge that this method is rudimentary; however, it reflects the most systematic approach we could come up with to synthesize across both qualitative and quantitative studies in order for the results of the evaluations to be shared more broadly.

Results

All calculated mean scores indicated positive effects. The outcome with the highest mean score was parenting ($n = 24$, $M = .85$), followed by father involvement ($n = 27$, $M = .78$), coparenting ($n = 24$, $M = .63$), child support ($n = 36$, $M = .44$), and employment ($n = 31$; $M = .39$). Although there is no test of significance, and these mean scores do not reflect the magnitude of the effects, there is still a general indication of positive impact according to the mean scores.

Coders also included an "other" category for any outcomes outside of the five primary categories listed previously. These outcomes varied widely across studies. Mean scores were calculated if outcomes were reported across at least three studies. Outcomes with sufficient data for mean scores included father's perception of self (e.g., confidence, self-esteem; $n = 4$, $M = .75$), anger management ($n = 3$, $M = .67$), and education (e.g., school enrollment, having a GED or high school diploma; $n = 3$, $M = .67$). Outcomes with insufficient overlap to calculate mean scores included custody and visitation, community involvement, racial and social barriers, empathy, masculinity, staff participation, social support, and mother's welfare. Overall, all outcomes indicated positive impact from participating in a diverse array of fatherhood programs.

Factors That Encourage Program Participation and Retention

Identifying what draws fathers to responsible fatherhood program is an important factor in both recruiting and retaining participants. Researchers reported that participants were obtained through partnering with local court systems and parole offices along with child support agencies. Some also used community outreach, diverse media outlets, and word of mouth. Evaluations differed regarding the best way to obtain participants with some promoting the usefulness of local agencies and the court, while others found most of their success through word of mouth. Reasons for fathers' decisions to attend the programs were not as well documented. However, many of the fathers did express a desire to be more involved in their children's lives.

Not all fathers completed the programs, despite their initial decision to participate. Of the evaluations that reported retention rates, the range varied between 40% and 87% completion. Program staff were an important influence on a father's decision to participate and complete the program. Fathers reported the importance of feeling supported and encouraged by staff who did not stigmatize them as "deadbeat dads." African American fathers in particular benefited from having staff and group leaders who were from their local community, who were examples of successful fathers, and/or were sensitive to the social and cultural pressures they experienced. Having the opportunity to interact with other men going through similar experiences, whether staff or fellow participants, was generally helpful for many of the fathers included in these studies. The information provided by the program also had an impact on fathers' decisions to continue attending. Many fathers reported that while they wanted to learn about coparenting and fathering, their greatest struggle was centered around how to obtain access to and visitation with their children. Fathers consistently reported that inadequate information and help in these areas was a reason for not completing the programs.

Qualitative Findings

Multiple articles presented qualitative quotes from fathers, mothers, and professionals participating in fatherhood programs. For our analysis, we focused primarily on quotes from fathers that exemplified the five primary outcomes listed above: father involvement, coparenting, parenting, employment and economic well-being, and child support. They reveal strong consistencies.

TEXT BOX 2.2 WHAT FATHERS SAY ABOUT FATHERHOOD PROGRAMS

I don't know, there's a lot of people to help the mom with the kid because she was the one that had the baby…it helps to think that a child needs his father just as much as he needs his mother…It's like…the perfect opportunity to learn more about how you can develop a better relationship with your child.

(Parra-Cardona et al., 2006)

It's great to finally have a program that's nurturing to fathers. You got a lot of programs that's nurturing to mothers. Nothing wrong with it, but in [this community]…there's not really too many programs that cater to fathers, so I found it to be pleasant and great.

(Sandstrom et al., 2015)

The valuable part was that you get a chance to learn how to put up with your baby's mama if you all don't get along, and you learn how to compromise with' em.

(Kotloff, 2005)

They haven't just talked about parenting. I'm learning childcare strategies, getting help with my daughter's addiction. Every one of them is willing to listen.

(Soriano, 2013)

This program gave me something more valuable than getting me a job. They gave me information on how to keep a job…how to work along with other people in my work area and [develop] good relations with these people and respect for my supervisor … Because I always could get a job. I had many jobs over the years but for some reason I always ended up losing 'em. And I learned … that nobody every [sic] fires you … you fire yourself.

(Anderson et al., 2002)

People be calling us deadbeat dads, but I never seen a deadbeat volunteer for anything. Nobody is twisting our arms here. When some of the guys from the program told me that I could have custody of one of my kids, I almost laughed at them. I actually didn't

> know that there were so many people going through what I was going through. I used to sit back and say, man, how in the hell can men even have a chance in court.
>
> *(Roy & Dyson, 2010)*

Father Involvement

Most of the fathers reported greater involvement in their children's lives as well as better quality. As one father put it, "I've become better at learning how to play with my child and teach her how to play and learn at the same time" (Wakabayashi et al., 2011). Fathers reported increased knowledge, skills, and confidence in their abilities to interact in positive ways with their children and further develop their relationships. Another father described how his attitude and behavior toward involvement with his child changed. He stated that the program "taught me more to listen to my kids and pay more attention to them and play with them when they wanna be played with—even if I didn't feel like it. So, it helped me change my attitude towards them" (Anderson et al., 2002).

Many fathers not only learned how to be involved, but they learned that their involvement is important for their children. One father explained how the fathering program helped to change his perspective on the importance of his role as a father. He said,

> I don't know, there's a lot of people to help the mom with the kid because she was the one that had the baby…it helps to think that a child needs his father just as much as he needs his mother…I mean, like there isn't a lot of things out there for teenage fathers…It's all about the mothers…It's like… the perfect opportunity to learn more about how you can develop a better relationship with your child.
>
> *(Parra-Cardona et al., 2006)*

As the fathers learned that their role was important for their children, it inspired them to work harder to be involved in their children's lives. One father stated, "For me it increased my desire to want to be a dad and want to be involved in my child's life despite all the odds" (Sheppard et al., 2004). Overall, fathers learned both how and why they could be more involved with their children. As a result, reports of increased involvement were high among fathers in these programs.

Coparenting

Closely connected to father involvement is the outcome of coparenting. Many quotes from fathers and mothers included statements about both improved father involvement and improved communication between parents. One example of this is a father's statement:

> When [the home visitor] started coming, I was like, I'm starting to realize I'm not doing my job. I'm not being a father. Really just being a bum. It helped me interact with [my son]...If he's crying, I try to solve it. I used to not. I used to be, "[Partner], I don't know what he wants." That's great. I interact with [partner] better...I'll help her if she needs something. We actually sit down, we talk better now.
> *(Sandstrom et al., 2015)*

As he learned what it means to be a father, to be involved with his child, he learned how to better interact with the mother of his child as well. Even for nonresident fathers, they found their relationship with their child's mother improve through the fathering programs. One father said, "The valuable part was that you get a chance to learn how to put up with your baby's mama if you all don't get along, and you learn how to compromise with' em" (Kotloff, 2005). Improved communication quality and frequency helped both resident and nonresident fathers develop better relationships with their child's mother and in turn improve their ability to parent together.

Parenting

A common theme shared by fathers was learning better ways to discipline their children. Many of the fathers talked about how they previously resorted to yelling and violence when they wanted their children to do anything. However, after participating in fathering classes, they learned to be more patient and understanding with their children. As one father explained, "When you have a child, you have to have patience ... Oftentimes, I have to remind myself, even though he's smart, he's still only three" (Sandstrom et al., 2015). The classes also taught fathers to find new ways to discipline and handle their children's behaviors. For example, one father said,

> You ain't got to scream and holler at your kids. You ain't really got to spank them. You take one little thing from them, say like a videogame. You take that from them that's going to make them think "No, I want to play my game. So I know I got to do this here in order for me to get this game." It's like a swap...Usually I be ready to whoop them—I ain't even going to lie—I be ready to whoop them. But now I know another way around it...that I didn't know before I come to these classes.
> *(Holcomb et al., 2015)*

Fathers were not only able to stop their own negative parenting behaviors, but they were also able to replace those behaviors with positive parenting. Through changing their own behaviors, they learned how to better change the behaviors of their children and improve their abilities to properly parent their children.

Employment and Economic Well-Being

The participating fathers often discussed the benefits of learning step by step how to apply for jobs, do interviews, fill out a resume, and even keep the jobs they were offered. One father put it best when he said,

> This program gave me something more valuable than getting me a job. They gave me information on how to keep a job…how to work along with other people in my work area and [develop] good relations with these people and respect for my supervisor … Because I always could get a job. I had many jobs over the years but for some reason I always ended up losing 'em. And I learned … that nobody every [sic] fires you … you fire yourself.
> *(Anderson et al., 2002)*

Although most of the fathers expressed gratitude for the help they received with employment and furthering their career, other fathers felt torn between financially providing for their family and spending time with their children. For example, one father said, "This program has done me a lot of good—it got me back in school, helped me get a job, they're teaching me how to be a better person…except now I don't have that much time to spend with the baby and my girl, you know" (Achatz & MacAllum, 1994). Although the fathers wish they had more time to spend with their children, and some quit school or jobs they received through the program in order to have more time with their children, most of the fathers felt that their economic well-being improved.

Child Support

Most programs assessing child support focused on reducing arrears, modifying existing child support orders, or helping fathers better understand the child support enforcement system. In some cases, the program assessed fathers' satisfaction with the information they were provided but did not directly assess child support payments (see, e.g., Foust, 2007). In other programs minimal weekly payments were required for participation in fatherhood programs; thus, 100% of fathers in the program were making some form of child support payment in order to participate (see, e.g., Davis et al., 2014). The complexities of these distinctions meant that while child support payment activity existed in most programs, arrears balances might also still be growing when those were assessed. It also meant that while fathers could be satisfied with the program and the skills it offered them, participation in the program might not increase their actual child support payments.

These differences in assessments provided mixed results when trying to synthesize across studies. Despite some of these mixed results, many fathers discussed how the fathering program helped them to feel more empowered in the courtroom. One father shared his experience of going to court to have his child support payments dramatically cut down because of the assistance provided by his case worker in the program. Another father emphasized that he did not need a court order to pay child support, saying, "There's no need for that because I'm doin' it on my own. I don't understand why the system do that" (Achatz & MacAllum, 1994). Overall, the qualitative findings pertaining to child support payment were mixed, though there is evidence of fathers feeling empowered by acquiring a greater understanding of their child support situation and the advocacy that program staff provided regardless of their payment status.

Discussion and Implications for Practice

The purpose of this chapter was to systematically synthesize the results of reports previously excluded from a meta-analysis and to increase our understanding of how effective fatherhood programs are at increasing unmarried, low-income, nonresident fathers' positive father involvement, parenting, coparenting, employment/economic prospects, and child support payment.

Our initial meta-analysis demonstrated that fatherhood programs have small but significant effects on father involvement, coparenting, and parenting (Holmes et al., 2020). The current synthesis continues to support those earlier findings with participating fathers exhibiting positive father involvement, coparenting, and parenting improvements. This synthesis also added richness to the meta-analysis by providing participant stories of how meaningful fathering programs can be. Together, our meta-analysis and this synthesis represent a very large body of work on fatherhood programs and their efforts to work with low-income, unmarried, nonresident fathers; combined, these studies represent 62 reports, containing a total of 77 studies. We encourage practitioners who are looking for information on programs, or who are hoping to evaluate their own programs, to explore the list of reports in our reference sections since they represent the result of our exhaustive review of the literature on programs for low-income, nonresident fathers.

Also, though our meta-synthesis could not determine which type of program is more successful than others, it did help us document that a variety of effective program options exist, including formats that are solely educational; solely support-group oriented; or that combine education, support groups, and case management/employment services in some way. Program lengths also varied widely, ranging from four weeks to a year or more. The audience to whom the programs were offered differed, consisting of fathers alone, parents (including fathers and mothers not related to one another), and fathers and their coparenting partners. We hope that presenting all of these options will help program practitioners to consider which options might best suit their interests, the needs of their clients, and the resources available to them. We also encourage researchers to continue to test how program options, program lengths, and the audience to whom the program is offered all impact program outcomes so practitioners can implement the most effective courses.

Though our prior meta-analysis did not demonstrate statistically significant effects in employment/economic prospects and child support payments, this synthesis suggests that efforts to improve employment and economic prospects should continue. Though we could not create an overall effect size that assessed statistical significance, or the magnitude of the effects, our synthesis did demonstrate that fatherhood programs are having a positive impact on employment/economic prospects for unmarried, nonresident, and low-income fathers. Findings for child support payments are still mixed, though qualitative reports clearly demonstrate that even if consistent patterns of payment did not increase, fathers who participated felt they understood their rights and felt they had an advocate to support them in navigating the court system.

As we coded these reports, we once again saw consistent evidence that fathers need help and attention as much as mothers do; they should not be forgotten or neglected. One father's words capture this sentiment well. He said, "It's great to finally have a program that's nurturing to fathers. You got a lot of programs that's nurturing to mothers. Nothing wrong with it, but in [this community] ... there's not really too many programs that cater to fathers, so I found it to be pleasant and great" (Sandstrom et al., 2015). Another father captured the negative stereotype about nonresident or low-income fathers that can be a real barrier when he said, "People be calling us deadbeat dads, but I never seen a deadbeat volunteer for anything. Nobody is twisting our arms here ... I actually didn't know that there were so many people going through what I was going through" (Roy & Dyson, 2010).

It is also evident from our meta-analysis and this current synthesis that fathers can be inspired to improve their fathering, coparenting, and parenting behaviors when they are given the knowledge, tools, and resources to make those changes. As one father said,

> I was gonna be like one of them guys where she be down there and I'll be here, you know, just be like I give money and go see my kid every once in a while, that's the type of view I had...It changed though when I heard the guys in the program talkin' that they got their kids, they're with their kids. I see how it really means something to be with your kid, I mean really be with your kid and girl and try and work it out.
> *(Achatz & MacAllum, 1994)*

Our synthesis also exposed us to other outcomes that future evaluations might consider, including custody and visitation, community involvement, racial and social barriers, social support, fathers' perception of self (e.g., confidence, self-esteem), empathy, anger management, education (e.g., school enrollment, having a GED or high school diploma), masculinity, staff participation, and mother's welfare. Based on individual reports, these appear to be potentially valuable effects of fathering programs worth continued assessment, which would allow future meta-syntheses or meta-analyses to aggregate these effects across multiple studies.

In conclusion, we are encouraged by all of the good work fatherhood programs are currently performing, and we hope this synthesis will provide support and resources for practitioners who want to improve their efforts and evaluate the effectiveness of their programs.

References

*Indicates a study included in the meta-synthesis

*Achatz, M., & MacAllum, C. (1994). *Young unwed fathers: Report from the field*. Public/Private Ventures. https://eric.ed.gov/?id=ED374172.

Administration for Children and Families. (2009). *How to implement promising practices: Peer Guidance from the responsible fatherhood program*. https://www.fatherhood.gov/sites/default/files/resource_files/e000001908.pdf.

Amato, P. R. (2005). The impact of family formation change on the cognitive, social, and emotional well-being of the next generation. *The Future of Children, 15*, 75–96.

Amato, P. R., & Gilbreth, J. G. (1999). Nonresident fathers and children's well-being: A meta-analysis. *Journal of Marriage and the Family, 61*(3), 557–573.

*Anderson, E. A., Kohler, J. K., & Lettiecq, B. L. (2002). Low-income fathers and "responsible fatherhood" programs: A qualitative investigation of participants' experiences. *Family Relations: An Interdisciplinary Journal of Applied Family Studies, 51*(2), 148–155.

Arnold, L. S., & Beelmann, A. (2019). The effects of relationship education in low-income couples: A meta-analysis of randomized-controlled evaluation studies. *Family Relations, 68*, 22–38.

*Aronson, R. E., Whitehead, T. L., & Baber, W. L. (2003). Challenges to masculine transformation among urban low-income African American males. *American Journal of Public Health, 93*(5), 732–741.

*Barthelemy, J. J., & Coakley, T. M. (2017). Fathering attitudes and behaviors among low-income fathers. *Journal of Family Social Work, 20*(5), 399–415.

Carlson, M. J., McLanahan, S., & Brooks-Gunn, J. (2008). Coparenting and nonresident fathers' involvement with young children after a nonmarital birth. *Demography, 45*(2), 461–488.

Cherlin, A. J. (2010). Demographic trends in the United States: A review of research in the 2000s. *Journal of Marriage and Family, 72*, 403–419.

*Davis, L., Pearson, J., & Thoennes, N. (2014). *Building assets for fathers and families in Tennessee: BAFF final report*. Center for Policy Research. https://centerforpolicyresearch.org/wp-content/uploads/TNBAFFF.pdf.

*DeMaria, R., & Isserman, N. (2010). *The executive report: The Philadelphia healthy marriage project*. Care Center of the Advancement of Relationship Education. http://www.frpn.org/file/371/download?token=MzObPBc8.

*Dickinson, J., & Murphy, P. (2000, July 24–26). "Mums and Dads Forever": A cooperative parenting initiative [Conference presentation]. Australian Family Studies Conference, Sydney, Australia. https://webarchive.nla.gov.au/awa/20010122130000/http://www.aifs.org.au/institute/afrc7/papers.html.

Fagan, J. (2008). Randomized study of a prebirth coparenting intervention with adolescent and young fathers. *Family Relations, 57*(3), 309–323.

Fagan, J., Cherson, M., Brown, C., & Vecere, E. (2015). Pilot study of a program to increase mothers' understanding of dads. *Family Process, 54*(4), 581–589.

Fagan, J., & Kaufman, R. (2015). Coparenting relationships among low-income, unmarried parents: Perspectives of fathers in fatherhood programs. *Family Court Review, 53*(2), 304–316.

Fagan, J., & Palkovitz, R. (2011). Coparenting and relationship quality effects on father engagement: Variations by residence, romance. *Journal of Marriage and Family, 73*(3), 637–653.

*Fagan, J., & Stevenson, H. (1995). Men as teachers: A self-help program on parenting for African American men. *Social Work with Groups, 17*(4), 29–42.

Fagan, J., & Stevenson, H. (2002). An experimental study of an empowerment-based intervention for African American Head Start fathers. *Family Relations, 51*(3), 191–198.

*Ferguson, S., & Morley, P. (2011). Improving engagement in the role of father for homeless, noncustodial fathers: A program evaluation. *Journal of Poverty, 15*(2), 206–225.

*Fischer, R. L. (2002). Gaining access to one's children: An evaluation of a visitation program for noncustodial parents. *Families in Society, 83*(2), 163–174.

Florsheim, P., Burrow-Sanchez, J. J., Minami, T., McArthur, L., Heavin, S., & Hudak, C. (2012). Young parenthood program: Supporting positive paternal engagement through coparenting counseling. *American Journal of Public Health, 102*(10), 1886–1892.

*Foust, J. J. (2007). *An evaluation of the fatherhood program at Middle Georgia Technical College* (Publication No. 3245287). [Doctoral dissertation, Capella University]. ProQuest Dissertations Publishing.

*Gearing, R. E., Colvin, G., Popova, S., & Regehr, C. (2008). Remembering fatherhood: Evaluating the impact of a group intervention on fathering. *Journal for Specialists in Group Work, 33*(1), 22–42.

*Hanks, D. E. (1995). *An implementation and evaluation of the curriculum, "taking care", designed to address the needs of young adult and adolescent unwed fathers* (Publication No. 9610502) [Doctoral dissertation, University of Delaware]. ProQuest Dissertations Publishing.

*Holcomb, P., Edin, K., Max, J., Young, A., D'Angelo, A. V., Friend, D., Clary, E., & Johnson, E. J. (2015). *In their own voices: The hopes and struggles of responsible fatherhood program participants in the parents and children together evaluation* (OPRE Report No. 2015-67). U.S. Department of Health and Human Services, Administration for Children and Families, Office of Planning, Research and Evaluation. https://www.acf.hhs.gov/sites/default/files/opre/pact_qualitative_report_6_17_2015_b508_3.pdf.

Holmes, E. K., Galovan, A. M., Yoshida, K., & Hawkins, A. J. (2010). Meta-analysis of the effectiveness of resident fathering programs: Are family life educators interested in fathers? *Family Relations, 59*(3), 240–252.

Holmes, E. K., Egginton, B., Hawkins, A. J., Robbins, N. L., & Shafer, K. (2020). Do responsible fatherhood programs work? A comprehensive meta-analytic study. *Family Relations: An Interdisciplinary Journal of Applied Family Studies, 69*(5), 967–982.

*Kost, K. A. (1997). The effects of support on the economic well-being of young fathers. *Families in Society: The Journal of Contemporary Social Services, 78*(4), 370–382.

*Kotloff, L. J. (2005). *Leaving the street: Young fathers move from hustling to legitimate work.* Public/Private Ventures. https://www.reentry.net/ny/search/item.86017.

*Lanier, P. (2017). *Final evaluation report: Enhancing social support for low-income fathers.* Fatherhood Research and Practice Network. https://www.frpn.org/asset/frpn-grantee-report-enhancing-social-support-low-income-fathers.

*Lewin-Bizan, S. (2015). *24/7 Dad program in Hawai'i: Sample, design, and preliminary results.* Center on the Family. https://cdn2.hubspot.net/hubfs/135704/Program%20Assets/24-7%20Dad/247-Dad-Evaluation-Lewin-Bizan-06102015.pdf.

*Martinson, K., Nightingale, D. S., Holcomb, P. A., Barnow, B. S., & Trutko, J. (2007). *Partners for fragile families demonstration projects: Employment and child support outcomes and trends.* Urban Institute. https://www.urban.org/sites/default/files/publication/46816/411567-Partners-for-Fragile-Families-Demonstration-Projects.PDF.

*McDaniel, M., Simms, M. C., Monson, W., & de Leon, E. (2014) *The CUNY fatherhood academy: A qualitative evaluation.* Urban Institute. https://www.urban.org/sites/default/files/publication/41721/2000109-The-CUNY-Fatherhood-Academy-A-Qualitative-Evaluation.pdf.

McHale, J. P., & Coates, E. E. (2014). Observed coparenting and triadic dynamics in African American fragile families at 3 months' postpartum. *Infant Mental Health Journal, 35*(5), 435–451.

*Mordaunt, E. (2005). *Young fathers project: Evaluation report.* Trust for the Study of Adolescence.

*Parra-Cardona, J. R., Wampler, R. S., & Sharp, E. A. (2006). "Wanting to be a good father": Experiences of adolescent fathers of Mexican descent in a teen fathers program. *Journal of Marital and Family Therapy, 32*(2), 215–231.

*Pearson, J., Davis, L., & Thoennes, N. (2007). *Colorado parenting time/visitation project.* Center for Policy Research. https://centerforpolicyresearch.org/wp-content/uploads/COParentingTimeVisitation.pdf.

Pearson, J., & Fagan, J. (2019). State efforts to support the engagement of nonresident fathers in the lives of their children. *Families in Society, 199*(4), 392–408.

*Pearson, J., & Thoennes, N. (1999). *An evaluation of the parent opportunity project.* Center for Policy Research. https://centerforpolicyresearch.org/wp-content/uploads/POPFINAL.pdf.

*Pearson, J., Thoennes, N., Davis, L., Venohr, J., Price, D., & Griffith, T. (2003). *OCSE responsible fatherhood programs: Client characteristics and program outcomes.* Center for Policy Research. https://www.frpn.org/asset/ocse-responsible-fatherhood-programs-client-characteristics-and-program-outcomes.

*Roy, K. M., & Dyson, O. (2010). Making daddies into fathers: Community-based fatherhood programs and the construction of masculinities for low-income African American men. *American Journal of Community Psychology, 45*(1/2), 139–154.

*Saleh, M. F., Buzi, R. S., Weinman, M. L., & Smith, P. B. (2005). The nature of connections: Young fathers and their children. *Adolescence, 40*(159), 513–523.

*Sandstrom, H., Gearing, M., Peters, H. E., Heller, C., Healy, O. & Pratt, E. (2015). *Approaches to father engagement and father's experiences in home visiting programs* (OPRE Report 2105-103). Office of Planning, Research and Evaluation, Administration for Children and Families, US Department of Health and Human Services. https://www.acf.hhs.gov/sites/default/files/opre/20151130_fahv_report_finalized_b508.pdf.

*Schock, A. M. (2002). *Father participation in family-based programming: The sample case of a program targeting at-risk adolescents* (Publication No. 3039521) [Doctoral dissertation, Ohio State University]. ProQuest Dissertations Publishing.

*Schroeder, D., Looney, S., & Schexnayder, D. (2004). *Impacts of workforce services for young, low-income fathers: Findings from the Texas bootstrap project*. Ray Marshall Center for the Study of Human Resources. https://raymarshallcenter.org/files/2004/10/Bootstrap_Final_Impacts.pdf.

*Schroeder, D., Walker, K., & Khan, A. (2011). *Non-custodial parent choices PEER pilot: Impact report*. Ray Marshall Center for the Study of Human Resources. https://raymarshallcenter.org/files/2005/07/NCP_Choices_PEER_Sep2011final.pdf.

*Scourfield, J., Allely, C., Coffey, A., & Yates, P. (2016). Working with fathers of at-risk children: Insights from a qualitative process evaluation of an intensive group-based intervention. *Children and Youth Services Review, 69*, 259–267.

*Sheppard, V. B., Sims-Boykin, S. D., Zambrana, R. E., & Adams, I. (2004). Low-income African American fathers' perceptions and experiences in a fatherhood support program. *Journal of Applied Sociology, 21*(1), 30–50.

*Smith, L. A. (1989). *Windows on opportunities: An exploration in program development for black adolescent fathers* (Publication No. 9009784) [Doctoral dissertation, City University of New York]. ProQuest Dissertations Publishing.

*Sorensen, E. S. (2011). *New York initiative helps fathers increase their earnings and child support payments*. Urban Institute. https://www.urban.org/sites/default/files/publication/26681/412443-New-York-Initiative-Helps-Fathers-Increase-Their-Earnings-and-Child-Support.PDF.

*Soriano, J. (2013). *Program evaluation of family enhancement programming*. (Publication No. 3365423) [Doctoral dissertation]. Adler University. ProQuest Dissertations Publishing.

Tollestrup, J. (2018). *Fatherhood initiatives: Connecting fathers to their children*. Congressional Research Service. https://fas.org/sgp/crs/misc/RL31025.pdf.

*Turbiville, V. P., & Marquis, J. G. (2001). Father participation in early education programs. *Topics in Early Childhood Special Education, 21*(4), 223.

*Wakabayashi, T., Guskin, K. A., Watson, J., McGilly, K., & Klinger, L. L., Jr. (2011). *The parents as teachers promoting responsible fatherhood project: Evaluation of "Dads in the Mix," an exemplary site*. Parents as Teachers. https://www.fatherhood.gov/sites/default/files/resource_files/e000002466.pdf.

Zaveri, H., Baumgartner, S., Dion, R., & Clary, L. (2015). *Parents and Children Together: Design and implementation of responsible fatherhood programs* (OPRE Report 2105-76). U.S. Department of Health and Human Services, Administration for Children and Families, Office of Planning, Research and Evaluation. https://www.acf.hhs.gov/sites/default/files/opre/pact_initial_rf_implementation_report_9_11_15_508b.pdf.

3

DOES CURRICULUM MATTER? A RANDOMIZED CONTROL STUDY OF THE "DEVELOPING ALL DADS FOR MANHOOD AND PARENTING PROGRAM (DAD MAP)" CURRICULUM

Bright Sarfo and Vernon Wallace

Rationale for the Study

Although social service organizations have made efforts to address challenges faced by low-income fathers, there are many questions that remain unanswered in the fatherhood field. First, few approaches to working with fathers have been rigorously tested, leaving questions about their efficacy in improving outcomes. Second, structured curricula have not been compared to other fatherhood program approaches that use a free-flowing, open group format where fathers receive services that emphasize peer group relationships rather than those designed to build skills and knowledge. These unstructured programs are widely used by many fatherhood programs and operate much like a support group, allowing fathers to identify the topics of discussion and express any experiences they wish to share. Although support group formats are often popular and can be helpful for getting fathers to engage in group activities, it is unknown if these methods of engaging fathers are any more or less effective at reaching outcomes than fatherhood programs that include a structured component to their approach.

Description of the Current Study

The current study describes the results of an impact study testing the *Developing All Dads for Manhood and Parenting(DAD MAP)* curriculum, which is used by the Baltimore Responsible Fatherhood Program (BRFP) at The Center for Urban Families (CFUF).[1] CFUF is a community-based organization located in Baltimore, MD. CFUF serves Baltimore residents by providing an array of services aimed at empowering low-income families. CFUF services include case management as well as employment readiness, healthy relationship education, and fatherhood workshops. CFUF's programs generally aim to improve families by enhancing the ability of men and women to be strong sources of support for their families. The BRFP is a three-month program designed to strengthen families by empowering fathers with the skills, knowledge, attitudes, and opportunities necessary to become better parents. BRFP integrates case management with curriculum-driven workshops. The *DAD MAP* curriculum was developed by a team of researchers and practitioners and includes skill development, guided discussion, and interactive activities to promote responsible parenting and healthy relationships among fathers. CFUF created the *DAD MAP* curriculum based on their experience working in low-income African American communities in the city of Baltimore.

The *DAD MAP* curriculum is representative of a common method of implementing best practices for fatherhood group formats (National Responsible Fatherhood Clearinghouse, 2013). Specifically, it addresses four key challenging areas for fathers: promoting father economic and emotional support of children; emphasizing healthy relationship skills building; and including opportunities and discussion around job searching and the development of soft skills such as interviewing for a job or communicating in the employment setting. Fatherhood programs provided in groups allow for peer learning and can provide fathers with an opportunity to identify common struggles in a safe environment. This method of program delivery, when provided in an open group format, can also be less expensive than one-on-one parental education interventions, and more convenient for fathers—who are juggling multiple demands.

The current study aims to answer the following research questions:

1. To what extent are changes in fatherhood outcomes associated with participation in the *DAD MAP* curriculum compared to enrollment in an unstructured support group among low-income fathers?
2. What is the extent to which impacts associated with participating in groups that use the curriculum versus an unstructured format vary for participants with different levels of employment status, criminal background, coparenting relationship quality, income, and attendance?

Method

Implementation of the *DAD MAP* evaluation began in April 2015, with recruitment ending in May 2017. The study was conducted using a randomized experimental design in which fathers were randomly assigned to either 1) the treatment group which received the *DAD MAP* curriculum workshops, or 2) the control group that received the unstructured peer-led support group instead of the *DAD MAP* curriculum. IRB approval for this study was provided by Temple University.

Participants were fathers who enrolled in BRFP during the study period, were at least 18 years old, and reported having children under the age of 12. Fathers who were eligible for the study and expressed interest in participating in the fatherhood program were consented to be in the study by a responsible fatherhood specialist. Participants were recruited from external community-based agencies serving men and fathers as well as internal CFUF programs such as the employment initiative known as STRIVE. BRFP staff also used street recruitment strategies, such as posting literature describing the program in barbershops, convenience stores, and other local businesses. Finally, BRFP staff recruited fathers from the local child support offices by distributing literature and collecting contact information from walk-ins.

Fathers who sought services from CFUF were instructed to complete an application form that asked fathers for basic information, including demographics and an indication of which services they were interested in receiving. Fathers who indicated an interest in receiving fatherhood services were directed to a responsible fatherhood specialist, who provided case management and implemented *DAD MAP* workshops for the BRFP.

These fatherhood specialists screened applicants to ensure they were fathers who were 18 years old or older before explaining the study procedures. Fathers were then randomly assigned to either a treatment group of fathers participating in *DAD MAP* curriculum sessions or a peer-led support group.

We contacted fathers by phone to complete two follow-up surveys at three and six months after enrollment. The follow-up surveys were conducted by a research assistant, and fathers' responses were entered in the MIS system by a responsible fatherhood specialist. Fathers in the control group were not permitted to enroll in the treatment condition until after they had either completed their six-month follow-up assessment or after the window to complete the six-month follow-up survey had closed.

Research Groups

The *DAD MAP* curriculum contains four modules, with each one corresponding to one of the four key objectives of the *DAD MAP* curriculum. Each topical module contains four curriculum sessions exploring different subtopics for a total of 16 sessions. Each session is delivered in 60–90 minutes, beginning with a group welcome activity and ending with fathers sharing key concepts they have learned during the session. The curriculum is delivered in an open group format, with rolling enrollment allowing fathers to join the group at any time during the four modules. Fathers who enroll late are expected to continue attending with a new cohort after their original cohort ends to receive material they missed. See Figure 3.1 for an example of a welcome activity and Figure 3.2 for an example of elements relating specifically to the target population.

The unstructured, peer-led support group, unlike the treatment group, covered a range of topics that were not addressed in the *DAD MAP* curriculum. Rather than include specific topics on parenting, healthy relationships, or employment

THE D.A.D. M.A.P

RESPONSIBLE FATHERHOOD SESSION 2

FATHERHOOD PLEDGE

For instance Handout A2-3 corresponds to the third handout for session 2 of module 1.
Each handout is also appropriately titled to aid in identification.
I am a man.
My roots run deep and embrace the earth
My spirit flows free through the universe.

The divine intelligence has touched me
And the sacred seeds grow in the fields of heaven.
I am blessed because I am potent.
I am blessed because I am virile.
I am blessed because I am earning the secrets of love.

May my energy be increased for fatherhood!
May my heart be more loving for fatherhood!
May my thoughts be wise for fatherhood!
May my health be protected for fatherhood!
May my work be fulfilling for fatherhood!
May my senses be sharpened for fatherhood!
May my mind become deeper for fatherhood!

Now, so my sons and daughters know and respect my name,
So the work of my hands shall bless our table and strengthen our roof,
So the mother is assured that she is not alone on the long road,
I pledge and vow to think and act and strive to be the kind of father my ancestors will be proud to see.
When I show them our children, bright strong healthy and free.

So I say
And so you have heard.
Let my deeds be testimony
To the power of the word.
Ashe.

FIGURE 3.1 Fatherhood Pledge call-and-repeat handout from the *DAD MAP* curriculum

facilitated by a fatherhood specialist, control group members chose the topic of discussion while a part-time staff person guided the group discussion and enforced group rules emphasizing respect for other members, participation, and confidentiality. The staff person was instructed to refrain from engaging in any instruction associated with skill development in parenting, communication, anger management, or workforce readiness. Furthermore, staff guiding the unstructured support group was not trained in the *DAD MAP* curriculum. The staff person did not provide guidance on the topic of the day and allowed fathers the freedom to

ENHANCING EMPLOYABILITY OVERVIEW SESSION 1

"In Their Eyes"

The growing emphasis on soft skills already disadvantages black male job applicants, and will continue to do so. This is because many employers see black men as lacking in precisely the skills that they consider increasingly important.
What's behind the employers' views of black men?
Stereotypes about Black men based in American racism.

- Cultural gap between the middle-class, mailny White culture in which most employers live their lives and the low-income, Black male culture that employers see in the media and in their travels through the Inner Cities.
- Contact with low-skilled Black men who have shown they are less-educated than the type of people employers are looking to hire.
- Media portrayals of a Thug-Gangsta lifestyle based on crime and drugs and dominated by Black males who speak aggressively and advocate violence.
- Previous experience with Black males who proved to be "difficult to control" in the workplace.
- The Black male speech pattern that includes a lot of slang and expresses low communication skills in Standard English.
- A perception that the Black male "has a chip on gis shoulder" and a "sense of entitlement" to something he has not earned by his work.
- Low motivation among Black male employees as shown by their lazy attitudes, hostility to take on assignments, disregard for completing tasks well and on time, and lacking pride in their own work.

FIGURE 3.2 Handout outlining perceptions White employers may have about low-income Black men

talk in a nonjudgmental environment. Although the groups were open and unstructured, staff took attendance and held fathers to the same attendance standards as fathers enrolled in the treatment group. The staff was instructed to provide a summary of what was discussed in the unstructured peer-led support groups and reported to researchers how the groups operated.

Measures

To assess study outcomes, several items and subscales were included in the baseline, three-month, and six-month follow-up surveys administered to fathers, including father involvement, coparenting relationship quality, child well-being, and workforce participation/job seeking. This study used *The Father Engagement Scale*, which includes two subscales measuring *Parental Care* and *Parental Support*. The items in this scale ask about parenting behaviors targeted to the father's youngest child in the last 30 days using a 5-point scale ranging from *never* to *very often* (Dyer, Kaufman, et al., 2018).

Informal and formal child support provided by the father were assessed by asking participants to report the degree to which they have contributed resources towards the care of their children. We asked fathers seven questions assessing the degree to which they have contributed towards the purchase of various items for their youngest child in the last 30 days (e.g., food, clothing, school supplies, toys). We asked fathers to indicate the frequency of their contribution on a scale ranging from 0 = *never* to 3 = *often* for six items. We also asked fathers to report the dollar amount of contributions they made and whether it included formal child support payments. The questionnaire also included an item asking fathers whether they had children for which they made no contribution.

Survey items also included questions regarding how many nights fathers have spent with any of their children in a typical week in the last 30 days as well as how many days they spent with the father's youngest child (the focal child) in the last 30 days.

We measured coparenting cooperation using the *Coparenting Relationship Scale* with items assessed on a 5-point "agree" to "disagree" Likert scale (Dyer, Fagan, et al., 2018). Although listed as an outcome, coparenting cooperation was also explored as a moderator. This scale includes three subscales measuring concepts of "alliance," "undermining," and "gatekeeping". Child well-being was measured using the *Brief Infant Toddler Social & Emotional Assessment* (BITSEA) scale and the *Behavioral Problems Checklist* (BPC) (Briggs-Gowan et al., 2004; O'Malley & Qualls, 2016). We used three items to assess attempts to pursue employment. We asked fathers how often they engaged in employment-seeking behaviors in the last 90 days, such as filling out applications, attending job interviews, or submitting a resume. Fathers indicated whether they had engaged in behaviors to pursue employment "sometimes," "rarely," or "never," with higher scores indicating greater frequency of pursuits.

To assess the effectiveness of the *DAD MAP* curriculum, we compared outcomes at three- and six-month follow-up (controlling for baseline measures of outcomes) from those receiving the *DAD MAP* curriculum sessions and those in the unstructured control group, whether they completed/attended the program or not. We used ANOVA models comparing group differences on each individual measure.

Results

See Table 3.1 for the distribution of baseline characteristics for study participants. In total there were 164 fathers included in the analysis, with 89 fathers in the treatment group and 75 in the control group. The average age of the fathers was approximately 35 years. Fathers identified predominantly as African American/Black (96%). A majority of fathers had at least a high school education (68%),

TABLE 3.1 Baseline Characteristics for Total Sample and Study Groups

	Total N = 164	Treatment n = 89	Control group n = 75	p-value
Age mean (SD)	35.2 (8.5)	34.5 (8.2)	36 (9)	.57
Race				.29
• African American	96.3%	97.8%	93.8%	
• Non-African American	3.6%	2.2%	2.5%	
Education				.69
• Less than high school	33%	30.3%	33.3%	
• High school or GED	39%	39.3%	40.7%	
• Some college/tech	23.7%	25.8%	21%	
• Associates or four-year degree	4.2%	4.5%	4.5%	
Housing				.72
• Own home/apartment	25.6%	28.09%	23.46%	
• In a relative's home/apartment	42%	41.57%	44.44%	
• Intimate partner's home	18%	16.85%	20.99%	
• Someone else's home/apartment	5.3%	4.49%	7.41%	
• Transitional housing	5.3%	6.74%	7.41%	
• On the streets or other	1.2%	2.24%	0	
Economic stability				
• Employed	24.4%	23.86%	25.93%	.68
• Income > $400/month	29.8%	25.84%	35.80	.22
• Any monthly income	44%	40.45%	50.62%	.25
Number of children mean (SD)	2.4 (1.72)	2.70 (1.72)	2.26 (1.63)	.09
Nights spent with any of your children in a typical week mean (SD)	4.28 (2.9)	4.24 (2.99)	4.44 (2.85)	.67
Days spent at least one hour with focal child in the last 30 days mean (SD)	14.04 (12.78)	15.05 (13.04)	12.91 (12.47)	.32
Lives with any of his children	39.02%	42.69%	34.67%	.29
Parental Care subscale score	27.86 (14.46)	29.05 (15.57)	26.44 (15.31)	.28
Parental Support subscale score	7.84 (3.94)	7.2 (4.09)	8.3 (3.74)	.06
Informal child support contribution score	9.58 (5.67)	10.28 (5.55)	8.8 (5.73)	.09
Total $ spent on child in last 30 days	$241 (297.35)	$270 (345.78)	$206 (224.42)	.18

with few fathers having less than (33%) or greater than a high school diploma or GED (27%). The largest group of fathers reported they were living in a relative's home or apartment most of the time in the last 30 days (42%) while a majority of remaining father lived in their own apartment or home (26%) or in an intimate partner's home or apartment (18%). Only about a quarter of fathers reported being employed at baseline, with most of these fathers (89%) working on the books with recorded compensation. Over half of fathers reported having no income in the last 30 days (55%), with just under a third reporting incomes over $400 per month from all sources in the past 30 days.[2] The average monthly income from all sources was approximately $450 a month. No significant differences were observed between the control group or treatment group on the demographic variables assessed for this study.

Most fathers were nonresident, with just under 40% reporting that they lived with at least one child. Fathers tended to have more than one child, and when asked how many nights they spent with their children in a typical week, fathers reported spending about four nights in a typical week with their child on average. When asked how many days in the last 30 days they spent with their youngest child, fathers shared that they spent 15 days with the focal child on average. Bivariate analyses comparing treatment and control group characteristics did not suggest any significant differences on these measures at baseline.

Results indicated that participants had relatively low attendance in the peer-led support group and *DAD MAP* workshops. Fathers who were randomized to the *DAD MAP* curriculum condition attended about a quarter of all sessions at roughly 3 of 12 sessions, while those in the control group attended approximately 4 sessions on average. Approximately 95 fathers out of the 164 fathers participating in the program completed at least one session. There were no significant dosage differences between the treatment or control on any of CFUF programs, including the BRFP.

Impacts on Fatherhood Engagement Measures

See Table 3.2 for a summary of key outcome differences between the treatment and control groups on fatherhood engagement. The results indicated that fathers in the *DAD MAP* group scored significantly higher than fathers in the support group at the three-month follow-up on the following measures: Parental Support, nights spent with children in a typical week, and money spent on children in the last 30 days. There was also a trend for *DAD MAP* fathers to self-report making more informal child support contributions than fathers in the support group. It is important to note that the effect sizes for Parental Support, nights spent with children in a typical week, and money spent on children in the last 30 days, while significant, were small. Fathers in the *DAD MAP* group did not score significantly higher than fathers in the support group on any of these measures at the six-month follow-up, although there was a trend for *DAD MAP* fathers to report spending more money on children in the last 30 days and to self-report providing more informal support.

Analyses examining treatment effects on employment, job application completion, resume submission, job searching, coparenting cooperation, and child behavior problems or emotional symptoms at three-month and six-month follow-up, did not yield any significant *DAD MAP* impacts. In other words,

TABLE 3.2 Treatment Group Effects on Fatherhood Engagement at Three- and Six-Month Follow-Up

3 Month Follow-Up	Treatment n = 52 Mean (SD)	Control n = 42 Mean (SD)
Parental Care Subscale Score	19.99 (19.98)	17.21 (18.92)
Parental Support Subscale Score	6.50 (4.96)	3.89 (5.15)*
Nights spent with children in a typical week	4.55 (2.94)	3.16 (2.98)*
Days spent at least one hour with focal child	14.94 (13.18)	11 (12.42)
Informal child support contribution score	12.48 (4.84)	10.45 (5.77)†
Total $ spent on child in last 30 days	$273.69 (246.55)	$173.69 (213)*
6 Month Follow-Up	Treatment n = 43 Mean (SD)	Control n = 35 Mean (SD)
Parental Care subscale score	17.67 (16.74)	18.57 (18.61)
Parental Support subscale score	5.55 (5.11)	5.54 (5.15)
Nights spent with children in a typical week	4.02 (3.0)	4.32 (12.84)
Informal child support contribution score	12.53 (5.08)	10.06 (6.33)†
Total $ spent on child in last 30 days	316.79 (329.54)	206.28 (156.63)†

†$p < .10$ *$p < .05$

fathers in the group exposed to the *DAD MAP* curriculum and fathers who participated in the support group exhibited similar outcomes in reported behaviors concerning employment and engagement in a variety of job search activities at the three- and six-month follow-up data collection time points. In addition, the effect of the *DAD MAP* curriculum was not significantly different from the effect of the support group on fathers' reports of child behavior problems or emotional symptoms.

Subgroup Analysis

We examined whether the effects of *DAD MAP* on the outcome measures were influenced by fathers' reported number of times arrested, BRFP attendance, employment status, residence with coparent, coparenting alliance scores, and income. The findings (see final report for details, Sarfo, 2018) showed that *DAD MAP* fathers scored significantly higher on coparenting alliance subscales at three month follow-up when they reported higher income at baseline.

Our analyses did not show that the effects of the two interventions on coparenting, employment, and father engagement outcomes were influenced by lifetime arrests or level of attendance in the program.

Discussion and Conclusion

The current study examined whether participation in the *DAD MAP* curriculum was associated with improvements in key outcomes associated with father involvement, coparenting relationship quality, and job-seeking behavior. We also examined whether any observed impacts differed for fathers with various characteristics, including criminal justice involvement, initial coparenting relationship quality, employment status, and income. Findings yielded from this study hold implications for practice and ongoing evaluation and research.

Improvements in Parental Support and time spent with children are consistent with the content delivered in the *DAD MAP* curriculum, which emphasizes the importance of encouragement in the development of children. Module 2 of the *DAD MAP* curriculum, which emphasizes fatherhood and parenting, focuses particularly on using encouragement as a method of teaching children. The module also reviews short- and long-term effects of fathers spending more time with their children, emphasizing that even fathers with few resources can have a strong impact on the lives of their sons and daughters when parents are consistently present. The results support the program theory of the BRFP in general, which assumes that fathers will modify their behavior to achieve positive parenting outcomes learned in the curriculum.

The absence of significant impacts on some outcomes in general may have also been a result of low treatment differential regarding the supportive services available to fathers enrolled in the study. While the *DAD MAP* and unstructured support group were quite different, members of both groups had access to a case manager that is considered one of the main sources of support for fathers participating in the BRFP. If fathers demonstrated a need in any area of fatherhood engagement associated with getting parenting time, parental rights, or mediation services to form a legal agreement with the coparent, a responsible fatherhood specialist was there to provide assistance.

Results did not suggest program impacts on any dimensions of the childhood well-being measures. The absence of observable impacts on childhood well-being measures may be explained in several ways. One possibility is that fathers may not be able to recognize the specific behavioral symptoms in their focal child that the assessments were referring to. The *DAD MAP* curriculum does not emphasize noticing and diagnosing behaviors in children. A majority of fathers did not live with their children and may not have had sufficient opportunities to recognize negative behavioral anomalies or patterns within their youngest child. Future studies may benefit from collecting secondary sources of information, perhaps from the coparent, assessing changes in the child's behavior as a function of the father's participation in fatherhood programs.

Findings from the current study did not suggest evidence of *DAD MAP* effects on coparenting cooperation. This finding was not surprising given the structure of the curriculum and the method used to improve coparenting relationship quality. Specifically, the curriculum is designed to improve interpersonal, communication, and anger management skills to help the father manage challenges he is having with his coparent rather than prioritize improving the relationship. For instance, activities and discussion around healthy relationships may encourage fathers to walk away from conflicts when feelings of anger arise in order to prevent any negative repercussions associated with allowing arguments or fights to escalate. Although this may prevent severe conflicts from taking place, it may not necessarily improve the quality of the coparenting relationship in all cases. For instance, the father's coparent may continue to engage in undermining or gate keeping behaviors despite the father's attempts at using the interpersonal, communication, and anger management skills learned in *DAD MAP* sessions. Effects on coparenting outcomes may also be improved if the program engaged mothers as well as fathers. It is also not clear whether fathers attended the sessions on healthy relationship skills, and coparenting is not a topic that blends as easily into the other modules of the *DAD MAP* as parenting topics do. Given the low rate of program attendance, it is also reasonable to assume that many fathers were not exposed to the healthy relationship skills that were presented in only 4 of the 16 *DAD MAP* sessions. To contrast, parenting and responsible fatherhood topics are covered exclusively in half the total curriculum sessions and are consistently brought into the discussions of the remaining curriculum. With that said, there may be a more complicated path between exposure to coparenting skills and reports of relationship improvements that is not captured in the current study. Future studies may benefit from assessing whether fathers learn the skills presented in the curriculum and measure the frequency with which they attempt to implement new behaviors with a coparent.

Limitations

Although the current study used a rigorous randomized control design to assess program impacts, the results should be interpreted with caution. One factor that may have had an impact on fathers in the *DAD MAP* and the informal support group is the case management that fathers in both groups received at CFUF. Information on the degree of case management each father received was unknown, and accurate methods of capturing this data were not available at the time of the current study. Case managers could have assisted fathers in a variety of ways, ranging from expunging criminal records, to connecting fathers to mental health services or contacting the coparent on the father's behalf in an effort to mediate conflicts. The tasks performed by case managers can be difficult to quantify and are often not collected beyond entering case notes in narrative form. It would be valuable to also get some idea as to the extent to which *DAD MAP* discussion may have informed how fathers interacted and sought assistance from case managers. For instance, fathers may learn of a variety of child support payment programs through their discussions in the *DAD MAP* groups, and in turn, inquire about such services from their case managers. Knowledge gained in a session may alter service-seeking behavior, which can improve a host of key outcomes among fathers. In a similar fashion, case management may have afforded to fathers in the informal support group opportunities for assistance that reduced the differences in outcomes between the two groups observed in this study.

Another limitation lies in the treatment–control contrast that was limited only to the curriculum sessions. While fathers in the treatment and control groups experienced vastly different topics of discussion in their respective groups, all other services received as a part of the BRFP were uniform across research participants. Thus, in addition to receiving case management from a trained responsible fatherhood specialist, all participating fathers in both groups developed services plans and had opportunities to participate in family events and activities sponsored by CFUF. The current study was unable to fully assess the effectiveness of the BRFP program as a whole. Future studies would greatly benefit from gaining a full understanding of the impacts of other crucial aspects of fatherhood programs that go beyond curricula and target case management and other methods of engagement and retention.

As with many studies and program initiatives with vulnerable populations, attrition was high, and there was a great degree of drop off between baseline and three-month follow-up survey data collection. Given the length of the *DAD MAP* curriculum workshops, there are several points at which a father may have been lost to follow-up. The average attendance was low, with 68 out of the 164 (41%) failing to attend any curriculum or unstructured support groups at all. The staff report some reasons behind poor attendance, including the multitude of financial, employment, and social barriers participating fathers often face that makes a parenting program like the *DAD MAP* and its research-related tasks much less of a priority. As the report shows, a large proportion of fathers have had frequent interactions with the criminal justice systems and have had virtually no income in the 30 days prior to enrollment. Adverse events like arrest or incarceration may not only discourage fathers from continuing with fatherhood programs but can be a physical barrier to participating in any social service program. CFUF staff have attempted to address this problem in a number of ways, including offering incentives for perfect attendance each month, and have now moved to provide such incentives for every four sessions attended. CFUF has also engaged in previous efforts to visit the homes of fathers when they have failed to show for several sessions in a row. Although attrition was high, the analysis did not suggest any difference in participation rates between the treatment and control condition, which provides evidence against any potential participation bias.

We also acknowledge that our measures of informal and formal child support payments relied fully on self-reports, which may not always be accurate. Future studies may benefit from collecting child support payment history from local administrative data sources.

Implication for Practice

Results from the current study suggest that fatherhood programs using a group-based approach with structured activities and discussion aimed at helping fathers understand the impact of their decision making on their child's lives can result in changes in behavior. Specifically, changes in parenting behavior associated with praise and encouragement can be gleaned from peer discussion and guided group interaction focusing on the benefits of parental support on children. Fathers, in particular, may have some challenges around this dimension of parenting as it may be associated more with mothering and be less normative among men in general. While providing parental care may seem essential to most adults, providing signals of love and encouragement to children may seem less intuitive. Fatherhood programs that incorporate messages that emphasize the importance of support may observe changes in outcomes in an area where fathers have room for improvement. Results from the current study also suggest that messaging associated with the importance of providing informal child support can still be effective, even for low-income fathers. The *DAD MAP* curriculum not only emphasizes the importance of providing support but also provides tools and strategies for budgeting and managing funds to make room for contributions to the development of one's child.

The lack of program effects on coparental subscale scores supports the need for efficacious approaches to address the interpersonal challenges faced by fathers attempting to work with their coparents. Although the *DAD MAP* curriculum includes topics to help fathers address the conflicts of their coparenting relationships and builds skills around anger management and communication, such efforts may not work unless the coparent is able to build skills with the father. Improvement in interpersonal relationships often requires a systems-level intervention that focuses on behavioral changes of both parties. Fathers may learn skills to communicate effectively with their coparent, but if their coparent is not learning the skills to effectively work with the father, then the skills participants pick up may be ineffective in practice. Moreover, facilitators and instructors may not understand the full circumstances associated with coparenting conflict when the perspective of the coparent is often absent. Crucial information that may inform effective methods of intervening may be missing when the facilitator is not able to verify or expand upon any information provided by participating fathers concerning coparenting challenges. Addressing coparenting challenges can be especially difficult with coparents who are romantically involved with new partners. Designing and implementing coparenting interventions will necessarily come with challenges, but such programs could fill a deep void in the field of fatherhood, especially when it comes to nonmarried, low-income parental dyads.

In an effort to build a systems-level approach to fatherhood, specifically with interventions aimed at the quality of parenting or coparenting relationship quality, CFUF has brought in a mother engagement specialist to assist with the BRFP initiative. In cases where responsible fatherhood specialists identify a father is having challenges with his coparent, they refer the client to the mother engagement specialist, who will assist the father in a multi-stage process towards improving his relationship with the coparent or at least building a functional relationship between the two. These mother engagement specialists use coaching and feedback and may engage the mother to help communicate on the father's behalf.

Fatherhood programs also may need to adopt other practices to improve outcomes associated with child well-being. For example, they may benefit from including children and coparents in sessions and providing fathers with opportunities to learn and practice parenting skills with members of their families in dyads or groups. Facilitators may in turn provide real-time feedback to fathers based on observations rather than second-hand reports. For instance, MDRC is currently testing a program with fathers with young children that includes a play session component where fathers interact with their child based on lessons learned in an initial parent training activity (Manno et al., 2019). Fathers then receive feedback based on observations made during the play session. This approach can expose strengths and/or weaknesses in parenting that fathers would otherwise be unable to express or recognize and can represent a powerful teaching tool for facilitators.

A great deal of work remains in improving the approaches to fatherhood programs. Programs can still benefit from improving areas of retention, recruitment, and implementation. Researchers and practitioners should prioritize rigorous evaluations to identify best practices and approaches to yield benefits for children, fathers, and families.

Notes

1 Learn more about CFUF at www.cfuf.org.
2 Sources included public benefits, money from friends and relatives, and panhandling.

References

Briggs-Gowan, M. J., Carter, A. S., Irwin, J. R., Wachtel, K., & Cicchetti, D. V. (2004). The Brief Infant-Toddler Social and Emotional Assessment: Screening for social-emotional problems and delays in competence. *Journal of Pediatric Psychology, 29*(2), 143–155.

Dyer, J., Fagan, J., Pearson, J., & Cabrera, N. (2018). Self-perceived coparenting of nonresident fathers: Scale development and validation. *Family Process Institute, 57*(4), 927–946.

Dyer, J., Kaufman, R., Fagan, J., & Cabrera, N. (2018). A measure of father engagement for nonresident fathers. *Family Relations, 67*(3), 1–18.

Manno, M., Mancini, P., & O'Herron, C. (2019). *Implementing an innovative parenting program for fathers: Findings from the B3 study* (OPRE Report 2019-111). U.S. Department of Health and Human Services, Administration for Children and Families, Office of Planning Research, and Evaluation. https://www.acf.hhs.gov/sites/default/files/opre/innovative_parenting_b3_findings_dec_2019.pdf.

National Responsible Fatherhood Clearinghouse. (2013). *Responsible fatherhood toolkit: Resources from the field*. U.S. Department of Health and Human Services. https://www.fatherhood.gov/sites/default/files/resource_files/e000002752.pdf.

O'Malley, K., & Qualls, S. H. (2016). Development and preliminary examination of the psychometric properties of the Behavior Problem Checklist. *Clinical Gerontologist, 39*, 263–281.

Sarfo, B. (2018). *Final evaluation report: The DAD MAP evaluation*. Fatherhood Research and Practice Network. https://www.frpn.org/asset/frpn-grantee-report-the-dad-map-evaluation-randomized-controlled-trial-culturally-tailored.

4

FACTORS ASSOCIATED WITH FATHERHOOD PROGRAM EFFECTIVENESS

A Randomized Controlled Trial of TYRO Dads

Young-Il Kim, Sung Joon Jang, and Brenda J. Oyer

Rationale for the Study

Historically, it was thought that mothers were more important in their children's lives than fathers. Now, the growing cultural consensus, as well as the scholarly view, is that fathers are just as important in their children's lives as mothers (LaRossa, 1988). Fathers today are expected to provide not only financial, but also emotional support for their children (Cabrera et al., 2000). Some fathers from economically disadvantaged backgrounds, however, have difficulty in meeting these expectations. Besides economic hardship, these fathers have many barriers to effective fathering, including incarceration, not co-residing with their children and their children's mother, and physical and mental health problems (Coley, 2001).

In an attempt to help fathers who face these challenges, the U.S. government has allocated federal dollars to fatherhood programs across the nation. One of them is TYRO Dads, a 20-hour class delivered by trained facilitators in ten 2-hour sessions over five weeks. Since 2006, it has been run by The RIDGE Project based in McClure, Ohio. Despite its decade-long history, it has never been rigorously evaluated as to its effectiveness in achieving its goal—teaching participants to take responsibility for their actions and to become responsible fathers (The RIDGE Project, n.d.). Accordingly, we evaluated the effectiveness of the TYRO Dads program by conducting a randomized controlled trial, where we randomly assigned some of the program participants to take the class (intervention group) and others, not to take the class (control group). By comparing the outcomes of these two groups, we were able to determine whether TYRO Dads generated positive outcomes for participants.

> **TEXT BOX 4.1 THE RIDGE PROJECT—BUILDING A LEGACY OF STRONG FAMILIES**
>
> At The RIDGE Project, we believe strong families produce strong and healthy children who will then pass that legacy on to future generations. We are in the business of rescuing families who others have deemed disposable. theridgeproject.com

Description of Current Study

The current study has three objectives. First, we evaluate the effectiveness of TYRO Dads by looking at fathers' satisfaction with parenting and the frequency of father–child activities. We expect that, to the extent that TYRO Dads is successful in helping the fathers become more responsible, fathers who took the class (intervention group) will feel more satisfied with their parenting and be more involved in their child's life than those who did not (control group). This hypothesis is stated formally as follows:

> HYPOTHESIS 1: Compared to the control group, the intervention group is more likely to show increased parenting satisfaction and father–child activities over the four-month period of evaluation.

Second, we expect that fathers who took the class are likely to learn the importance of various roles they ought to play as father, which will enhance their confidence as father. These fathers will also work together with the mother of their children as coparents. These predictions are stated formally in the following hypothesis:

> HYPOTHESIS 2: Relative to the control group, the intervention group is more likely to show increasing parenting efficacy (i.e., a belief that they will be able to perform parenting tasks), growing perception of the importance of their role as father, and an increase in coparenting with the child's mother.

Third, we examine whether there are changes in any of the outcomes—satisfaction, frequency of father–child activities, parenting efficacy, role identity, or coparenting relationship—between participants who were residing with their child and those who were not. Because resident fathers enjoy more proximity to their children, we expect them to experience stronger fathering outcomes than nonresident fathers. This prediction is stated formally as follows:

> HYPOTHESIS 3: The intervention effects are likely to be greater among resident than nonresident fathers.

In addition to examining program effectiveness by comparing outcomes for the intervention and control groups, we explore dosage effects by examining outcomes for fathers in the treatment group who attended at least eight sessions (the minimum required to receive a TYRO pin and be eligible to attend a completion ceremony). We expect the effect of TYRO Dads to be greater among fathers who attended more sessions than those who attended fewer or none. In doing so, we are able to determine whether the minimum attendance required by RIDGE is a key threshold for reaping the full benefit of the program.

Research Design

We conducted a randomized controlled trial to test whether fathers who took the TYRO Dads class, compared with those who did not, improved their relationship with their child over time. We collected survey data at three time points (baseline, five weeks later [at the end of the five-week class), and three months after baseline). All data were collected between February 2015 and September 2016. The study participants were recruited in nine cities in Ohio (Canton, Cincinnati, Cleveland, Columbus, Dayton, Lima, Mansfield, Toledo, and Wooster). Eligibility criteria for study participation included: being male, 18 years or older, a biological father of at least one child under the age of 19, and having household income at or below 200% of the 2014 federal poverty level ($47,700 for a family of four).

We randomly assigned applicants eligible for the study to intervention and control groups. A list of random assignments then was emailed to the RIDGE program coordinator, who distributed it to class facilitators at 17 research sites in the nine cities. All eligible applicants were blinded to the randomization, and the trained facilitators administered pre- and post-test surveys to all study participants. Approximately three months after the post-test s urvey, an interviewer called all fathers of both groups and asked them to participate in the final follow-up survey by telephone.

Study Participation and Attrition

We randomly assigned 469 eligible applicants to control and intervention groups, 212 and 257, respectively. Of the 469 randomized applicants, 252 fathers (115 in the control group and 137 in the intervention group) completed the pretest survey. A total of 177 (90 in the control group and 87 in the intervention group) participated in the post-test survey, and 140 fathers (59 in the control group and 81 in the intervention group) completed the follow-up survey. About 48% (120) of the 252 fathers completed all three surveys, whereas the remaining 132 fathers did one or two.

Attrition from the randomization to the pretest (46.3%) was more than twice as high as what was anticipated, while subsequent attrition became smaller, 29.8% (from the pretest to the post-test) and 20.9% (from the post-test to the follow-up). Many eligible fathers were reluctant to participate in the study because they did not want to take the risk of being assigned to the control group. Members of the control group for this study could not attend the class until the study concluded. Despite the attrition, the control and intervention groups were found to be not significantly different in their characteristics, thereby maintaining the integrity of the study.

Measures

We constructed composite measures of key variables based on exploratory factor analysis—a statistical method used to identify the underlying relationships between measured variables. (Factor loadings were mostly higher than .500, and all Cronbach's alphas were acceptable.)

Parenting Satisfaction

We constructed a scale of parenting satisfaction by averaging the four items: how happy and satisfied the father was with his relationship with the child, how good the relationship was, and how close the father felt with the child. They were all measured based on a 5-point Likert scale, although the content of response options differed among the items (i.e., 1 = *not at all happy*, 5 = *extremely happy*; 1 = *not satisfied*, 5 = *extremely satisfied*; 1 = *not good*, 5 = *great*; 1 = *not at all close*, 5 = *extremely close*).

Frequency of Father–Child Activity

We selected items from the Fatherhood Research Practice Network (FRPN) Father Engagement Scale to measure how often fathers have engaged in activities with the child during the last month (Dyer, Kauffman, et al., 2018). The items varied depending on the age of child: 12 months or younger (e.g., played with toys), older than 12 months but younger than 12 years old (e.g., read with the child), 12 years old or older (e.g., assisted the child with sports). Each item was measured using a 5-point Likert scale (1 = *rarely or never*, 5 = *almost every day*). For each age group, we constructed a scale of father–child activities by averaging the items at pretest, post-test, and follow-up.

Parenting Efficacy

We constructed a scale of parenting efficacy by averaging the seven items adopted from the parenting self-efficacy scale developed by FRPN. The items on this scale assess fathers' perceived sense of competence in providing parental care for the child, such as, "Helping the child when he/she is upset or distressed" and "Understanding what the child wants or needs." Each item was measured using a 4-point Likert scale (1 = *definitely not true*, 4 = *definitely true*).

Parenting Role Identity

We asked fathers how important different parental roles—for example, "Being a good financial provider for my child," "Being always available to my child," and "Meeting my child's physical and emotional needs" (1 = *not at all important*, 4 = *extremely important*)—were to them. We averaged the seven items and constructed our own scale of parenting role identity.

Perception of Coparenting Relationship With the Child's Mother

We constructed a scale by averaging the eight items taken from FRPN-validated Coparenting Relationship Scale (Dyer, Fagan, et al., 2018). It measures the extent to which parenting partners trust each other and have quality communications between them. Each item was measured using a 5-point Likert scale (1 = *strongly disagree*, 5 = *strongly agree*).

Besides these composite measures, we measured fathers' resident status (i.e., whether the father was living with the child or not), employment status, current housing or living situation (e.g., whether the father was living in a halfway house, homeless, or in shelters), and sociodemographic characteristics (e.g., age, race and ethnicity, education, income, marital status).

Analysis Plan

We used a statistical method known as latent growth curve analysis to test our hypotheses and determine whether they were supported or rejected by the data we collected from members of the treatment and control groups. This is a longitudinal analysis technique that estimates growth over a period of time. For details on our analysis, please see our final report (Kim & Jang, 2018).

Results

Descriptive Statistics

On average, participants are in their mid-30s. About two-thirds of the participants had previously been incarcerated. The majority of the participants are non-White. Two-thirds or more of fathers were never married, while about 10% to 15% of them were cohabiting when they participated in the study. The participants typically lived with two people in the same household that had an average annual income of about $6,000 and had no high school diploma or GED.

Table 4.1 shows descriptive statistics between control and intervention groups. *T*-tests were conducted to compare sociodemographic characteristics of 120 fathers who completed all three surveys (55 in the control group and 65 in the treatment

TABLE 4.1 Comparisons of Sociodemographic Characteristics between Control and Intervention Group: T-Tests

Variable	Control Group (n = 55)		Intervention Group (n = 65)		p-value
	Mean	SD	Mean	SD	
Age	38.691	11.159	36.523	10.253	.270
Previous incarceration	.709	.458	.688	.467	.800
On parole	.188	.394	.319	.471	.144
Ever convicted of sex offense	.056	.231	.077	.269	.646
Hispanic	.115	.323	.050	.220	.220
Black	.740	.443	.707	.459	.705
White	.180	.388	.259	.442	.327
Other race	.000	.000	.017	.131	.356
Non-White	.827	.382	.750	.437	.322
Never married	.673	.474	.554	.501	.185
Married	.073	.262	.215	.414	.024
Divorced	.255	.440	.215	.414	.617
Widowed	.000	.000	.015	.124	.360
Cohabitation	.236	.429	.154	.364	.263
# people in the household	1.815	1.275	2.492	1.768	.018
Household income (in $1,000)	6.083	15.154	7.099	11.738	.706
Personal income (in $1,000)	2.370	5.977	4.733	9.830	.140
Education	2.037	.910	1.969	.809	.668

group). We found the two groups to remain generally equivalent with a couple of exceptions: Fathers in the control group were less likely to be married (7.3%) than those in the treatment group (21.5%). Fathers in the control group were more likely to live with a smaller number of people in their household (1.815) than those in the treatment group (2.492).

Effectiveness of the Intervention

To test Hypotheses 1 and 2, we estimated growth in parenting satisfaction and father–child activities, parenting efficacy, perception of the importance of their role as father, and coparenting relationship with the child's mother. The model controls for the two time-invariant baseline covariates: being married and number of people living in the household, in which the control and intervention groups were found significantly different. Estimated models all had an acceptable fit to data (see Kim & Jang, 2018, for details).

Hypothesis 1

There was no significant difference in the primary outcomes between control and intervention groups. In other words, if we simply ask if there was a difference between those who participated in the program and those who did not, with respect to parenting satisfaction and frequency of father–child activities, the answer is "no."

When class attendance level was considered, however, we found a significant intervention effect. The results are presented in Appendix 4.1. First, the top panel shows the number of sessions attended was significant in the model of parenting satisfaction (.009), while it was not in the frequency of father–child activities (−.005). That is, the more sessions intervention group fathers attended, the more likely their parenting satisfaction was to increase over the four-month period, although the number of sessions attended had no significant effect on how frequently the fathers did things with the child. In other words, what made a difference in parenting satisfaction was the number of the class sessions attended, not simply being in the intervention group.

There was a threshold for the intervention effect when we examined four different levels of dosage: no (zero sessions), low (one to four sessions), medium (five to seven sessions), and high dosage (eight to ten sessions). Using no dosage as the reference category, we found the threshold to be eight, which coincided with the minimum requirement for the completion of TYRO Dads (see the bottom panel). The intervention effect for parenting satisfaction was observed for the high dosage (.091) but not the low or medium dosage (.048, and .044), while no effect was found again for the frequency of father–child activities (−.015, −.045, and −.044).

TEXT BOX 4.2 INTERVIEW WITH A CLASS FACILITATOR

Once they make it to my classroom, maturity level is the biggest challenge that I deal with because if a person is not mature enough, he's not going to be committed. And I work hard trying to spend extra time working with those people as I notice. Sometimes they're just not ready and they've got personal things that they're dealing with, and to be honest with you, a lot of them need some life counseling, to deal with some mental health issues.

Figure 4.1 shows patterns of change for mean scores of parenting outcomes across Times 1, 2, and 3 (when pretest, post-test, and follow-up surveys were conducted) separately for three groups: control group, fathers who attended less than eight sessions, and fathers who attended 8 or more sessions. The patterns tend to be consistent with the results presented in Appendix 4.1. Specifically,

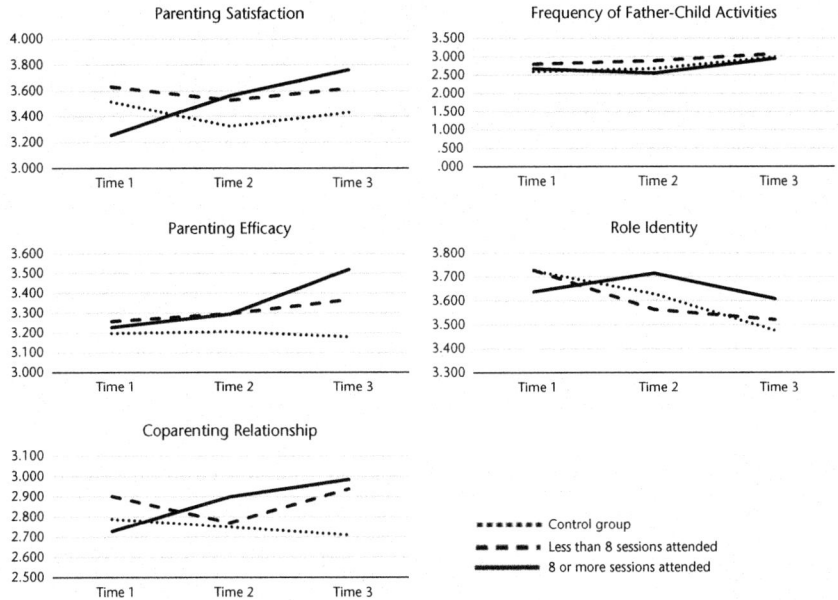

FIGURE 4.1 Group means of parenting outcomes at the time of pretest (Time 1), post-test (Time 2), and follow-up survey (Time 3)

fathers who attended 8 or more sessions showed a pattern of increase in parenting satisfaction, parenting efficacy, and coparenting relationship, unlike the other two groups of fathers who showed no clear pattern, though such contrast was not observed for role identity. On the other hand, the three groups of fathers showed no distinct pattern of change in the frequency of father–child activities (see Appendix 4.1).

Hypothesis 2

Unlike the primary outcomes of parenting satisfaction and frequency of father–child activities, two of the three secondary outcomes were significantly different between control and intervention groups: parenting efficacy and coparenting relationship, though not role identity. As was the case for parenting satisfaction, we found the more sessions fathers attended, the more likely it was for fathers to report increased parenting efficacy (.008) and coparenting relationship (.007), though not role identity (.005). Furthermore, attending at least eight sessions was found crucial for improvement in all three outcomes: parenting efficacy (.066) as well as role identity (.048) and coparenting relationship (.077).

In sum, Hypotheses 1 and 2 received empirical support for parenting satisfaction, parenting efficacy, coparenting relationship, and, to a lesser extent, role identity but no support for the frequency of father–child activities.

Hypothesis 3

To test whether the intervention effects were greater among resident than nonresident fathers, we conducted a series of multi-group analyses of the linear latent trajectory model[1] and found only two significant differences. Specifically, intervention group fathers who were not living with their child were found to have higher levels of parenting role identity at the time of pretest and were also more likely to report a greater increase in parenting satisfaction at the follow-up, compared to their resident counterparts. While the former finding simply shows significant group difference in role identity at the baseline, the latter finding was not consistent with our hypothesis that the intervention effects on parenting outcomes were likely to be greater among resident than nonresident fathers. Specifically, contrary to our predictions, nonresident fathers experienced a greater increase in parenting satisfaction as compared with their resident counterparts.

We also found the intervention effect on coparenting relationship was significant among nonresident fathers at the post-test and follow-up but not among resident fathers. We speculate that nonresident fathers were bigger beneficiaries of TYRO Dads, perhaps because they were more motivated to improve their parenting so they might overcome their structural disadvantage (i.e., fewer opportunities for parenting than resident fathers).

In sum, the present finding may indicate that nonresident fathers are not necessarily disadvantaged in experiencing improvements in coparenting relationships following participation in a fatherhood program compared to those who live with their children.

Discussion

The present study provides evidence that TYRO Dads is effective in making a difference in the lives of low-income fathers in several ways. First, TYRO Dads improved the parenting satisfaction of fathers who participated in the program regularly and attended most sessions, specifically, 80% and above. Second, TYRO Dads helped fathers enhance their parenting efficacy, perception of coparenting relationship with the child's mother, and, to a lesser extent, perceived importance of their role as parent over the course of the study. Intervention group fathers who attended at least eight of ten sessions reported a significant increase in parenting efficacy over the four-month period. This finding makes sense as the more sessions fathers attended, the more parenting principles and skills they learned and practiced, and, as a result, the more sense of self-efficacy in parenting they eventually gained. Lastly, we found some indication that nonresident fathers might be more likely than their resident counterparts to report positive outcomes of the treatment, such as parenting satisfaction, role identity, and perception of coparenting relationship. While this finding was not consistent with what we expected, the heightened benefits that nonresident fathers appear to experience is a positive finding for fatherhood programs given that most fathers who participate in those programs do not live with their child.

Implications for Practice

One of the primary implications of our findings is that program dosage is important to the effectiveness of responsible fatherhood programs. Therefore, organizations implementing such programs would do well to optimize fathers' amount of participation in the program, evaluate program outcomes in relation to dosage, and identify the optimum levels of attendance for achieving desired outcomes (although not all outcomes may be impacted by attendance levels). Accomplishing this might require analysis not only of quantitative data but also of qualitative data such as feedback from program facilitators who have direct experience interacting with participating fathers. In the case of TYRO Dads, The RIDGE Project had implemented the program for more than a decade at the time of this study, and had previously determined that participating fathers must attend at least eight of ten sessions to be considered a program completer and to receive a "TYRO" pin, signifying the adoption of a new identity as a responsible father. Similarly, other responsible fatherhood program providers should consider providing some type of honor or recognition to participants who meet the data-based attendance threshold for program completion.

Qualitative data from this study revealed two specific barriers to program participation: class schedules and transportation (For more details, see our final report [Kim & Jang, 2018]). RIDGE staff who facilitated TYRO Dads classes reported that many fathers assigned to the intervention group were not able to attend classes scheduled during the daytime because they were working, or looking for work, while classes were being held. RIDGE staff also reported that some fathers did not have a means of transportation to get to the TYRO Dads class location. Thus, we suggest that programs may maximize participant attendance by offering evening classes and transportation assistance, such as gas cards or bus tokens, when possible.

TEXT BOX 4.3 INTERVIEW WITH A CLASS FACILITATOR

...For those who have completed the class...they've become more successful in reaching their goals. They might have [become] a truck driver and [completed] CDL training...Stronger relationships with their family...is the most rewarding thing that I hear. Stronger relationships with their family and their children. That just really makes my day.

Surprisingly, however, the number of sessions attended had no effect on how frequently the fathers did things with the child (i.e., frequency of father–child activities). This finding provides fruitful ground for future research. Practitioners should be aware that multiple factors influence the amount of time fathers spend with their children. Fathers may have the desire to spend more time with their children but may face obstacles in doing so, such as managing multiple priorities or (for nonresident fathers) navigating visitation schedules with the child's mother or other caregiver. Thus, responsible fatherhood programs should help fathers recognize and develop a plan for overcoming these obstacles to child contact.

> **TEXT BOX 4.4 SELECTION FROM THE TYRO DECLARATION**
>
> I AM A TYRO. I AM a father. I AM a man of honor…I do not embarrass my family nor do I cause them pain and suffering…I AM a man of integrity…I AM trustworthy…I protect those that I love and defend those who are weaker than I…Pain and suffering have been my greatest teachers. I will not use them as an excuse to fail. I AM free. I am free to dream and to create a better world for myself and all those around me…I AM patient. I do not lose my temper when I do not get my way or give up when I encounter resistance. I understand that those things worth having are worth waiting for…I love my family…I AM responsible. I can be depended upon to do what I say I will do. I AM a leader. I AM a man worth following. I AM A TYRO!

Another unexpected result of this study was that nonresident fathers experienced better outcomes than did resident fathers who participated in TYRO Dads. We can only speculate that nonresident fathers may be more motivated to improve their parenting so they may overcome their structural disadvantage. Regardless of the reason for this difference, practitioners should be aware that programs can be more helpful and impactful for nonresident fathers than even for resident fathers and have the benefit of making them feel more effective, engaged, and rewarded as fathers.

Note

1 We first estimated a trajectory model without equality constraints and then with a constraint on the treatment effect to see whether the constraint resulted in a significant chi-square difference of 3.841 (i.e., the critical value of chi-square distribution with one degree of freedom at the level of .05) or larger (which would indicate significant moderation) between the two models. For the test of difference in chi-square, we used Satorra-Bentler scaled chi-square because the model was estimated using MLR instead of ML. Complete results are available from the lead author upon request.

References

Cabrera, N., Tamis-LeMonda, C. S., Bradley, R. H., Hofferth, S., & Lamb, M. E. (2000). Fatherhood in the twenty-first century. *Child Development, 71*(1), 127–136.

Coley, R. L. (2001). (In)visible men: Emerging research on low-income, unmarried, and minority fathers. *American Psychologist, 56*(9), 743–753.

Dyer, W. J., Fagan, J., Kaufman, R., Pearson, J., & Cabrera, N. (2018). Self-perceived coparenting of nonresident fathers: Scale development and validation. *Family Process, 57*(4), 927–946.

Dyer, W. J., Kauffman, R., Fagan, J., Pearson, J., & Cabrera, N. (2018). Measures of father engagement for nonresident fathers. *Family Relations, 67*(3), 381–398.

Kim, Y.-I., & Jang, S. J. (2018). *Final evaluation report: A randomized controlled trial of the effectiveness of a responsible fatherhood program: The case of TYRO Dads*. Fatherhood Research and Practice Network. https://www.frpn.org/asset/frpn-grantee-report-randomized-controlled-trial-the-effectiveness-responsible-fatherhood.

LaRossa, R. (1988). Fatherhood and social change. *Family Relations, 37*(4), 451–457.

The RIDGE Project. (n.d.). *TYRO curriculum*. https://theridgeproject.com/tyro-suite/.

APPENDIX 4.1 Conditional Linear Latent Trajectory Models of Parenting Variables Regressed on Class Attendance and Covariates ($n = 252$)

Exogenous Variables	Parenting satisfaction		Frequency of father–child activities		Parenting efficacy		Role identity		Coparenting relationship	
	Intercept	Slope	Intercept	Slope	Intercept	Slope	Intercept	Slope	Intercept	Slope
# sessions attended	-.017 (.020)	.009** (.004)	-.005 (.021)	-.005 (.006)	-.004 (.011)	.008** (.003)	-.006 (.007)	.005 (.003)	-.003 (.012)	.007** (.003)
(Constant)	-.356 (.426)		-.077* (.046)		-.017 (.018)		-.016** (.007)		-.032** (.015)	
Married	.099 (.209)	-.024 (.062)	.412 (.251)	-.066 (.071)	.010 (.101)	.008 (.052)	-.188** (.092)	.024 (.031)	.213 (.154)	-.028 (.044)
Household size	.176** (.042)	-.003 (.009)	.230** (.050)	-.018 (.013)	.051** (.022)	.014* (.008)	.038** (.014)	.005 (.006)	.083** (.027)	-.009 (.006)
1–4 sessions attended	-.240 (.220)	.048 (.057)	-.293 (.243)	-.015 (.083)	-.064 (.147)	.051 (.047)	.006 (.073)	.025 (.028)	-.220 (.138)	.101** (.046)
5–7 sessions attended	.113 (.268)	.044 (.054)	.247 (.298)	-.045 (.107)	-.135 (.181)	.042 (.045)	-.014 (.093)	.011 (.042)	.228 (.159)	.048 (.035)
8–10 sessions attended	-.236 (.189)	.091** (.042)	-.107 (.201)	-.044 (.061)	-.045 (.102)	.066** (.032)	-.075 (.067)	.048* (.028)	-.095 (.120)	.077** (.031)
(Constant)	-.102 (.090)		-.076 (.047)		-.016 (.017)		-.016** (.007)		-.030** (.014)	

Endogenous Growth Factors

Married	.129	−.027	.457*	−.070	.018	.005	−.191**	.023	.244	−.035
	(.210)	(.061)	(.245)	(.071)	(.103)	(.052)	(.094)	(.031)	(.149)	(.042)
Household size	.181**	−.004	.235**	−.016	.051**	.013	.039**	.004	.088**	−.011
	(.041)	(.009)	(.049)	(.014)	(.022)	(.008)	(.014)	(.006)	(.027)	(.007)

Note: All models showed acceptable levels of fit. Specific model fit indices are available from the authors. Coefficients in the box are correlations and their standard error (in parentheses) between intercept and slope factors of each parenting variable.

* $p < .05$ (one-tailed test), ** $p < .05$ (two-tailed test).

5

ENGAGING FATHERS IN PERINATAL HOME VISITING

Early Lessons From a Randomized Controlled Study of Dads Matter-HV

Jennifer L. Bellamy, Justin S. Harty, Aaron Banman, and Neil B. Guterman

Rationale

We begin this chapter with a brief overview of the advantages of, and barriers to, engaging fathers in perinatal home visiting.

Perinatal Home Visiting as a Platform to Serve Fathers

Perinatal home visiting (HV) programs are early intervention services primarily serving pregnant women and children under five years old. These programs address the diverse needs of disadvantaged, socially isolated, or historically underserved families (Peacock et al., 2013; Sharps et al., 2008). Most perinatal HV programs consist of (1) preparation materials, (2) an evidence-based parenting curriculum, (3) psychosocial support to parents, and (4) collaboration with or referrals to community-based resources (Sharps et al., 2008). Perinatal HV programs expanded notably in the United States after federal funding became available through the Maternal, Infant, and Early Childhood Home Visiting Program (MIECHV) in 2010 (Finello et al., 2016). In the fiscal year 2018, the 55 perinatal HV programs under the MIECHV Program served approximately 150,000 parents and children in 76,000 families across all 50 states, the District of Columbia, and five U.S. territories (Health Resources and Services Administration, 2019).

HV programs represent a promising service platform with broad reach from which to engage fathers and families. Research indicates that fathers impact children's educational outcomes (e.g., McWayne et al., 2013) as well as maltreatment risk (e.g., Lee et al., 2009), two primary service goals for HV services. Engaging fathers and mothers in HV services may improve long-term fathering trajectories (e.g., Bellamy et al., 2015) and boost child and family service outcomes (Cowan et al., 2009). Children benefit from the positive involvement of both parents as well as a strong coparenting relationship (Cabrera et al., 2012). Furthermore, fathers tend to exhibit their greatest involvement in families when their children are very young (Reichman et al., 2001).

Barriers to Engagement of Fathers in Perinatal Home Visiting

Unfortunately, HV services have not served fathers well. As our research team has conducted trainings with HV workers and focus groups with fathers, we have gathered anecdotal examples of these barriers. Most perinatal HV models were developed for mothers and babies. Sometimes casework forms do not direct HV workers to collect information from, or about, fathers. Communications and parenting curricula used in many HV programs are directed to mothers. Images in offices and on brochures mostly focus on mothers and babies. The content of HV interventions often excludes fathers. For example, content designed to support breastfeeding may fail to provide parallel information for fathers who wish to support breastfeeding or bond with babies through skin-to-skin contact.

Women primarily staff the field, and some female HV workers hold negative attitudes about working with fathers. In our work with HV programs across Chicago, all but one of over 200 workers we trained were women. During our trainings, several workers characterized fathers as "absent" or "uninvolved." Other workers said many of the fathers they work with bring only risks like domestic violence and substance abuse. Not all workers have negative attitudes about fathers, but even those who wish to engage fathers may lack the time, skill, or comfort to do so effectively. Supervisors often do not train, supervise, or otherwise support efforts to work with fathers. It is also more complicated to serve two parents than one. Mothers and fathers have different needs and schedules, and they may not get along well together. Some workers may worry that efforts to engage fathers will compromise their relationship with mothers. Others may make an initial effort to engage fathers but cease efforts if they perceive fathers as disinterested or challenging to engage.

These examples are described as mostly anecdotal because little research has examined barriers to father engagement in perinatal HV, and even fewer studies have tested the effectiveness of approaches designed to address them. This chapter describes a newly developed father engagement intervention for perinatal HV called Dads Matter-HV. Dads Matter-HV is designed to leverage HV as a service platform to serve fathers and mothers together, and address many of these barriers.

Current Study

In this section of the chapter, we describe the development, testing, and content of the Dads Matter-HV intervention.

Dads Matter-HV Intervention Development and Pilot Testing

The research team carried out a series of steps to develop and pilot test the Dads Matter-HV intervention, including a literature review and focus groups with HV workers and their supervisors, mothers receiving HV services, and biological fathers. The intervention is grounded in family systems, coparenting, stress, and social support theories, and also draws from prior empirical work on service engagement. A pilot study of the intervention indicated very promising trends in promoting the quality of the mother–father relationship, perceived stress of both parents, father involvement, child maltreatment risk, and fathers' verbalizations with their infants (Guterman et al., 2018).

Dads Matter-HV Intervention Content

Dads Matter-HV is a manualized intervention delivered by HV workers over the initial four to eight home visits. The intervention does not replace the content of standard HV programs but is layered into existing HV services using a flexible modular approach. The intervention is presented in modules that can be integrated into any standard HV program and flexibly ordered to fit the needs of each family. The content of the intervention is focused on the parents' shared responsibility to care for their child(ren) regardless of their legal, residential, or romantic status. The research team designed the intervention so that it can be delivered either conjointly or separately with mothers and fathers, and adapted to the diversity of family structures, roles, and quality of existing relationships. Dads Matter-HV can be delivered in-person or over the phone. Figure 5.1 provides an overview of the modules included in the intervention. Copies of the manual can

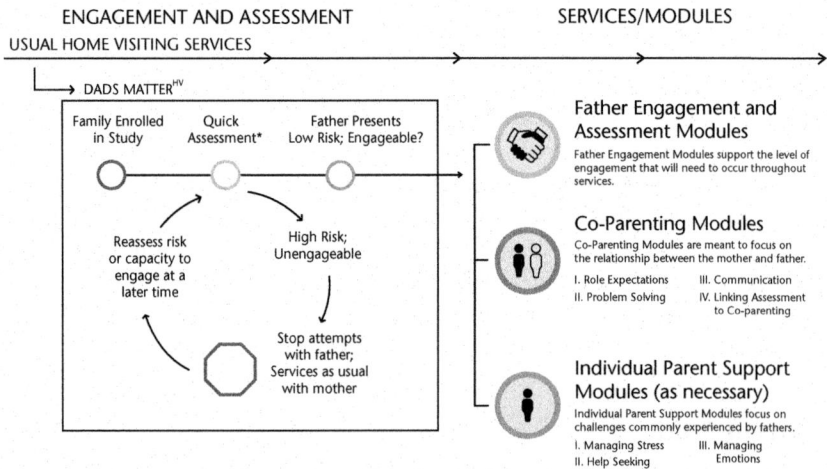

FIGURE 5.1 Dads Matter-HV modules service flowchart

be obtained from the authors of this chapter, and a more detailed explication of the Dads Matter-HV and our evaluation can be found in the full evaluation report (Bellamy et al., 2020), located on the Fatherhood Research and Practice Network website (www.frpn.org).

The first two modules in the manual specifically focus on engagement and assessment. The overarching engagement approach in the manual broadly directs workers to (1) engage fathers as early as possible in services and assess the potential of working with fathers and mothers together; (2) continuously and creatively use multiple engagement strategies and address barriers to fathers' engagement; (3) revise the processes and content of services (e.g., referrals, intake procedures) to be inclusive of fathers; and (4) provide supervision to HV workers as they engage fathers. The first engagement module focuses on preparing for, and carrying out, initial contact with fathers. Strategies include explicitly and frequently inviting both mothers and fathers to visits; considering both parents' schedules; and leaving information, activities, or personal notes to fathers who do not attend visits. Workers are guided to continuously attempt new ways to engage fathers through direct outreach and by working with mothers.

The engagement modules also include assessment tools designed to aid engagement, better understand the father's role, and identify potential risk. Assessment questions help HV workers include the father in early visits, and include strategies to start conversations with fathers and ease HV workers into working with this new group of clients. In cases where fathers should not be engaged due to risks they present to the family, the worker is guided to provide HV services as usual with the mother alone, while continuing to assess the viability of engagement with the father. This approach is designed to avoid engaging fathers for whom the service is not appropriate, but also continue to check back with the family in case the father may appropriately participate at a later point. The second engagement module focuses on strategies for workers' ongoing engagement of fathers in services. These strategies include explaining to the father why it is important for him to participate in services, inquiring into how the worker might help facilitate the father's participation in services, and identifying and resolving barriers to the father's participation in services.

The second section of Dads Matter-HV consists of four modules organized around key aspects of coparenting that can strengthen the father's and mother's work together as a team for their child. Topics include roles and expectations of mothers and fathers, shared problem solving, communication, and linking assessments to coparenting. The third section of Dads Matter-HV focuses on topics specifically designed to support individual parent issues that commonly pose challenges to the father's engagement in services and his positive involvement with the child and family. These modules include content on managing stress, help-seeking, and managing emotions. These modules can also be used with mothers.

Dads Matter-HV can be delivered by professional or paraprofessional HV staff. Training for Dads Matter-HV, as delivered within the current study, includes participation in a one-day in-person training, two- to three-hour booster training sessions for staff, consultation meetings or phone calls with HV supervisors, and email reminders and tips for HV workers on how to implement Dads Matter-HV.

Method

This study was conducted in partnership with five agencies that provide HV services in Chicago, including Metropolitan Family Services, Family Focus, Catholic Charities, SGA Youth and Family Services, and ChildServ. All five organizations utilized as their standard HV model one or more of three nationally prominent evidence-informed HV models: Healthy Families America (HFA), Parents as Teachers (PAT), and Early Head Start (EHS). In randomly assigned clusters of cases, all five organizations agreed to embed Dads Matter-HV within their standard HV curricula.

Dads Matter-HV was tested using a clustered randomized controlled trial (RCT) study design in which groups (supervised teams), rather than individuals, are randomly selected to receive the intervention or not. Eighteen HV program teams from the five agencies agreed to participate in the study and were randomly assigned to deliver standard services plus Dads Matter-HV, or to deliver services as usual, without Dads Matter-HV. Figure 5.2 depicts the randomization and the number of teams,

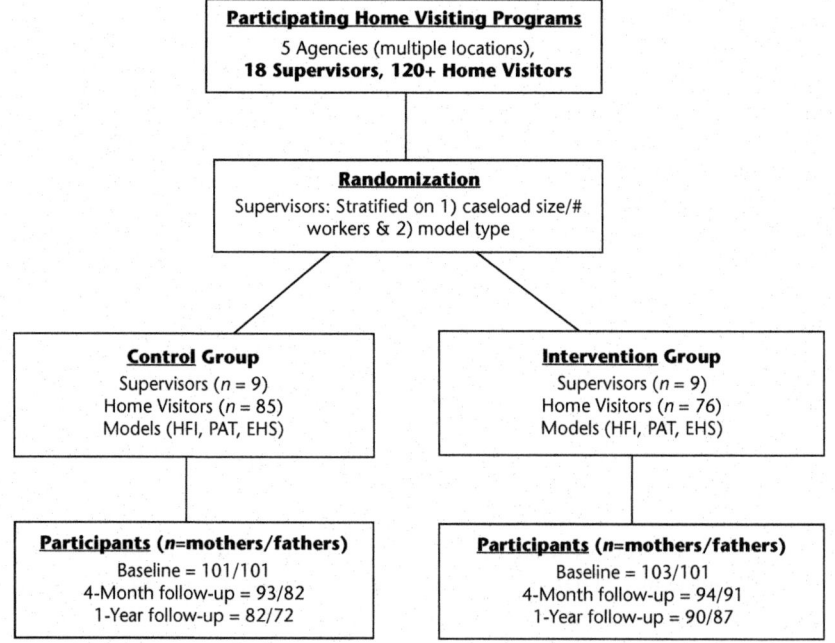

FIGURE 5.2 Dads Matter-HV study flow chart

supervisors, fathers, and mothers that participated in the study at each data collection time point. Data were collected from 204 families recruited to be in the study at three time points: baseline (i.e., at the point of intake into services), four months post-baseline, and one year post-baseline. Overall, 92% of families (both mothers and fathers were retained at four months, and 84% of families (both mothers and fathers) were retained at one year post-baseline. Families were recruited into the study over 30 months. In this chapter, we present descriptive and qualitative findings on workers' attitudes about and strategies for engaging fathers. We also present correlations among these variables, family demographics, and fathers' perceived relationships with their workers. We compare patterns for workers who delivered standard services using the above-noted curricula (the "control group") with those in the intervention group that used Dads Matter-HV in addition to standard services.

During the study, data were also collected from HV workers by survey and qualitative interviews. In total, 113 workers participated in a survey at the start of the study. Qualitative data were also collected from a subgroup of 28 workers by telephone at the end of the study recruitment period.

Sample of Participating Families

Table 5.1 describes the characteristics of the baseline sample of participating families. There was a slightly greater proportion of Hispanic or Latino fathers in the control group, and a slightly greater proportion of Black or African American fathers in the intervention group ($F = 7.1$, $p < .008$). No other significant differences were observed on demographic and relationship characteristics across intervention and control groups. Nearly three-quarters of participating parents were married or living together; 85% of mothers were recipients of public assistance, but 78% of fathers were employed.

Quantitative Methods

Home Visitor–Reported Measures

We constructed a measure of home visitor attitudes about working with fathers based on self-reports by HV workers. We asked workers to indicate their agreement with statements such as "I enjoy working with fathers during visits" and "I know how to include fathers in home visiting services." The entire list of items is presented in Table 5.2. Overall, the scale showed strong reliability, meaning that the measure was consistent and dependable. We also asked workers to self-report services they provided to families using a *Parent Services Log* (PSL)—a brief self-report tool that was developed to determine whether different workers delivered Dads Matter-HV material and services in a consistent way (Guterman et al., 2018). Using the form, workers noted the identity of the family members they met with and the specific Dads Matter-HV activities they delivered.

TABLE 5.1 Demographic Characteristics of Mothers and Fathers at Baseline ($n = 204$)

Characteristic	Mothers		Fathers	
	n	% or Mean (SD)	n	% or Mean (SD)
Race/Ethnicity	204		202	
Hispanic/Latino		67%		68%
African American/Black		28%		26%
Other		5%		5%
Relationship Status of Mother with Father	204			
Married or living together		72%		–
Romantically involved or friends and not living together		25%		
Not romantically involved and not living together or "friends only" and not living together		3%		–
Age of Parent (years)	204	25.66 (7.53)	202	27.9 (8.7)
Age of Child (months)	151	14.07 (10.89)	–	–
Prenatal Case (child not yet born)	53	26%	–	–
Receipt of Public Assistance	204	85%*	202	37%*
Father Employment Status	204			
Employed		–		78%
Unemployed		–		15%
Enrolled in school		–		7%

Note: *Many noted that the child's mother/father received public assistance or was unemployed and did not specify income.

Parent-Reported Measures

Mothers' and fathers' perceptions of the quality of the relationship between parents and their worker were measured using the *Relational Health Index—Mentor Scale* (RHI) (Liang et al., 2002) at four-month and one-year follow-ups. We asked mothers and fathers to rate their agreement with statements like "I can be genuinely myself with my home visitor" and "I believe my home visitor sees me as a whole person." This measure also demonstrated good reliability. The RHI measures three qualities of the parent–worker relationship: engagement (mutual feelings about involvement in the relationship), authenticity (feeling genuine in the relationship), and empowerment/zest (feeling strengthened or built up by the relationship) (Liang et al., 2002).

We also created two new scales for the study to capture mothers' and fathers' beliefs about fathers' participation in HV services. The scales were designed to measure parents' beliefs about the value of the father's participation, his desire to participate in services, and his expected participation in services. We asked fathers to rate their agreement on items such as "It is important that I be at home visits," "I want to be at home visits," and "I would enjoy participating in home visits with the mother of my child." We asked mothers similar questions about fathers' participation in HV such as "It is important that the father of my child be at home visits," "The father of my child wants to be at home visits," and "I would enjoy participating in home visits with the father of my child." These measures also demonstrated good reliability.

Home Visitor Data Analysis

We analyzed HV worker survey data using descriptive statistics. We also conducted bivariate analyses to assess whether attitudes varied by worker demographics such as worker age, race, and years of experience. We analyzed PSLs to compare the proportion of visits in which workers noted they had interacted with fathers and the proportion of visits that manual-specified components were delivered to each parent. We used bivariate analyses to analyze differences in service delivery by intervention versus control group, and for mothers versus fathers. All quantitative analyses were completed using R version 3.5.2. Quantitative analyses are defined by the use of numbers to describe the characteristics of study participants.

Parent Data Analysis

Scales and subscales were calculated for all measures, and bivariate t-tests were conducted to test for differences between intervention and control group with regard to the parent–worker relationship at the follow-up interview. We also calculated correlations indicating the relationships between mothers' and fathers' beliefs about fathers' participation in HV services, the quality of the relationship of home workers with mothers and fathers, and demographic factors.

Qualitative Methods

Interviews

The research team selected a sample of 28 HV workers representing a wide range of training and practice experiences for qualitative interviews conducted after all 204 families had been recruited into the study. Workers were interviewed over the telephone using a semi-structured question format. The interviews included questions about how the workers engaged fathers and barriers to engagement. The interviews lasted from between 25 to 90 minutes, with most interviews lasting around 45 minutes.

Analysis

All interviews were audio-recorded, transcribed, and checked for quality prior to analysis. The research team analyzed the transcripts using a qualitative data analysis software program (Dedoose, 2018). The research team analyzed the interview data using interpretive description (Thorne et al., 1997). Interpretive description is a method that is used to generate knowledge relevant for the clinical or practice context. The research team also shared results of the data analyses with a subgroup of workers and supervisors to get their input on the accuracy of our description and interpretation of the data.

Results

In this next section of the chapter, we share the results of our current study relating to engaging fathers in perinatal home visiting.

Home Visitor Attitudes About Working with Fathers

Table 5.2 summarizes the attitudes of the workers surveyed at the start of the study, prior to their training on Dads Matter-HV. Each of the items ranged from 1 to 5, with 1 = *Strongly Disagree* and 5 = *Strongly Agree*. On average workers indicated that they enjoyed working with fathers, felt that they

TABLE 5.2 Home Visitor Baseline Attitudes About Working With Fathers ($n = 113$)

Subscale	Mean	SD
Barriers		
I enjoy working with fathers during visits.	4.08	1.01
Mothers want fathers to participate in visits.	3.86	.92
Fathers want to participate in visits.	2.90	1.02
It is hard to include fathers in home visits.	3.23	1.25
I do not have enough time to work with fathers during visits.	2.32	1.25
If I include fathers in home visits I will be less able to serve mothers.	2.05	1.23
Knowledge		
I know how to include fathers in home visiting services.	3.78	1.02
I feel confident in my knowledge about the level of father involvement in the families I work with.	3.69	.94
I have been trained to work with fathers in home visiting.	3.12	1.23
Priority		
As a home visitor I should work with both mothers and fathers.	4.35	.97
I am encouraged to work with fathers during visits.	4.04	.97
The home visiting program I use is appropriate for fathers.	3.91	1.94
Home visiting services are designed for mothers more than fathers.	3.60	1.29
Value		
Children will benefit if fathers are included in home visiting services.	4.62	.82
Fathers can benefit from home visiting services.	4.61	.90
It is important that fathers participate in home visits.	4.50	.81

should work with both mothers and fathers, and felt encouraged to do so. Home visitor attitudes were generally positive about fathers' engagement in HV services. Overall, workers strongly endorsed the value or benefits of including fathers. On average, workers perceived that mothers were more interested in having fathers participate in visits than fathers were interested in participating. In general, workers were relatively less confident about their knowledge of father involvement and their training on how to work with fathers. Our analyses did not reveal any statistically significant differences in attitudes based on home visitor demographic characteristics, including age, race, and years of experience.

Father Participation in Services

Parent Service Log (PSL) data indicate that fathers in the control group attended 20% of home visits. To contrast, fathers' attendance in home visits for the intervention group was 33%. This difference was statistically significant. Although the intervention increased fathers' participation in visits, most visits (67%) did not include fathers.

Barriers

When workers were asked in qualitative interviews about barriers to fathers' participation in services, the most common barriers reported were lack of time or scheduling conflicts with work. For example, one home visitor said, "With my dads that were in Dads Matter, a lot of them worked and were not in the home." Other workers described how families did not understand that the father was supposed to be part of services. Still others reported that the mother tends to take the lead. For example, some workers described fathers as shy or looking to mothers for answers or cues as to what to say. One home visitor said, "It's hard for dads to feel like they are actually a client." Others noted changes in the parents' relationship as a barrier, especially if the father was at first residing with the mother and child and then later moved out. For workers that were more successful in engaging fathers, they described being unsure of how to work with fathers at first, but once they tried some strategies and had some successes, they felt more confident with engaging fathers.

Worker Strategies to Engage Fathers

Workers trained in Dads Matter-HV employed a larger variety of engagement strategies as compared to workers who were not trained in the intervention. Table 5.3 summarizes father engagement strategies described by workers in each study group. Some strategies reported by workers were not specifically prescribed in the Dads Matter-HV manual or training, such as making eye contact, using

TABLE 5.3 Father Engagement Strategies by Study Group ($n = 28$)

Intervention Group Strategies ($n = 15$)	Control Group Strategies ($n = 13$)
Talk to father	Provide incentives
Make eye contact	Leave information for father
Leave things for father	Tell father he is needed/important
Communicate through mother	Communicate through mother
Specifically/explicitly invite father	
Tell father he's needed/important	
Provide referrals (jobs, etc.)	
Use hands-on activities	
Use technology	
Being there for fathers when needed/consistent relationship/building trust	
Give him information	
Provide opportunities to interact with other fathers	
Explain benefits of his involvement	
Use "other" activities: holiday parties, family events, etc.	
Respect/acknowledge father's expertise	
Consider schedules of both parents	

technology, "being there," being consistent, building trust, using incentives, as well as using other activities like holiday parties or family events.

In general, workers said the keys to successful engagement of fathers in services involved using a variety of relatively straightforward approaches and making efforts to engage fathers consistently and explicitly, from the earliest stage of services and continuously in visits. Workers described the shift in the ways they approached including fathers after training in Dads Matter-HV in the following ways:

> In general, I just want to invite the fathers in more and that's a wonderful thing. It's made me, maybe not less afraid of fathers, but I'm kind of, I'm more willing to be happy and playful and joking with them...as well as knowing some more of their fears now...Nobody's offered you any of this before. Okay, this is cool. We'll do this together.

> It has changed how I am in home visits in general...I'm gonna bring two sets of paperwork when I have an inkling that Dad's going to be there. Or, I'm going to, when I do these parent assessments, I'll ask Mom's opinion and I'll ask Dad's opinion and make sure I actually really write both of them down.

Parent–Worker Relationships

Father

The Relational Health Index (RHI) total score, which measured relationships between fathers and workers, indicated that fathers exposed to the Dads Matter-HV intervention reported more positive RHI scores at the four-month follow-up as compared with their counterparts in the control group, but the difference was not statistically significant (Control: $M = 39.09$, $SD = 13.27$; Intervention: $M = 42.02$, $SD = 13.33$, $t = 1.5$, $p > .05$). At the one-year follow-up, the RHI scores for fathers were highly similar across intervention groups.

Mother

The RHI scores for mothers in the intervention and control group were virtually identical at four-month and one-year follow-ups (Four-month: Control: $M = 47.13$, Intervention: $M = 47.26$, $t = 0.2$, $p > .05$; One-year: Control: $M = 45.37$, Intervention: $M = 46.92$, $t = 1.1$, $p > .05$). This suggests that workers in the intervention group who tried to cultivate relationships with fathers did not jeopardize their relationships with mothers.

Relationship between Clinical Content and Parent Beliefs, Home Visitor–Parent Relationship, and Demographics

We examined the associations between mothers' and fathers' beliefs about fathers' participation in HV services, workers' relationship with mothers and fathers based on RHI scores, and parent demographics. We found that mothers' and fathers' positive attitudes about father participation in HV are related to one another, but not strongly ($r = .24$, $p < .001$). In addition, fathers who have positive attitudes about being involved in HV tend to have a better relationship with the home visitor, including feelings of empowerment ($r = .24$, $p < .01$), engagement ($r = .25$, $p < .001$), and authenticity ($r = .24$, $p < .001$). Mothers' beliefs about fathers' participation in HV did not affect the quality of his relationship with the home visitor (empowerment: $r = .05$; engagement: $r = .07$; authenticity: $r = .10$). No other variables that we examined were significantly related to the quality of the workers' relationships with the parents or parents' attitudes about fathers participating in HV services.

Discussion

In this final section of the chapter, we discuss important implications and limitations of our current study as well as offer suggestions for future research.

Home Visitor Attitudes About Working with Fathers

In a survey administered to workers prior to receiving training on Dads Matter HV, workers reported positive attitudes about fathers' participation in HV services. They particularly endorsed the importance and value of father's engagement. Since the survey was confidential and workers have been open with us about their concerns about father engagement in HV, we feel confident about this finding. Worker hesitancy about father engagement appears to stem from their concerns about being successful and doing a good job. Workers primarily report that they lack skills and training in strategies to engage fathers, and that they are working from service models or program curricula that were designed for mothers and are not well suited to fathers. Training for workers and implementing adjustments to program communications, activities, and materials to explicitly include fathers may be particularly fruitful ways to improve father engagement.

Workers who were trained in Dads Matter-HV were better able to engage fathers, with the percentage of fathers who participate in visits increasing from 20% to 33%. Although modest, such improvement was statistically significant, suggesting that the intervention had an observable effect on participation. This certainly leaves room for improvement, and more intensive worker training, supervision, and other supports may be needed to further increase rates of participation. Also, given the scheduling challenges reported by workers, it may not be a practical goal to get all mothers and fathers to physically participate in visits together. Some workers were creative in using technology to reach fathers, bringing them into visits virtually rather than in person, which may be another particularly helpful strategy.

Dads Matter-HV, Parents' Beliefs, and Home Visitors' Relationship with Mothers and Fathers

Mothers' and fathers' beliefs about fathers' participation in HV services appear to be related, although the association is small. This suggests that parents can hold independent views about father participation. More importantly, although workers were initially concerned that mothers would oppose father participation and that mother's opposition would inhibit their ability to work with fathers, our analysis found that only fathers' beliefs about his participation are associated with the quality of his relationship with the home visitor. Fathers who are more positive about participating in HV report better quality relationships with the home visitor four months after the HV intervention begins. Mothers' beliefs do not strongly relate to workers' relationships with fathers. Because fathers' beliefs are significantly correlated with the quality of his relationship with the worker, trying to improve fathers' beliefs early on may improve their engagement with their HV worker. Finally, despite fears expressed by some workers that their relationships with mothers might be compromised if they include fathers, the implementation of Dads Matter-HV did not seem to impact the quality of the relationship between workers and mothers.

The modest improvements in fathers' perceptions of the quality of their relationships with workers in the intervention group were not maintained at the one-year follow-up and at that point relationships between workers and fathers in the control and intervention groups were identical. Because Dads Matter-HV was designed to be provided in the first four months of HV services, it may be that initial differences in RHI scores were not sustained as the intervention was concluded. Although the research team hoped any improvements in the home visitor–father relationships would be sustained or even amplified over time, this did not occur. Achieving improvements that last over a longer period of time may require additional interventions or the extension of the intervention over a longer period of time. Additional interventions might include opportunities to engage fathers more frequently, perhaps through technology, peer support groups, or father-focused events or activities.

Worker Strategies to Engage Fathers

The qualitative data presented in this study illustrates the variety and innovative father engagement strategies employed by workers who were trained in Dads Matter-HV. Workers reported using many of the engagement strategies noted in the Dads Matter-HV manual and intervention training, suggesting that the program changed workers' behavior in ways that were intended. Workers also improvised and went beyond the techniques outlined in the manual. It may be that both identified engagement strategies and worker creativity are needed to improve father engagement in HV services.

Limitations

Staff turnover was perhaps the biggest challenge in this study. Of the 17 teams that actively participated in the study, 59% experienced changes at the supervisor level during the study, and 41% of the teams experienced a 50% or greater turnover rate during the study. New workers must be trained, and the experience and relationship of the former worker in working with fathers and families is lost. Another limitation of the study is that we did not measure the quality of the father's participation in the home visits. Although we did track whether the content of material designated for each home visit was delivered as planned using the PSL data, we did not capture the depth of fathers' and mothers' engagement with intervention content. In other words, the PSL measures whether or not content was delivered, but not the degree to which fathers and mothers interacted with, understood, or learned from the content. Another limitation of this study is the limited external validity or ability to replicate these findings with other HV programs and curricula. Although the study was carried out in partnership with five agencies delivering three different HV models, other models may or may not pair as well with the Dads Matter-HV intervention. Similarly, the study was located in one specific metropolitan area, and most participants identified as either Hispanic or Latino. The intervention needs to be tested in other regions, in rural areas, and with other racial and ethnic groups to determine whether or not it is consistently effective.

Conclusion

Study findings suggest that fathers' participation in HV can be improved with an enhancement to existing HV service models, rather than by requiring a wholly separate model designed only for fathers and that fathers and mothers can participate in services together. Offering an enhancement to the existing HV models, rather than developing a completely new father-inclusive model for the HV field is relatively more efficient and cost-effective. This service enhancement approach may be a promising strategy for increasing fathers' engagement in other types of child and family interventions where father engagement has been limited. The research team has also used the data collected from this study to further develop the Dads Matter-HV intervention, and these intervention adaptations should be evaluated in future research, with the potential for further improved father engagement outcomes.

References

Bellamy, J., Harty, J., Guterman, N., Banman, A., Morales-Mirque, S. & Massey Combes, K. (2020). *The engagement of fathers in home visiting services: Learning from the Dads Matter-HV study*. Fatherhood Research and Practice Network. https://www.frpn.org/asset/frpn-grantee-report-the-engagement-fathers-in-home-visiting-services-learning-the-dads-matter.

Bellamy, J. L. Thullen, M. J. & Hans, S. L. (2015). The effect of fathers' presence at birth on involvement over time. *Journal of Marriage and Family, 77*(3), 647–661.

Cabrera, N. J., Scott, M. E., Fagan, J., Steward-Streng, N., & Chen, N. (2012). Co-parenting in married and cohabiting families and children's school readiness: A mediational model. *Family Process, 51*(3), 307–324.

Cowan, P. A., Cowan, C. P., Pruett, M. K., Pruett, K. & Wong, J. J. (2009). Promoting fathers' engagement with children: Preventive interventions for low-income families. *Journal of Marriage and Family, 71*(3), 663–679.

Dedoose. (2018). *Version 8.0.35, web application for managing, analyzing, and presenting qualitative and mixed method research data*. SocioCultural Research Consultants, LLC. www.dedoose.com.

Finello, K. M., Terteryan, A., & Riewerts, R. J. (2016). Home visiting programs: What the primary care clinician should know. *Current Problems in Pediatric and Adolescent Health Care, 46*(4), 101–125.

Guterman, N. B., Bellamy, J. L., & Banman, A. (2018) Promoting father involvement in early home visiting services for vulnerable families: Findings from a pilot study of "Dads Matter." *Child Abuse & Neglect, 76*, 261–272.

Health Resources and Services Administration. (2019). *The maternal, infant, and early childhood home visiting program: Partnering with parents to help children succeed.* Administration for Children and Families, U.S. Department of Health and Human Services. https://mchb.hrsa.gov/sites/default/files/mchb/MaternalChildHealthInitiatives/HomeVisiting/pdf/programbrief.pdf.

Lee, S. J., Bellamy, J. L., & Guterman, N. B. (2009). Fathers, physical child abuse, and neglect: Advancing the knowledge base. *Child Maltreatment, 14*(3), 227–231.

Liang, B., Tracy, A., Taylor, C. A., Williams, L. M., Jordan, J. V., & Miller, J. B. (2002). The relational health indices: A study of women's relationships. *Psychology of Women Quarterly, 26*(1), 25–35.

McWayne, C., Downer, J. T., Campos, R., & Harris, R. D. (2013). Father involvement during early childhood and its association with children's early learning: A meta-analysis. *Early Education & Development, 24*(6), 898–922.

Peacock, S., Konrad, S., Watson, E., Nickel, D., & Muhajarine, N. (2013). Effectiveness of home visiting programs on child outcomes: A systematic review. *BMC Public Health, 13*(1), 1–14.

Reichman, N., Teitler, J., Garfinkel, I., & McLanahan, S. (2001). Fragile families: Sample and design. *Children and Youth Services Review, 32*(4/5), 303–326.

Sharps, P. W., Campbell, J., Baty, M. L., Walker, K. S., & Bair-Merritt, M. H. (2008). Current evidence on perinatal home visiting and intimate partner violence. *Journal of Obstetric, Gynecologic & Neonatal Nursing, 37*(4), 480–491.

Thorne, S., Kirkham, S. R., & MacDonald-Emes, J. (1997). Interpretive description: A noncategorical qualitative alternative for developing nursing knowledge. *Research in Nursing & Health, 20*(2), 169–177.

6

A MIXED-METHODS EVALUATION OF *KEY TO KANE*, A TEXT-MESSAGING INTERVENTION FOR FATHERS IN HAWAII

Selva Lewin-Bizan, David "Kawika" Mattos, and Edeluisa "Edel" Baguio-Larena

Introduction

Fatherhood interventions have been designed to support men in their parenting role (Bronte-Tinkew et al., 2012), but rates of in-person attendance are frequently low. Among the reasons are scheduling conflicts and competing time demands (see Fagan & Pearson, 2020). With these barriers to participation in mind, alternative modes to improve the reach of interventions for parents have been developed. These include interventions using mobile phones, computers, and video conferencing (for reviews see Breitenstein et al., 2014; see Hall & Biernan, 2015) that offer participants opportunities for consultation with professionals, learning parenting skills, and social support (for a review see Nieuwboer et al., 2013), either as standalone interventions or as enhancements to standard face-to-face interventions (for a review see Jones et al., 2013).

Text-Messaging Parenting Interventions

Existing evaluations of text-messaging interventions for parents show that they generally produce gains in outcomes of interest. For example, an evaluation of an intervention for parents of overweight and obese preschoolers showed parental gains in knowledge and healthy lifestyle following face-to-face meetings with health care providers augmented by text messaging (Militello et al., 2016). But the use of text messaging in conjunction with clinical care without a control condition makes it hard to determine how text messaging performs in relation to other delivery formats. Other evaluations of interventions that also sought to improve children's health demonstrated that, compared to participants in control conditions, pregnant and new mothers who received text messages about prenatal and postpartum health were more likely to believe that they were prepared to be new mothers (Evans et al., 2012); that for adolescents needing vaccination, those whose parents received text messages or postcards were more likely to get vaccinated (Bar-Shain et al., 2015); and that for infants lacking a scheduled one-year doctor's appointment, those whose parents received text-message reminders were more likely to undergo timely vaccination (Hofstetter et al., 2015a). To better understand what is the most effective message type to increase vaccination rates, another similar study compared the effectiveness of text-message vaccination reminders versus the same reminders with options to request more information about the vaccine, and found that the interactive texts were more effective in increasing vaccination rates from infancy through adolescence (Hofstetter et al., 2015b).

Evaluations of interventions that aim to promote parental involvement have also sought to understand what the most effective intervention is. For example, an evaluation of an intervention for mothers of preschoolers that aimed to increase engagement compared the effectiveness of home visits versus home visits plus text messaging and showed that mothers who received the enhanced intervention were more likely to use the newly learned parenting strategies (Carta et al., 2013). An evaluation of an intervention that aimed to increase parental educational involvement found that parents who received text messages about educational resources and activities and the positive effects of reading were more likely to attend parent-teacher conferences than parents who received nonliteracy text messages (Kraft & Monti-Nussbaum, 2018).

In all these studies, most participants have been mothers, either because the intervention was designed for them or because they were more likely to participate than fathers. An evaluation of an intervention intended to promote activity engagement of mothers and fathers found that the effect of the texting intervention varied by parent gender: there were no differences for mothers, but fathers who received text messages completed more activities with their children, such as pretend play or storytelling or singing, than fathers who did not receive the texts (Hurwitz et al., 2015). While this evaluation has demonstrated that a text-messaging intervention that delivered activity suggestions and words of encouragement was effective for fathers, it included a relatively small sample of men. Clearly, more intervention-effectiveness research is needed.

The Current Study

Key to Kane—a pilot fatherhood intervention that uses text messaging in Hawaii—was designed to further understand the impact of delivering parenting information and support via text messaging on fathering behaviors. This study used mixed-methods research, drawing on potential strengths of both quantitative and qualitative methods. Using this methodology in the study of *Key to Kane* adds to the breadth and depth of our understanding of the program. While the quantitative portion of our study found no association between the receipt of text messages and fathering behaviors and attitudes (Lewin-Bizan et al., 2020), the qualitative portion allowed us to uncover participants' individual perceptions of the intervention and learn that they saw some value in it.

We begin the chapter by summarizing the intervention and the methods and findings from the quantitative portion of the study. We then present the qualitative portion in which we focused on what participants had to say about their reasons for enrolling in the intervention, satisfaction with it, perceived parenting changes they associate with participation, and suggestions to improve the intervention. The use of text messaging for fatherhood programs is also discussed.

The Intervention

Key to Kane is a pilot, technology-assisted, 12-week text-messaging intervention for fathers of children age 0–12 that aims to help men become more involved with their children as well as increase their levels of parental self-confidence. *Kane* is the father of living creatures in Hawaiian mythology and represents the god of procreation. The study was conducted at Maui Family Support Services, Inc. (MFSS), a social services organization founded in 1980 in Wailuku, HI. MFSS offers family services such as outreach and resources for new mothers and Early Head Start centers. MFSS also offers evidence-based fatherhood programs delivered by trained facilitators in weekly group sessions and one-on-one home visits. Piloting the efficacy of a new text-messaging intervention was a natural next step in the organization's fatherhood programming as it sought ways to engage hard-to-reach fathers.

Recruitment efforts included personally reaching out to families known at MFSS; spreading the word through community organizations, nonprofits, and government agencies; and posting flyers throughout Wailuku and in social media. Fathers who expressed interest in the intervention were invited to a group meeting at MFSS. These meetings were held on a rolling basis, included an informational dinner, and culminated in the enrollment of interested fathers. A total of 120 men enrolled and received a demonstration on how to use the functions of the phone application for the program.

As part of the 12-week intervention, men were sent three weekly messages at a prescribed schedule with a different topical focus on fathering, for a total of 36 messages. On Mondays, the messages had information about normative child development; on Wednesdays they offered concrete and simple engagement ideas; and on Fridays they highlighted words of encouragement for men in their role as *Na Makua Kane* (fathers). Although messages were automated, they were delivered based on the age of the focal child, and language was tailored to the sex and name of this child to enhance the relevance of the content. In addition, messages were tailored to the Hawaiian culture, using Hawaiian language and proverbs to enhance cultural relevance.

Quantitative Portion of the Evaluation

There are few evaluation reports with data on fathers' participation dosage in programs (Fagan & Pearson, 2020), so one of the goals of the quantitative portion of the study of *Key to Kane* was to assess whether participation dosage differentially affects two outcomes: levels of father engagement and parental self-confidence (Lewin-Bizan et al., 2020). Participation was measured as reading dosage, or how many text messages participants read during their time in the intervention. As in prior studies (Fagan & Iglesias, 1999; Kim & Jang, 2018), we created four reading dosage groups and followed Fagan and Pearson's (2020) recommendation for cutoffs: no-dosage (zero texts read, 19% of the sample), low-dosage (less than 40% of the texts, or 1–14 texts, 11% of the sample), moderate-dosage (40%–69% of the texts, or 15–25 texts, 13% of the sample), and high-dosage (70% of the texts or more, or 26–36 texts, 57% of the sample, with 23% of the sample reading all the texts).

There were two quantitative data-collection points: baseline (paper-and-pencil at time of study enrollment) and 12 weeks later (over the phone at intervention completion). One hundred and nineteen participants completed the baseline questionnaire, and 87 completed the post-intervention questionnaire. Participants were given gift cards for their time and effort completing each questionnaire and a bonus gift card for completing both.

Contrary to quantitative findings of previous research that demonstrated that it is possible to modify parenting behavior using text-message interventions (Carta et al., 2013; Hurwitz et al., 2015; Kraft & Monti-Nussbaum, 2018), the quantitative portion of the evaluation did not obtain statistically significant results. That is, pre- and post-intervention measures did not yield any evidence that higher reading dosage in *Key to Kane* encouraged higher levels of fathers' engagement with their children or increased parental self-confidence.[1]

Qualitative Portion of the Evaluation

Study Design and Participants

Including participants' subjective responses is recommended in research (Ansay et al., 2004). We chose to use focus groups rather than individual interviews to understand reactions to the intervention because the group setting facilitates conversations between participants and allows to build on each other's points of view (Kitzinger, 1995).

Men enrolled in *Key to Kane* who read at least 40% of the text messages (moderate- and high-dosage groups, $n = 84$, or about 70% of all the men) were invited to participate in a 90-minute focus group session designed to elicit their perspectives on the program, and three groups were conducted with a total of 17 men. We decided on this cutoff so participants were familiar enough with the content to share their experiences. Seven of the 17 participants read all messages, and seven others read almost all.

Demographic characteristics of these 17 men were similar to those of the full sample in the quantitative portion of the study. Thus, most lived with the mother of the child (47% of fathers in the qualitative study and 41.4% of fathers in the quantitative study were married; 28.4% and 23.5%, respectively, were non-married cohabiting); most had attended at least some college (76.5% and 57%, respectively); most were employed full time (64.7% and 63.6%, respectively); and among the single-race participants, the largest group was the Native Hawaiian/Pacific Islander (29.4% and 27.7%, respectively) followed by White (17.6% and 19.3%, respectively) and Asian (11.8% and 10.1%, respectively). This was the first fatherhood intervention for most, but men who participated in the focus groups were less apt to be first-time users of a fatherhood intervention (58.8%) as compared with the full sample in the quantitative study (70.4%).

Procedure and Analysis

Each group was conducted on a different weeknight at the meeting room of MFSS and was audio-recorded and transcribed. Participants signed a consent form, received a gift card in appreciation for their time, and were served dinner. The groups were moderated by the director of fatherhood programing for MFSS and a researcher, using a semi-structured interview guide with open-ended questions designed to elicit information about participants' expectations and needs from the intervention, and their likes and dislikes.

Our analysis of the content of the transcriptions involved identifying emergent themes. Content was identified as a theme when it was discussed more than once or for more than a few minutes. Major themes that emerged and offer insight into *Key to Kane* are discussed in the results section and include satisfaction with content of the intervention, convenience of the delivery mode, and the absence of human connection. The quotes included in the chapter were chosen for their exemplification value, as were the text messages.

Results

The Content and Perceived Changes in Fathering

The Basics of Child Development

Parenting interventions can help fathers gain critical knowledge of child development, and this was a reason for men to enroll: "It's always good to have information, especially as a new parent. I've never done this before… You want as much information as you can get. From trusted adults."

In general, fathers may be more knowledgeable in some areas of child development than in others and want to know more about specific developmental milestones, such as language and communication:

> I have also a 16-year-old, a seven-year-old, and a 22-year-old. But I wanted to do [this for] my two-year-old, to sharpen up my skills. This is not my first rodeo, but I don't know everything. So, I'd like to know how to have conversations with a two-year-old. Ask questions… get them to talk rather than just a yes-or-no answer.

Some fathers remembered messages about milestones that were especially helpful in knowing whether their children were developing properly:

> My daughter, she's a baby … and when I started the … program, it mentioned … by this age she'll be doing this, she says a word… It helped me with the progression of where she should be at, so I can check. So, I read [the texts] during the week, and when I see her on the weekend, I practice a lot of what the texts are telling me.

Sample text message: normative child development

> Did you know…? Your child's speech develops gradually. Your almost-one-year-old responds to simple requests, shakes her head for "no," and says "dada" and "mama."

Men were also curious about optimal caregiving strategies, such as how to manage their child's behavior: "For me [the reason to enroll], [was] disciplinary action. Growing up, that was 'Go stand in a corner'. [My] middle daughter is the hardest one, she's like the rebel. Learn how I can make [her] stop."

Sample text message: tips for discipline (ages 10–12)

> Hello [name of participant]. Here are some ideas about what to do when you need to engage in [name of child]'s discipline. Set realistic, short-term goals together with your child. For example: "By the end of 2 weeks, my child will be picking up [his/her] clothes 4 days a week" (as opposed to never picking up clothes). Acknowledge your child's efforts, even when [he/she] doesn't fully meet expectations. Reconsider the goals and adjust them when your child is consistently unable to meet your expectations.

Some fathers remembered messages about caregiving that were especially helpful for routines:

> The sleeping habits that we can incorporate... I like to roughhouse, so I have [a] blast, and then there's the calm time that you need before bedtime... I appreciate that. I look forward to... the ideas and some of the new challenges.

Fathers in general may need specific information on health-related topics and wish for coverage of health issues, an area not included:

> If it's 100 degrees [of fever], is this emergency room status or can this wait until the morning?... We were just like 'Okay, maybe we should go'... I [know] you can't just [specifically tell me what to do in advance]... [but] at least give like a tip.

Nevertheless, they agreed that the information about normative child development positively affected their parenting behavior:

> It was definitely something that impacted me... gave me more patience, reading a lot of tips... and because I'd be at times getting upset at my daughter, but then I stop to think about it. You know, she's one... I would read the text, it makes sense. Definitely it would be a good reminder for me.

And they would like to continue receiving information about what to expect in new developmental stages:

> My [son is] still growing, I could still use some information... We have messages for different age groups... My son now is between the ages of 0 and 2, and then we have messages for ages 3 to 5... Maybe find the way to continue doing that.

Engaging With One's Child

Parenting interventions can help parents become more involved in their children's lives, and men appreciated receiving practical tips:

> My girls are off-island... with a limited amount of time to see and talk to them, this was just a great tool... to maximize that time... I... start[ed] reading them books over FaceTime... It was encouraging. I need constant reminding because I would just go off somewhere.

Men remembered messages about engagement that were helpful, such as singing songs to their children:

> Singing to your child... I remember all that. I have a song... [if she] cries... there's this magic song that you'll just sing, it's kind of crazy... because 99% of the time she'll just stop crying... I didn't realize the [impact] of music.

They also remembered messages about dealing effectively with their children's challenging behaviors:

> You can't just fix them the food and then leave them at the table and do other things, actually have dinner with them. Get them to talk. Ask them, "Do you like your food?" Not just yes-no, "What do you like about your food?" Instead of scolding them, "Don't use your hands, use a fork!"

Messages about the benefits of involvement for children were especially significant, as they encouraged men to continue investing in their parenting role:

> Even though I'm not with my son right now... [paternal involvement] is a thing I didn't have as a child... I want to make sure that I make every effort and this... message hit me big time... Is true... more involvement of a father with your child makes them less likely to abuse alcohol... that I know from my own experience.

Sample text message: words of encouragement

Children with involved fathers are less likely to abuse alcohol and other substances in the future. Be involved with your children in positive ways, even if you don't live with them. This is your *kuleana* (responsibility) as a parent. *I ka wa mamua, ka wa mahope* (the future is in the past).

Participants wished for more depth than what was offered within each subject:

> You gotta make... one suggestion... for me to absorb that one thing... Maybe not introducing more concepts or more suggestions, but maybe an option to go a little bit deeper. Especially reading, like ok, read to your child... What's a good length? What kind of stuff should I read?

But, nevertheless, they agreed that the concrete and simple ideas they received positively affected their engagement, including plans for the future: "I don't have my son. But... it doesn't stop me from reading this... role-playing in my head as a father, and just once again, reinforcing... reading the messages."

Confidence in the Fathering Role

Parenting interventions can give fathers confidence in their parental role, and men wanted to feel that they are doing the right things as a parent: "For me it's positive affirmation to reinforce... I do a check-in for myself, like a reminder. Whether it's daily or weekly or monthly, that's why I chose to do this... program."

Some remembered messages that were especially significant for them in terms of parental confidence:

> For me, it would be... language development... [Even before the intervention] I was like, "Let's go to school [and on the way] check up on reading, read signs"... Not just being able to be part of it but doing, it's like a win-win.

Men agreed that the words of encouragement they received positively affected how they see themselves in their role as fathers:

> Now [after] week 12, it just reconfirms again that I'm doing, as a father, that I'm not off track. I'm not perfect, but even failure and forgiving yourself, leave room for that. It just reconfirms that I'm not that off track. It supports my fatherhood.

The Convenience of the Delivery Mode

Since levels of fathers' attendance in in-person interventions are often low, it is important to understand how delivery mode affects participation. Men decided to participate because of the convenience of the technology-based delivery mode:

> I've a busy schedule and got four kids and you don't have time to commit to coming to a class, so it's kind of at your own leisure, you get a text and you can check it out when you get time... It just takes the stress off of having to get to a class and interrupting your day.

They agreed that the delivery mode met their needs in terms of what to focus on:

> It's just easy to have something sent to you a few times rather than trying to go look. The internet's so full of stuff if you specifically want something. But if you don't know what you want, it's hard to find something of value. So that was nice that way.

They appreciated the readily available information:

> Using technology in that way... was good. If you sit in a classroom, you go and listen, you can forget... Open up your phone you can read it. Over and over again. You have it with you at all times... I read some of the messages... over and over.

And they also acknowledged the personalized nature of the messaging, which was keyed to the sex, age, and name of the focal child:

> I only get to see my daughter... on Saturdays. And I'm like going to church feeling amazing on Sunday, and then on Monday, Tuesday, Wednesday, kind of going away... But... when I was getting the texts, on the day that they came in... as I'm reading it, it uses my daughter's name and everything... Just reading that, it made me feel closer to her.

The Lack of, and Need for, Human Interaction

Despite the strong support for *Key to Kane* voiced by fathers in the focus groups, men were disappointed with the lack of human interaction. Men had decided to enroll because of their trustful relationship with the director of fatherhood programming at MFSS, whom they knew either from a previous intervention or as a community member:

> For me it was based on [the director of MFSS' fatherhood programing] reference. I respect what he has to say. So, if he tells me "Hey, this program is something that may benefit you" I was of the mindset that I would have to check it out.

Nevertheless, once in the program, fathers missed this connection and would have liked a close contact with the director and the possibility to ask personal questions:

> I [would like a] personal coach, because then you can read them [the texts], and if you do actually need more... you can go to the one-on-one coach. So at least you know how to base your questions. So... if we still don't understand, we can talk to somebody for more information.

Although participants clearly valued the convenience of the text-messaging delivery mode, they would have liked to combine it with some sort of group forum to also benefit from interactions with other fathers with similar life experiences who can understand what they are going through:

> Do a small... group. And all the members we have numbers [and can] every day [write] to each other... And that's what actually keeps us afloat.... As we respond with the next guy, and somebody else picks that up. And it's the uplifting and concrete information that you can ask "Is there anybody else in this situation where they can see the baby once a week?"

Moreover, they believed that a community of fathers could reinforce their knowledge and confidence in what they do as parents:

> It was this [focus] group... all together, we all have different strong points... [Another group member's] strong point, that he made it aware to me... Group discussions bring up a lot of areas that I might have overlooked or skipped, that wasn't too important, but then when they brought it up again I said "I remember that."

Discussion

The qualitative analysis of *Key to Kane* suggests that the intervention may represent a valuable tool to provide factual information and to promote men's confidence in their parenting role as well as father involvement, but this stands in contradiction to findings from quantitative analysis that yielded no evidence that higher reading dosage in *Key to Kane* can effectively increase men's levels of engagement with their children or parental self-confidence from pre- to post-intervention. This is in a way consistent with previous studies that show that participants liked the interventions, and their quantitative analyses indicated significant changes from pre- to post-intervention, but that these changes were limited to only subgroups of participants (e.g., Cabell et al., 2019), to only a few selected outcomes among the many targeted (e.g., Kraft & Monti-Nussbaum, 2018), or the effect sizes were small (Holmes et al., 2018). With this discrepancy in mind, it is difficult to reach firm conclusions about the potential of *Key to Kane* to produce gains in the outcomes of interest. It is possible that the discrepancy reflects a disconnect between the study population and the measures of engagement and parental self-confidence that we used. Most of the fathers who participated in *Key to Kane* lived with their children either because they were married (41%) or cohabiting (28.4%). In addition, most were employed full time (64.7%) and had completed at least some college (76.5%). The outcome measures we used were developed and validated with an exclusively nonresident father population with much higher rates of unemployment and lower levels of educational attainment (Dyer et al., 2018). The discrepancy also may stem from the content of the text messages and target audience, delivery mode, and dosage.

Content and Target Audience

Parents may join parenting interventions looking for specific information or practical suggestions (Letourneau et al., 2012; Militello et al., 2016), and some *Key to Kane* participants wished for information on topics that the intervention did not cover or wished for more depth than what was offered within each topic. In addition, it targeted both resident and nonresident fathers, and some messages did not apply to nonresident fathers who lacked contact with their children. Based on their experiences, it is clear that while these men overall liked the intervention, a one-size intervention does not fit all participants, and those with individual needs not covered in text-messaging interventions may not benefit, even if they faithfully read messages. This apparent lack of match between content and needs of participants is consistent with findings from other studies in which parents also seemed to like the intervention. For example, an evaluation of a parenting intervention that aimed to improve prekindergartens' literacy found that children of parents who were in the comparison condition and received information about health and well-being had better literacy outcomes than those whose parents were in the treatment condition, possibly because the information on health and well-being was more important for participating families and may have facilitated academic performance, or because the literacy content was too difficult for the children of participating families (Cabell et al., 2019). Similarly, parents who received messages about educational resources, activities, and the value of reading in an attempt to increase parental educational involvement showed no better gains than parents in the control group, with the exception of increased engagement in one of the many expected outcomes. One possible reason for this is that the content of the intervention did not tap into other forms of educational involvement that were measured as outcomes (Kraft & Monti-Nussbaum, 2018). Expanding interventions like *Key to Kane* by adding themes for fathers to choose from could be a better way to ensure that participants have access to information that is relevant to their parenting and their children's needs, but this should be explored in future studies.

Delivery Mode

Previous quantitative studies of text-messaging interventions for parents that provided information, tips, and encouragement have found some positive effects of the interventions on their targeted outcomes. However, these studies found that, compared to static messages, texts were more effective when parents could interact with the service, for example, by soliciting more information about a topic (Hofstetter et al., 2015b), or by receiving personalized texts inquiring about whether they used the newly presented strategies (Carta et al., 2013). *Key to Kane* was not interactive, and although fathers were pleased with the convenience of the technology-based delivery mode of the intervention, most wanted social connections: a coach for close guidance and a community of fathers, the very things that in-person fatherhood programs afford. Specifically for fathers, qualitative studies indicate that men want to interact with other men in interventions and discuss their parenting needs and feelings (Salinas et al., 2011; Scourfield et al., 2016; Sicouri et al., 2018), and that the social interactions with other fathers is the most engaging aspect of parenting programs for many men (Pfitzner et al., 2020). It has been argued that effective fatherhood programs emphasize the development of strong bonds between participants, and between participants and program staff, to buffer against feelings of isolation (Baumgartner et al., 2020), and this raises the question of whether interventions like *Key to Kane* can ever be effective as standalone. Studies that compare the effectiveness of text messaging as standalone versus as enhancement to in-person interventions are needed.

Dosage

Findings from studies discussed above and others suggest that even when fatherhood programs produce statistically significant results, the effects are either on only a few of the desired outcomes or their magnitude is small (Baumgartner et al., 2020; Holmes et al., 2018). For example, a meta-analysis study reports that most programs included in the analysis delivered a maximum of 20 hours and about a third of them delivered 8 hours or less, and it found only small-size effects on father involvement (Holmes et al., 2010). This, coupled with the discrepancy between our quantitative and qualitative findings, may point to the importance of intervention intensity in making a difference in pre- and post-intervention measurement of father outcomes. More recently, an analysis of how outcomes can be achieved in fatherhood programs has emphasized the importance of intensity, arguing that 12 hours should be the minimum dosage (Baumgartner et al., 2020) and, in fact, the U.S. Department of Health and Human Services, Administration for Children and Families, has established that, to qualify for federal grants, fatherhood programs must provide at least 24 hours of curriculum-based workshops and at least eight individual meetings with a case manager (see https://www.acf.hhs.gov/grants). All in all, this suggests that to improve effectiveness, programs must be significantly more intensive than the 36 texts in 12 weeks offered in *Key to Kane*. These text messages may be useful and appreciated for some things, but not intensive enough to produce change, and more research on dosage is needed.

Conclusion

Text-messaging interventions should be designed with careful attention paid to the delivery mode, content, and dosage, especially as they pertain to helping specific groups of fathers. Our intervention delivered 36 messages that intended to increase fathers' engagement with their children and levels of parental self-confidence for men with children age 0–12 in Hawaii. Our findings from the quantitative and qualitative portions of the evaluation are mixed and do not allow to reach firm conclusions about the potential of *Key to Kane* to produce gains in the outcomes of interest. As such, and also considering that *Key to Kane* is a pilot intervention, an important next step in research would be to implement randomized trials, which would provide information about the comparative effectiveness of interventions in improving fathering. Naturally, a quantitative research approach should be combined with qualitative data collection and analysis for more understanding of factors that affect fathers' enrollment, learning, and satisfaction. As is the case with *Key to Kane*, by combining quantitative measures and participants' subjective responses, the understanding of program processes and outcomes is expanded and strengthened.

Note

1 For a full description of the quantitative evaluation of *Key to Kane* see Lewin-Bizan et al. (2020).

References

Ansay, S., Perkins, D., & Nelson, C. (2004). Interpreting outcomes: Using focus groups in evaluation research. *Family Relations, 53*(3), 310–316.

Bar-Shain, D., Stager, M., Runkle, A., Leon, J., & Kaelber, D. (2015). Direct messaging to parents/guardians to improve adolescence immunizations. *Journal of Adolescent Health, 56*(5), S21–S26.

Baumgartner, S., Friend, D., Holcomb, P., Clary, E., Zaveri, E., & Overcash, A. (2020). *Pathways-to-outcomes: How responsible fatherhood program activities may lead to intended outcomes*. Office of Planning, Research, and Evaluation, Administration for Children and Families, U.S. Department of Health and Human Services.

Breitenstein, S., Gross, D., & Christophersen, R. (2014). Digital delivery methods of parenting training interventions: A systematic review. *Worldviews on Evidence-Based Nursing, 11*(3), 168–176.

Bronte-Tinkew, J., Burkhauser, M., & Metz, A. (2012). Elements of promising practices in fatherhood programs: Evidence-based research findings on interventions for fathers. *Fathering, 10*(1), 6–30.

Cabell, S., Zucker, T., DeCoster, J., Copp, S., & Landry, S. (2019). Impact of a parent text-messaging program on pre-kindergarteners' literacy development. *AERA Open, 5*(1), 1–16.

Carta, J., Lefever, J., Bigelow, K., Borkowski, J., & Warren, S. (2013). Randomized trial of a cellular phone-enhanced home visitation parenting intervention. *Pediatrics, 132*(S2), S167–S173.

Dyer, W.J., Kauffman, R., Fagan, J., Pearson, J., & Cabrera, N. (2018). Measures of father engagement for nonresident fathers. *Family Relations, 67*, 381–398.

Evans, W., Wallace, J., & Snider, J. (2012). Pilot evaluation of the Text4baby mobile health program. *BMC Public Health, 12*(1), 1031–1041.

Fagan, J., & Iglesias, A. (1999). Father involvement program effects on fathers, father figures, and their Head Start children: A quasi-experimental study. *Early Childhood Research Quarterly, 14*(2), 243–269.

Fagan, J., & Pearson, J. (2020). Fathers' dosage in community-based programs for low-income fathers. *Family Process*, *59*(1), 81–93.

Hall, C., & Bierman, K. (2015). Technology-assisted interventions for parents of young children: Emerging practices, current research, and future directions. *Early Childhood Research Quarterly*, *33*(4), 21–32.

Hofstetter, A., DuRivagea, N., Vargas, C., Camargo, S., Vawdrey, D., Fisher, A., & Stockwell, M. (2015a). Text-message reminders for timely routine MMR vaccination: A randomized controlled trial. *Vaccine*, *33*(43), 5741–5746.

Hofstetter, A., Vargas, C., Camargo, S., Holleran, S., Vawdrey, D., Kharbanda, E., & Stockwell, M. (2015b). Impacting delayed pediatric influenza vaccination: A randomized controlled trial of text-message reminders. *American Journal of Preventive Medicine*, *48*(4), 392–401.

Holmes, E., Galovan, A., Yoshida, K., & Hawkins, A. (2010). Meta-analysis of the effectiveness of resident fathering programs: Are family-life educators interested in fathers? *Family Relations*, *59*(3), 240–252.

Holmes, E., Hawkins, A., Egginton, B., Robbins, N., & Shafer, K. (2018). *Do responsible fatherhood programs work? A comprehensive meta-analytic study*. Fatherhood Research and Practice Network. https://www.frpn.org/sites/default/files/FRPN_MetaAnalysis_Summary_121418_v3.pdf

Hurwitz, L., Lauricella, A., Hanson, A., Raden, A., & Wartella, E. (2015). Supporting Head Start parents: Impact of a text-message intervention on parent-child activity engagement. *Early Child Development and Care*, *185*(9), 1373–1389.

Jones, D., Forehand, R., Cuellar, J., Kincaid, C., Parent, J., Fenton, N., & Goodrum, N. (2013). Harnessing innovative technologies to advance children's mental health: Behavioral parent training as an example. *Clinical Psychology Review*, *33*(2), 241–252.

Kim, Y.-I., & Jang, S. (2018). *A randomized controlled trial of the effectiveness of a responsible fatherhood program: The case of TYRO Dads*. Fatherhood Research and Practice Network. https://www.frpn.org/sites/default/files/FRPN_Summary_TYRO_061518_v6.pdf.

Kitzinger, J. (1995). Qualitative research: Introducing focus groups. *British Medical Journal*, *311*(7000), 299–302.

Kraft, M., & Monti-Nussbaum, M. (2018). Can schools enable parents to prevent summer learning loss? A text-messaging field experiment to promote literacy skills. *The Annals of the American Academy of Political and Social Science*, *674*(1), 85–112.

Letourneau, N., Tryphonopoulos, P., Duffett-Leger, L., Stewart, M., Benzies, K., Dennis, C., & Joschko, J. (2012). Support intervention needs and preferences of fathers affected by postpartum depression. *The Journal of Perinatal & Neonatal Nursing*, *26*(1), 69–80.

Lewin-Bizan, S., Mattos, D., & Baguio-Larena, E. (2020). *Participation dosage in Key to Kāne: A pilot text-messaging intervention for fathers*. Fatherhood Research and Practice Network. https://www.frpn.org/sites/default/files/FRPN_Hawaii_ExecutiveSummary_020620_R3-1.pdf.

Militello, L., Melnyk, B., Hekler, E., Small, L., & Jacobson, D. (2016). Automated behavioral text messaging and face-to-face intervention for parents of overweight or obese preschool children: Results from a pilot study. *JMIR mHealth and uHealth*, *4*(1), e21.

Nieuwboer, C., Fukkink, R., & Hermanns, J. (2013). Online programs as tools to improve parenting: A meta-analytic review. *Children and Youth Services Review*, *35*(11), 1823–1829.

Pfitzner, N., Humphreys, C., & Hegarty, K. (2020). Bringing men in from the margins: Father-inclusive practices for the delivery of parenting interventions. *Child & Family Social Work.* https://doi.org/10.1111/cfs.12760.

Salinas, A., Smith, J., & Armstrong, K. (2011). Engaging fathers in behavioral parent training: Listening to fathers' voices. *Journal of Pediatric Nursing, 26*(4), 304–311.

Scourfield, J., Allely, C., Coffey, A., & Yates, P. (2016). Working with fathers of at-risk children: Insights from a qualitative process evaluation of an intensive group-based intervention. *Children and Youth Services Review, 69*, 259–267.

Sicouri, G., Tully, L., Collins, D., Burn, M., Sargeant, K., Frick, P., Anderson, V., Hawes, D., Kimonis, E., Moul, C., Lenroot, R., & Dadds, M. (2018). Toward father-friendly parenting interventions: A qualitative study. *Australian and New Zealand Journal of Family Therapy, 39*(2), 218–231.

7
CHALLENGES AND OPPORTUNITIES FOR ENGAGING UNMARRIED PARENTS IN COURT-ORDERED, ONLINE PARENTING PROGRAMS

Claire S. Tomlinson, Brittany N. Rudd, Amy G. Applegate, and Amy Holtzworth-Munroe

INDIANA UNIVERSITY

Introduction

Approximately two out of five births in the United States are to unmarried women (Wildsmith et al., 2011). Children with unmarried parents experience parental relationship instability, such as separation, at higher rates than those born to married parents (Osborne & McLanahan, 2007), a concern as parental relationship instability has significant implications for child well-being. On average, children whose parents separate experience greater difficulties with psychological adjustment and engage in more risky behaviors (e.g., substance abuse, early sexual initiation) than peers whose parents remain together (Amato, 2010).

Unmarried parents differ from their married counterparts in important ways. They tend to be younger, less educated, and have fewer children together (Insabella et al., 2003). In addition, unmarried parents are more likely to experience risk factors for lower levels of relationship stability and father involvement. For example, they are more likely to have children with other partners and to report depression, problems with drugs and alcohol, and intimate partner violence (McLanahan, 2011). Unmarried fathers are five times more likely than married fathers to report a history of incarceration at the time of the child's birth (McLanahan, 2011). Unmarried parents are more likely to be from economically disadvantaged backgrounds, as individuals with more resources are more likely to marry (Edin & Reed, 2005).

Parents who are not married may interact with the legal system to establish paternity and obtain child support and parenting time orders. Thus, family courts may be an important setting to increase unmarried parents' access to preventative services intended to build stronger coparenting relationships and high-quality father involvement (McHale et al., 2012). Parent education programs aim to meet these goals. Courts often offer such programs to families seeking to resolve parenting issues, with 46 U.S. states offering or requiring parent attendance at parent programs (Pollet & Lombreglia, 2008). Court-ordered parenting programs tend to use in-person formats and be short; 30% are three hours or less, and the majority are shorter than five hours (Fackrell et al., 2011).

Family court stakeholders, however, are concerned about low rates of parent program attendance (Cookston et al., 2002; Thoennes & Pearson, 1999). Parents, particularly those who are socioeconomically challenged, face many practical barriers to attendance. For example, young parents completing in-person parent programs report that their attendance would be enhanced by access to on-site childcare and public transportation, as well as making attendance voluntary and providing food (Taylor et al., 2012). A study of educational services offered through Head Start randomly assigned parents to either receive childcare and transportation or neither form of assistance; receiving those assistance programs increased the level of participation (Watterson, 2001).

Given that Internet and mobile device usage is widespread, and might overcome some of these access barriers, online versions of parent programs have flooded the marketplace. Indeed, court systems are beginning to encourage, and sometimes mandate, online parent programs. While these programs are touted as more time- and cost-efficient (Bowers et al., 2011), it is unclear whether they would be beneficial for unmarried parents. Thus, we evaluated barriers and facilitators to unmarried parents' access and completion of online parenting programs.

Method

The current study was conducted as part of a randomized controlled trial (RCT) comparing outcomes for parents assigned to one of two online parenting programs (i.e., Arbuthnot & Gordon, 1996; Caraway & Jones, 2011; Children in Between [CIB; https://online.divorce-education.com]; Two Families Now [TFN; https://www.twofamiliesnow.com]) or to a no-program control group. Both TFN and CIB are informational and skills-based online programs designed for separating and divorcing parents, with each program, on average, lasting three to five hours. Both include modules on topics such as interparental conflict, improving communication, coparenting, and improving the parent–child relationship. To engage parents, both use video scenarios (e.g., common coparenting problems, alternative responses), guided questions, skills practices, and quizzes. CIB also includes a brief section directed at never married parents, which highlights issues commonly encountered by this demographic (e.g., how younger parents react to situations).

The RCT study sample included both divorcing and unmarried parents, but here, we only focus on the experiences of unmarried parents. Eligible parties were unmarried parents scheduled for an initial court hearing for child-related issues (e.g., custody, parenting time; for unmarried cases, the issues could also include establishing paternity and/or child support). Eligible parents received a court order[1] that instructed them to access a court website that would inform them whether they were required by court order to complete an online parenting program. On the website, they also were invited to participate in the RCT, which involved completing online questionnaires for which they would be compensated.

The court order informed parties assigned to a program that they were allowed 30 days to access and complete the program, and that the online parenting programs could be completed on a variety of devices (e.g., smartphones). Parties were provided with information about using public library computers if they did not possess such devices. The order informed parents that the programs were free, took three to five hours to complete, and could be completed in sections and on one's own time. The order was signed by a judge. If the parent had not accessed the court website approximately one week after the court order, the parent was reminded to do so.

The RCT study was designed to examine an almost completely online process for a court to order parents to complete a parent program, for parents to do so, and for researchers to gather data on the effectiveness of the programs. Unfortunately, however, recruitment was challenging. Seventy percent of the way into the 30-month-long RCT study, only 28% of unmarried parents who had been sent a court order had accessed the court website, as ordered, to find out if they should complete a parent program. In addition, 37% of unmarried parents did not participate in an online parent program, even after accessing the court website and being court-ordered to do so. Looked at somewhat differently, only 10% of unmarried parents sent a court order both accessed the website and participated in a mandated online parent program. To assess facilitators and barriers to complying with the court order and participating in the parenting program, we implemented the current qualitative study, which involved interviews with small samples of participating and nonparticipating parents.

Study Participant Eligibility Criteria

At the time the current study was conducted, 380 RCT eligible unmarried parties had been sent a court order to access the court website. As noted above, eligible parties were initial cases involving unmarried parents and scheduled for a court hearing for child-related issues (e.g., to establish paternity, child support, custody, or parenting time) in Delaware County, Indiana. Eligible parties had to speak English, be 18 years of age or older, and not be incarcerated. Parties with attorney representation were excluded due to the complexity of obtaining consent for study participation from attorneys.[2] Also, parties had to meet one of the following conditions: had already had their court hearing to decide custody issues, had their case dismissed, or had waived their final hearing.[3] We recruited both parties who did and did not participate in a parenting program.

Recruitment Procedures

Participant recruitment for the current qualitative interview study occurred for almost one year during the course of the RCT. Undergraduate research assistants attempted to contact parties via mail, email, and phone (using whatever contact information was available) to invite them to participate in the study interview. We were able to interview 43 unmarried parties.

Subsample Sizes

There were two main points in the RCT study where we saw drop-off in parents' engagement in the online programs. The first was parents not complying with the court order to access the court website and see if they were ordered to complete a parenting program (i.e., 72% of unmarried parties did not access the website). The second involved parents who did not participate in the online parent program even after accessing the court website and being court-ordered to do so (i.e., 37% of unmarried parents). Among the 43 unmarried parties recruited and interviewed in the current study, there were seven parties who remembered receiving the court order but did not access the website. Further, 29 interviewees had not participated in a parenting program, so we asked them hypothetical questions about the parenting program. Finally, we asked the 11 parties who reported having participated in the parenting program questions about their actual experiences with a program.

Qualitative Interview and Interviewers

In the current study interview, we first asked questions regarding accessing the court website. Specifically, we asked parties who remembered receiving the court order but did not access the website about barriers to accessing the court website (i.e., "If you had been able to get online, would you have felt comfortable accessing the court website?"). We then inquired about barriers and facilitators to completing the online programs from the perspective of both parties who did or did not participate in a program. We asked interviewees who had not participated in a parenting program hypothetical questions about the parenting program (e.g., "Would you have been willing to participate in an online parenting program?"). For participants who participated in a parenting program, we asked questions about their actual experiences with a program (e.g., "Was doing the parenting program inconvenient?") and addressed party assessment of specific aspects of the program (e.g., content, length, videos, quizzes). Finally, we asked parties demographic questions, to describe our sample.

Interview Coding System and Coders

We developed an integrated, open coding system by examining the interviews part-way through the study and extracting recurring themes that were common both in the gathered data and the existing literature (Corbin & Strauss, 1990). Regarding accessing the court website, codes focused on barriers. Regarding parenting program participation, we divided codes into either barriers or facilitators. Here, we discuss only codes endorsed by more than 25% of the relevant subsample.

Results

Study Participant Demographics

We interviewed 31 female parties and 12 male parties. Parties were, on average, 32 years old, with approximately a high school education. They were primarily White (69%), and most worked either full or part time (81%). On average, they shared 1.5 children with the other parent in the court case, had lived with the other parent for 6 years, and had been separated for 2.5 years. Approximately a third of parties had a new partner. These findings are consistent with general information about the demographics of unmarried parents in the United States (Insabella et al., 2003).

Barriers to Accessing the Court Website

The seven parties who did not access the court website after receiving a court order to do so identified a variety of challenges. All reported that doing so would have been inconvenient (100%, 7/7), primarily due to being too busy (100%, 7/7), as a result of work (57%, 4/7) and/or children (57%, 4/7). For instance, one party noted, "[I] take care of children and grandmother and [I'm] working part time." Two parties (29%, 2/7) also endorsed that accessing the court website would have taken too long.

Despite the fact that they had not accessed the website, most parents held negative perceptions of it (71%, 5/7). Parties reported feeling that the court website would not be helpful (43%, 3/7) or feeling that they were already a good parent and thus did not need a court website or a program to help them improve their parenting (43%, 3/7).

Some parties identified technology issues as a barrier to accessing the court website (43%, 3/7). For example, one party indicated: "If I had had WIFI, and known I was supposed to get on the website, I would have done it." As reflected in that quote, parties also indicated that they did not understand why they were ordered to access the court website and expressed general confusion (43%, 3/7) and lack of awareness that they had been court ordered to do so (29%, 2/7). One party noted, "They could have made it more obvious whether I needed to go to do a parenting program if I was ordered to do so." Indeed, 29% (2/7) of parties stated that they would have preferred being notified about the court website in another manner. One party stated, "[I] would have liked them to tell [me] in the court room, not through written notice."

Only 28% of unmarried parents sent a court order to go to a court website did so, even with a reminder phone call. Our findings suggest that both the method of delivery and the content of the court order matters. If courts want parents to complete parenting programs, they should consider using multiple and varied forms of contact with parties rather than relying exclusively on a court order either mailed to parties or provided to parties' attorneys for transmission to their clients. In our study, the court order, and the reminder phone call to those who failed to comply, did not explicitly explain why the court wanted parents to participate in a program, the possible benefits of the program, or how the program might be particularly relevant to unmarried parties. Such additional information might increase compliance with court orders to complete online parent programs. When courts are particularly interested in reaching unmarried parents, using additional engagement strategies would be consistent with past research demonstrating the importance of strong judicial support for programs, particularly for unmarried parents (Insabella et al., 2003; Kusayeva & Miller, 2019; Thoennes & Pearson, 1999).

Facilitators and Barriers to Program Completion

Court Factors Related to Program Participation

Seventy-three percent of the 11 parties (8/11) who participated in an online parenting program stated that a court factor (e.g., the program was mandatory) facilitated their participation. All of those parties (8/11) reported completing the program because it was mandatory, while four of them (4/11, 36%) reported completing the program to look good for the judge. One party stated, "I was under the impression that it was required, a step in the process and could not continue the court [process] without it."

Just as almost half of parties who did not even access the court website expressed confusion about the court's communication to do so; 46% (5/11) of parties who participated in a program similarly endorsed a court-related factor that hindered their engagement in the program. Some parties indicated that they would have preferred a different form of communication from the court regarding the program (46%, 5/11), such as clearer presentation of information in the court order or details regarding the benefits of the program. One party suggested, "I think they could have made [the court order] more clear about what [the program] is, with something like a synopsis."

In sum, court actions might both help or hinder participation in a parenting program. For those who correctly understood that program completion was mandatory, the court order was a motivator. At the same time, many parents expressed dissatisfaction with the court's communication regarding the program and its possible benefits. Our findings indicate that unmarried parents may require (and benefit from) additional guidance, and clear messaging, from the court.

Positive and Negative Perceptions of the Program

Parents Who Participated in a Program. All 11 parties (11/11) who participated in a program characterized it favorably. When provided with a list of possible ways the program was helpful, each of the following was endorsed by 50% or more of the 11 parties: improved communication (9/11), improved parenting ability (7/11), and improved coparenting skills (6/11). In addition, four parties (4/11; 36%) felt that the program helped their child, while three (3/11; 27%) felt the program was interesting.

TEXT BOX 7.1

"i was resistant at first, but as I completed [the program], I personally wanted to get a better understanding of how to parent. It was beneficial to me, and it was eye opening. I really liked the parts about the effects of conversations with the kids and how I talk about the other parent in front of the kids. I also really, really enjoyed the collaborate [sic] part, because I really want my daughters to have two parents."

Parties who completed the programs were also asked if they enjoyed specific aspects of the program, with 91% (10/11) of parties who participated in a program giving a positive review of some aspect and generally liking multiple aspects, of the program. When given a list of program components, parties identified enjoying the quizzes (73%, 8/11) and videos (73%, 8/11).

TEXT BOX 7.2

"I liked [the videos] because it was real life stuff, and you'd get to see the situations in person...we feel kind of alone sometimes, but it was nice to see other people dealing with the same problems."

Indicating mixed feelings about the program, 27% of parties who actually participated in a program (3/11) had negative perceptions of it. For instance, one parent expressed, "I think if they cater to a single parent demographic it would be more helpful." Almost three-fourths (73%, 8/11) also disliked some specific aspect of the program (e.g., the quizzes, videos, or specific program elements).

Parents Who Did Not Participate in a Program. Of the 29 unmarried parties who did not participate in a program, 62% (18/29) characterized programs favorably after being given information about them. Most thought that online parenting programs would be helpful (55%, 16/29). When presented with a list of things they could have learned from the program, many parties identified that they would have liked to learn how to improve their parenting (48%, 14/29). For example, a parent reported, "With my four-year-old, I deal with a lot of fit throwing and anger, so I would love some information to help me out with that."

Among nonparticipants, 38% (11/29) held negative views of the program when it was described to them. Most expressing negative views felt that the program would not have been helpful (21%; 8/29). As one party stated, "I know everything to take care of a child."

Summary. The findings regarding actual and hypothetical perceptions of online parent programs suggest that once parents actually participate in a program, they perceive it positively. One strategy to increase initial program engagement is to improve potential participants' initial perceptions of online programs. Some researchers have successfully engaged parents by providing additional information regarding how the program would be relevant or beneficial[4], using a variety of methods, such as emailed newsletters, family testimonial flyers, teacher endorsement, and engagement phone calls (which troubleshoot barriers to attendance and discuss program relevance; Clarkson, 2014; Winslow et al., 2016). Others have used parental commitment to participation, such as through a written pledge, as individuals are more likely to carry out an activity if they have recorded their intended participation (Giné et al., 2010). While the current study used one reminder phone call, other researchers have used more consistent reminders across multiple platforms (e.g., texting) (Richburg-Hayes et al., 2014). Another method to increase participation may be to tailor programming to unmarried parents, as parents mentioned disliking aspects of the programs referencing divorcing parents that were not relevant to them. As noted previously, only one of the two programs, CIB, included a section targeted directly at unmarried parents. Other researchers have explored how to tailor programming to unmarried parents, such as including content emphasizing the importance of coparenting separately, reinforcing the role of both parents' relationships with their child, and providing resources for commonly encountered issues dealing with housing and employment services (Marczak et al., 2015). Program developers could consider beginning online parent programs with a brief online assessment that tailors the program to the unique needs of unmarried parents.

Consistent with adult learning theory (Collins, 2004), parents in our study reported enjoying the program videos and quizzes, which tend to be the most interactive and engaging parts of stand-alone digital interventions. Thus, incorporating strategies that increase parent opportunity for interaction may help with parent participation. Including clinician support may be one way to do that. For example, when Day and Sanders (2018) randomly assigned parents to an online self-guided parenting program with or without additional practitioner support sessions, they found that parents who had regular clinician contact were both more engaged in the program and showed greater symptom reduction in their children.

Online or In-Person: The Role of Social Support

Parents had mixed views about in-person versus online formats for parenting programs. Twenty-seven percent (3/11) of the 11 unmarried parties who participated in a program noted that they would have preferred an in-person class and would have liked some social support.

In contrast, 48% (14/29) of the 29 unmarried parties who did not participate in a program indicated that, hypothetically, they would have preferred an online course over a face-to-face course, often due to desire for privacy and confidentiality.

TEXT BOX 7.3

Two contrasting opinions of the role of social support in online parenting programs:
While one party stated, "I learn from other people, so I would have liked to have that interaction [with] other people," another party stated, "I, for one, don't like to share personal information with people that I don't know, and it would be more comfortable in a personal environment."

Thus, while some participants preferred the social support offered by an in-person program, others appreciate the privacy of an online program. In a systematic review of online parenting programs, Nieuwboer and colleagues (2013) found that the majority of programs offered some form of parent socialization, including through informational pages, group forums, discussion boards, email, or an online chat capability, and such services elicited parent satisfaction when offered. To boost parent engagement and program effectiveness, online program developers could include an optional form of online social support, such as a social media network or discussion board.[5] Doing so would honor the desire of both participants who want more social support as well as those who do not. It is also possible that, when resources are available to do so, offering parents a choice between an online program and an in-person program could increase engagement by allowing parents to select the format that best fits their needs for social support.

Convenience and Inconvenience of the Programs

Seventy-three percent (8/11) of the 11 parties who participated in a program felt that the program was convenient, and 55% (6/11) reported that the length of the program made completion easier. Similarly, the large majority of parties who did not actually participate in a program said that, hypothetically, they would have found program participation convenient (93%, 27/29), noting that the program would have been convenient due to its online nature, with 69% (20/29) of such parties noting the accessibility that technology offered.

On the other hand, 55% (6/11) of parties who actually participated in a program reported that it was inconvenient. Some parties took issue with the program length (46%, 5/11), while other parties reported that participating in the program was difficult given their busy schedules (27%, 3/11).

TEXT BOX 7.4

The program was "very lengthy, with two kids running around I couldn't sit down and complete the whole thing. I was trying to do it all at once, but it was too long."

Online parent programs were designed to increase convenience by eliminating the need for transportation and childcare associated with in-person formats. Thus, it is interesting that while the majority of parties find online programs convenient, some still experience inconveniences. Shorter programs may address the problem, particularly for unmarried parties. However, the programs in our study averaged only four hours in length, and the available literature shows effectiveness only for parent education programs that involve 10 in-person sessions with homework assignments (Sandler et al., 2020; Wolchik et al., 2002). Additional research is clearly needed about the impacts of short programs on child and parent well-being, parenting strategies, or other outcomes.[6] Indeed, through research on program effectiveness, we may begin to identify the active ingredients of parent programs and then "trim" programs to include only important components. In addition, the inconveniences reported by our unmarried participants indicate that online parenting programs can benefit from supplementary supports, such as allowing additional time to complete a program or alternative locations to participate in a program (e.g., offering computer access and childcare at the court).

Technology Associated With the Programs

Thirty-six percent (4/11) of the 11 unmarried parties who participated in an online program reported that doing the program on their available technology facilitated program participation. One party stated, "I could access [the program] through the internet and the answers and films were convenient and easy to understand and the options given were relevant." Further, the majority of the 29 parties who did not participate in a program noted that they possessed the technology that would have been required for program participation (66%, 19/29).

> **TEXT BOX 7.5**
>
> Completing the program would be "pretty convenient for me, I've always had a smart phone, and everyone in my family has a computer so it was pretty easy for me to get access to that."

Seventy-three percent (8/11) of those parents who participated in a program, however, encountered some problem related to technology use. Most commonly, parties reported a problem accessing or participating in a program due to the required technology (55%, 6/11) or confusion regarding how to navigate or access the program online (46%, 5/11).

> **TEXT BOX 7.6**
>
> "During the parenting program, one of the segments got stuck and wouldn't move on even after I completed it. I was clicking 'continue' or 'next' or whatever, but it wouldn't do anything."

In summary, while many parties reported that they enjoyed, or would have enjoyed, the use of technology and that they had, or would have had, the technology required to complete the programs, almost three-fourths of unmarried parties who actually participated in the program reported technological issues. Thus, methods to alleviate parents' technology issues or discomfort could be important to incorporate into programs. One study of barriers to parental education found that, although many parents were comfortable navigating an online program, some who were less familiar with technology relied more heavily on in-program prompts and online technology support (Robinson, 2018). Thus, program developers should consider providing technology support both prior to and throughout parenting program participation (e.g., a support line to assist parents).

Summary of Recommendations

The current study sought to understand barriers and facilitators to online parenting program access and participation among unmarried parents opening a court case to resolve child-related issues. To do so, we conducted qualitative interviews with 43 unmarried parents who had been court ordered to access a court website to learn whether the court was ordering them to participate in an online parent program or not. The following presents recommendations for courts, program developers, and researchers as informed by the current study results:

- To increase compliance with court orders to attend programming, courts could improve their messaging by providing parents with information about the program, why the court is ordering it, hypothesized or proven program benefits, and the possible relevance of the program to the parents and their children. Program developers should ensure that such information is available for courts to provide for families and, ideally, build it into both engagement materials and the programs themselves. Judges could consider explaining the parenting programs and their assumed utility to parents from the bench and urging parents to attend rather than relying exclusively on a written order.
- To optimize impact, courts and programs could consider developing programs exclusively for unmarried parents or including content tailored to unmarried parents. Unmarried parents may have unique needs that differ from those that divorced parents experience, that may include being younger on average, having potentially more complex coparental relationships, not having resided with the other parent, having children by multiple parties, and/or being more likely to face challenges such as unemployment and incarceration.
- Courts, in collaboration with researchers, could consider the costs and benefits of devoting additional resources to unmarried parties' engagement and completion of online parenting programs. There is evidence that positive parent engagement by unmarried, nonresident parents is usually associated with improved child well-being and child educational and emotional outcomes, and there may be some savings associated with reduced relitigation. Engagement strategies for online parenting programs could include supporting parents through the program initiation process (e.g., providing staff through the court to assist parents with accessing the online program, providing computers at the court and childcare for parents to complete the program). Also, program developers should make several key additions to

online programming to assist unmarried parents, including technical support, clinician support, and optional social support.

More work is needed to understand how to best support unmarried parents in their engagement of parent programs. However, there remains a lack of evidence-based online parent programs for unmarried parents engaged in the legal system. Parenting programs theoretically have great potential to decrease the risk of negative outcomes for parents resolving parental disputes and for their children. However, we lack empirical evidence that online programs meet that potential, nor do we know which program components are most effective for, and most appealing to, unmarried parents. Such work will help us meet the needs of the unmarried parents who are increasingly served by family court systems.

Acknowledgments

This work was supported by grants from two funders, the Indiana Supreme Court and the Fatherhood Research and Practice Network ("FRPN"), under grant #90PR0006 from the U.S. Department of Health and Human Services, Office of Planning, Research, and Evaluation (OPRE) to Temple University and the Center for Policy Research, Denver, Colorado. The Indiana Supreme Court and FRPN acted independently in funding the research studies referenced herein, and neither funder expresses any opinion as to the goals or mission of the other funder. These research studies were conducted through an academic judicial partnership with the Delaware Circuit Court, located in Muncie, Indiana. Any opinions, findings, and conclusions or recommendations expressed in this work are those of the authors and do not necessarily reflect the views of the Indiana Supreme Court, the Delaware Circuit Court, FRPN, or OPRE. We thank the Indiana Supreme Court, FRPN, OPRE, and the Delaware Circuit Court, particularly Delaware Circuit Judges Kim Dowling and Marianne Vorhees, and Delaware Circuit Court Administrator Emily Anderson, for their support of evidence-based research and practice. We also thank our research assistants, law interns, and the litigants who participated in these studies.

Notes

1 The court order was mailed to parties without an attorney; it was provided to the attorney for any party who had one.
2 Legally, we could not directly contact represented parties without the consent of their attorneys.
3 These criteria were intended to reduce the possibilities of parties perceiving any coercion from the court to complete the interview study or falsely believing that completing the study would affect their court outcome.
4 Assuming that empirical evidence demonstrates program effectiveness.
5 Such parent-to-parent interactions may require an online program moderator to identify and correct misinformation shared among parents.

6 It should be noted that longer, more intensive programs (e.g., the New Beginnings Program, which includes over ten in-person group sessions with homework assignments in between) are supported by research (Wolchik et al., 2002).

References

Amato, P. R. (2010). Research on divorce: Continuing trends and new developments. *Journal of Marriage and Family, 72*(3), 650–666.

Arbuthnot, J., & Gordon, D. A. (1996). Does mandatory divorce education for parents work? A six-month outcome evaluation. *Family Court Review, 34*(1), 60–81.

Bowers, J. R., Mitchell, E. T., Hardesty, J. L., & Hughes, R., Jr. (2011). A review of online divorce education programs. *Family Court Review,* 49(4), 776–787.

Caraway, N., & Jones, L. B. (2011). *Phase II final report: Parenting through divorce* (Grant #: 2R44HD050021-02). IRIS Media. https://study-reports.s3.amazonaws.com/Parenting%20Through%20Divorce-%20Phase%20II%20Report.pdf.

Clarkson, A. C. (2014). *Participation on a parenting website: Testing predictors of parents' passive and active site participation* (Publication No. 3635010) [Doctoral dissertation, the University of Wisconsin-Madison]. ProQuest Dissertations Publishing.

Collins, J. (2004). Education techniques for lifelong learning: Principles of adult learning. *Radiographics, 24*(5), 1483–1489.

Cookston, J. T., Braver, S. L., Sandler, I., & Genalo, M. T. (2002). Prospects for expanded parent education services for divorcing families with children. *Family Court Review, 40*(2), 190–203.

Corbin, J. M., & Strauss, A. (1990). Grounded theory research: Procedures, canons, and evaluative criteria. *Qualitative Sociology, 13*(1), 3–21.

Day, J. J., & Sanders, M. R. (2018). Do parents benefit from help when completing a self-guided parenting program online? A randomized controlled trial comparing Triple P Online with and without telephone support. *Behavior Therapy, 49*(6), 1020–1038.

Edin, K., & Reed, J. (2005). Why don't they just get married? Barriers to marriage among the disadvantaged. *The Future of Children, 15*(2), 117–137.

Fackrell, T. A., Hawkins, A. J., & Kay, N. M. (2011). How effective are court-affiliated divorcing parents education programs? A meta-analytic study: Divorce education meta-analysis. *Family Court Review, 49*(1), 107–119.

Giné, X., Karlan, D., & Zinman, J. (2010). Put your money where your butt is: A commitment contract for smoking cessation. *American Economic Journal: Applied Economics, 2*(4), 213–235.

Insabella, G. M., Williams, T., & Pruett, M. K. (2003). Individual and coparenting differences between divorcing and unmarried fathers: Implications for family court services. *Family Court Review, 41*(3), 290–306.

Kusayeva, Y., & Miller, C. (2019). *Tools for better practices and better outcomes.* MDRC. https://www.acf.hhs.gov/sites/default/files/programs/css/bics_final_report.pdf.

Marczak, M. S., Becher, E. H., Hardman, A. M., Galos, D. L., & Ruhland, E. (2015). Strengthening the role of unmarried fathers: Findings from the co-parent court project. *Family Process, 54*(4), 630–638.

McHale, J., Waller, M. R., & Pearson, J. (2012). Coparenting interventions for fragile families: What do we know and where do we need to go next? *Family Process, 51,* 284–306.

McLanahan, S. (2011). Family instability and complexity after a nonmarital birth: Outcomes for children in fragile families. *Social Science, 621*, 111–131.

Nieuwboer, C. C., Fukkink, R. G., & Hermanns, J. M. A. (2013). Peer and professional parenting support on the internet: A systematic review. *Cyberpsychology, Behavior, and Social Networking, 16*(7), 518–528.

Osborne, C., & McLanahan, S. (2007). Partnership instability and child well-being. *Journal of Marriage and Family, 69*(4), 1065–1083.

Pollet, S. L., & Lombreglia, M. (2008). A nationwide survey of mandatory parent education. *Family Court Review, 46*(2), 375–394.

Richburg-Hayes, L., Anzelone, C., Dechausay, N., Datta, S., Fiorillo, A., Potok, L., Darling, M., & Balz, J. (2014). *Behavioral economics and social policy: Designing innovative solutions for programs supported by the Administration for Children and Families*. (OPRE Report 2014-16a). Administration for Children and Families, Office of Planning, Research and Evaluation, U.S. Department of Health and Human Services.

Robinson, W. (2018). *Exploring parenting self-efficacy among parents of children in residential treatment: Evaluating a combined online psychoeducational intervention* (Publication No. 10793164) [Doctoral dissertation, Boston University]. ProQuest Dissertations Publishing.

Sandler, I., Wolchik, S., Mazza, G., Gunn, H., Tein, J. Y., Berkel, C., Joes, S., & Porter, M. (2020). Randomized effectiveness trial of the new beginnings program for divorced families with children and adolescents. *Journal of Clinical Child & Adolescent Psychology, 49*(1), 60–78.

Taylor, C., Mills, A., Schmied, V., Dahlen, H., Shuiringa, W., & Hudson, M. E. (2012). What works to engage young parents into services? Findings from an appreciative inquiry workshop. *Contemporary Nurse, 42*(2), 258–271.

Thoennes, N., & Pearson, J. (1999). Parent education in the domestic relations court: A multisite assessment. *Family Court Review, 37*(2), 195–218.

Watterson, K. J. (2001). Head Start parent education participation: A study of motivating factors. *Dissertation Abstracts International: Section B: The Sciences and Engineering, 62*(3–B), 1605.

Wildsmith, E., Steward-Streng, N. R., & Manlove, J. (2011). *Childbearing outside of marriage: Estimates and trends in the United States (Child Trends Research Brief, #2011–29)*. Child Trends. https://www.childtrends.org/wp-content/uploads/2013/02/Child_Trends-2011_11_01_RB_NonmaritalCB.pdf.

Winslow, E. B., Poloskov, E., Begay, R., Tein, J. Y., Sandler, I., & Wolchik, S. (2016). A randomized trial of methods to engage Mexican American parents into a school-based parenting intervention. *Journal of Consulting and Clinical Psychology, 84*(12), 1094.

Wolchik, S. A., Sandler, I. N., Millsap, R. E., Plummer, B. A., Greene, S. M., Anderson, E. R., Dawson-McClure, S. R., Hipke, K., & Haine, R. A. (2002). Six-year follow-up of preventive interventions for children of divorce: A randomized controlled trial. *JAMA, 288*(15), 1874–1881.

8

A MIXED-METHODS STUDY OF A MOTHER-ONLY PROGRAM TO ENHANCE COPARENTING RELATIONSHIPS

Jay Fagan, Jessica Pearson, and Abigail Henson

Positive coparenting relationships are necessary to realize the goals of enhancing nonresident fathers' long-term relationships with their children, increasing the financial support they provide, and improving child well-being. This observation is based on research finding that 1) positive forms of involvement by nonresident fathers are associated with children's social and emotional well-being, academic achievement, and behavioral adjustment (Adamsons & Johnson, 2013), and 2) the most salient predictor of nonresident father involvement is the quality of the father's relationship with the mother (Cowan et al., 2010; Sobolewski & King, 2005). Improving coparenting relationships, especially among unmarried, nonresident parents, however, is challenging.

While many programs attempt to improve coparenting relationships using father-only interventions, information on their effectiveness is mixed. For example, the *Caring for My Family* study found a moderate, positive effect on self-reported coparenting one week after program completion for nonrandomized treatment group participants compared to control group parents (Cox & Shirer, 2009). A recent randomized control trial of the Ridge program in Ohio also found that low-income, mostly nonresident fathers' self-reported coparenting relationships improved at post-test and three-month follow-up after participating in a fatherhood curriculum called TYRO DADS, which includes a coparenting component (Kim & Jang, 2018). However, the results of the PACT evaluation, an RCT of four Responsible Fatherhood Programs that each include substantial coparenting components, indicated no statistically significant difference on self-perceptions of coparenting alliance, support, or conflict among fathers in the experimental and control groups (Avellar et al., 2018).

Although researchers and practitioners have suggested that coparenting interventions would be more effective if both mothers and fathers were involved

(Fagan, 2008; Froehle, 2008), programs have had little success in recruiting mothers for coparenting interventions offered through fatherhood programs (Dion et al., 2015). For example, although three of the four fatherhood programs participating in the PACT evaluation encouraged current or past partners to join relationship workshops either with the father or by participating in a separate workshop for female partners, they were poorly attended (Dion et al., 2015). A research project that attempted to engage mothers in a coparenting intervention conducted through a fatherhood program sponsored by Talbert House in Ohio found mother recruitment to be virtually impossible due to poor parental relationships, mother's distrust of the fatherhood program to represent her interests, inconvenient class schedules and location, weaknesses in staff communication and outreach, and misunderstanding about the purpose of the coparenting service (Whitton & Sperber, 2018). Another evaluation of efforts to engage mothers in a single-session, mother-only coparenting intervention in Kentucky found that 53.6% of invited mothers agreed to participate (see chapter 9 in this volume).

These inconsistent findings on the effectiveness of fatherhood programs in producing coparenting outcomes and the difficulties of engaging mothers in coparenting interventions necessitate a closer examination of the myriad of issues pertaining to the context and needs of different groups of fathers and mothers. The current study draws from a mixed-methods evaluation of a National Fatherhood Initiative mothers-only coparenting intervention, *Understanding Dads*™, to determine the following: (1) Are mothers (whose child's father attends a fatherhood program [FP] interested in participating in a coparenting intervention? (2) What are the predictors of mothers' interest in participation? (3) What is the effect of mothers' participation on coparenting and father–child contact? and (4) What do mothers who participate (and the father of their children) have to say about the coparenting intervention and its effect.

The purpose of *Understanding Dads*™ is to enhance mothers' awareness and communication so they can more effectively coparent with the fathers of their children. The curriculum attempts to (1) help mothers understand why father involvement is important, (2) improve mothers' awareness of how her relationship with her own father impacts her relationship with the father of her child, (3) improve communication between the coparents, and (4) increase mothers' confidence as a parent and coparent.

In order to complete a sufficient number of cohorts of the intervention, the eight-session program was condensed into six sessions conducted over six consecutive weeks, with each session two hours in length. The first three sessions focused on the roles of mothers, the impact of one's own father on self, and the impact of one's own mother on self. The second half of the sessions focused on relationships with the fathers of their children, connecting the impact of these various relationships on their children, and healthy pro-relationship skills, such as building a foundation for effective communication, creating an open and safe environment for communication, and learning how to effectively listen to their partner. Each session included a range of activities, including handbook work, discussion, presentation, and role play. Additionally, each session provided opportunities for mothers to gain relationship knowledge and awareness as well as to learn about relationship skills they could use in their daily lives. At the end of each session, the participants reviewed the material learned and answered a couple of skills and attitude-specific questions.

Method

The coparenting research study attempted to answer research questions using both quantitative and qualitative research methods. Based on pilot research on *Understanding Dads*™ (Fagan et al., 2015), we hypothesized that mothers' participation in the intervention will be associated with mothers' reports of increased confidence in their ability to coparent, mothers' reports of increased coparenting alliance and father–child contact, and mothers' reports of decreased disagreements and undermining. The quantitative component employed a pretest/post-test/three-month follow-up design (there was no control or comparison group) with a total of 22 cohorts across six urban social service agency sites. Two cohorts took place in New York City, one in Colorado, two in Pennsylvania, two in New Jersey, eight in South Carolina, and seven in California. Each site was chosen due to their active fatherhood programs and interest in implementing mother education programs. The qualitative component consisted of semi-structured interviews (and one focus group) conducted with mothers who participated in *Understanding Dads*™ (total N of mothers = 17), and with fathers whose child's mother participated in the intervention ($N = 12$).

For the first nine cohorts, mothers and fathers were eligible if they were 18 years or older, lived separately, had a child 19 years or younger who lived mainly with the mother, did not have a restraining or protection order saying the father could not have contact with the mother, felt safe working together, could travel to the program, and if the father was an active participant in the fatherhood program at the service agency site. The next 14 cohorts held the same eligibility requirements; however, we started to allow coparents who lived together to participate, as well as fathers who expressed interest and were willing to participate in a fatherhood program but were not actively involved at the time of recruitment.

Mothers were recruited in one of three ways: (1) the father was recruited through advertisements at the urban agency sites or information sessions conducted at other community-based parenting programs and provided contact information for the mother, (2) the mother was recruited through advertisements in local and online mothering groups, or (3) the mother reached out to the coordinator after hearing of the class from a previous participant. Fathers who were recruited directly identified a "target mother" with whom they were interested in bettering their coparenting relationship and provided her contact information to the project coordinator, who later reached out to her. Attempts were made to reach 316 mothers to participate in the study. Sixty-three percent of the mothers were recruited via the father who was already enrolled in a fatherhood program.

The site-specific coordinator made multiple attempts to contact mothers via phone calls and text messages. For mothers who were recruited by way of fathers providing the project coordinator with her contact information, an average of 6 contact attempts were made to each mother, with a maximum of 20 attempts, a minimum of 1 attempt, and a standard deviation of 4.27. If the mothers were recruited in the latter two categories (e.g., advertisements in local and online mothering groups), they would provide the coordinator with the father's contact information and the coordinator would see if the father was (1) interested in enrolling in the fatherhood program, and (2) interested in participating in the coparenting study. Mothers were only deemed eligible to participate in the coparenting intervention if the father responded affirmingly to both.

For the first two cohorts, qualifying mothers were compensated $30 after completing each of the three surveys and $15 per class in addition to on-site childcare during the classes. However, after learning that mothers would prefer paying for their own child care, we increased the compensation to $45–$50 per class, depending on the site, and did not provide on-site childcare for the next 21 cohorts. Anywhere from six to ten mothers participated in each of the class cohorts. Most participating fathers attended fatherhood classes focused on parenting, coparenting, and employment readiness at the same time that mothers were attending *Understanding Dads*™ classes.

Of the 316 mothers who were reached out to for this study, 8 mothers were ineligible, 31 mothers could not be reached after multiple calls and voice mail messages (these mothers were treated as "disinterested"), 124 were disinterested, and 153 were interested in participating in the coparenting program. This represents an interest rate of 49.7%. Of the 153 eligible mothers who expressed interest in the program, 141 mothers completed the pretest survey. Of the 141 mothers who completed the pretest, 127 mothers (83% of those who were *interested*) attended at least one session, 105 of these mothers completed the post-test survey, and 81 mothers completed the pretest, post-test, and three-month follow-up. In analyzing the predictors of mother's interest in participating in the coparenting intervention, we conducted logistic regressions analyses using data collected from fathers and found that each additional level of education completed by fathers increased the odds that mothers were interested by 33%. We also found that each additional child shared by mothers and fathers increased the chances that mothers were interested by 54%, fathers' incarceration increased the odds of interest by 118%, and co-residing with the father decreased the chances of interest by 70%.

Quantitative Component

Participant Characteristics

Demographic characteristics are based on the sample of mothers who completed the pretest survey and attended at least one intervention session ($n = 127$). The average age of the mothers who were surveyed was 31.1 years ($SD = 7.3$ *years*, range = *18–34 years*). The average age of the fathers was 33.17 years ($SD = 7.97$ *years*, range = *18–36 years*). The average age of the participants' children was 4.63 years ($SD = 4.25$ *years*, range = *1 month–16 years*). About 54% of the mothers identified as being Black, 28.1% White, .8% Asian or Pacific Islander, 2.5% American Indian, and 14% identified as Other. About 25% of the all mothers identified as Hispanic. Of the surveyed mothers, 7.4% had not completed high school, 37.7%, completed high school or received their GED, 5.7% went to technical school following high school, 35.2% completed some college, 9.8% obtained a college degree, and the remaining 4.1% completed graduate school. Data on fathers showed that 23.5% had not completed high school, 47%, completed high school or received their GED, 4.3% went to technical school following high school, 18.1% completed some college, and the remaining 5.2% obtained a college degree. Mothers had an average of 2.3 biological children ($SD = 1.4$, range = 1–5). Mothers reported an average annual income ranging from $5,001–$15,000. Only 18.5% of mothers and fathers co-resided with each other.

Measures

The mothers' pretest survey included 170 items to gather demographic information and explore their coparenting experiences and attitudes. Mothers' post-test and follow-up questionnaires included items that appeared on the respective pretests in order to track any change in response. The items in all measures showed a high level of reliability (Cronbach's alpha above .65), suggesting a high level of consistency in the assessment of each concept. Measures at all three time points included a 12-item coparenting confidence scale relating to mother's confidence in her ability to coparent with the father ($\alpha = .88$ at pretest, .89 at posttest, and .96 at follow-up); a coparenting subscale representing behaviors relevant to alliance (pre/mothers $\alpha = .79$; post/mothers $\alpha = .77$; follow-up mothers $\alpha = .71$); a mother-reported undermining subscale addressing mothers' undermining of fathers (pre/mothers $\alpha = .79$; post/mothers $\alpha = .77$; follow-up mothers $\alpha = .71$); a list of nine issues regarding the care of children that mothers and fathers might have had disagreements about; and a question concerning father–child contact that elicited information from mothers on the frequency with which the father had contact with the child during the past month.

> **TEXT BOX 8.1**
>
> Sample Items from Measures
> *Coparenting confidence*
> "I am confident I can stay calm when I talk to [FATHER] about [CHILD],"
> "I am confident I can let go of unrealistic parenting expectations I have about [FATHER]."
> *Coparenting alliance*
> "[FATHER] and I share information about [CHILD] with each other."
> *Undermining*
> "I contradict the decisions he makes about my child."
> *Coparenting disagreement*
> "How much do you and father disagree about how to set limits and discipline [CHILD]?"

Moderation tests were conducted. Moderation examines the degree to which change on the outcome variables (e.g., change on coparenting confidence from pretest to post-test) is influenced by other factors. Four moderators were tested: program dosage, mother-father co-residence, race/ethnicity, and whether the mother was recruited first. The dosage variable was dichotomized into two categories and compared mothers who attended at least 5 out of the 6 coparenting classes (high dose, $n = 74$, 58.3%) to those who attended 4 or fewer classes (low dose, $n = 53$, 41.7%). The mother recruited first variable was also dichotomized and distinguished between mothers who were recruited independently ($n = 80$, 63%) and mothers who were recruited via fathers' attendance in a fatherhood program ($n = 47$, 37%). Co-residence was based on mothers' reports: $0 = $ *we do not live together*, $1 = $ *we live together all or most of the time*. Race/ethnicity of the mother consisted of the following categories: non-Hispanic Black, non-Hispanic White, Asian/Pacific Islander, American Indian, Hispanic, and other/not specified.

Quantitative Results

Preliminary Analyses

We conducted statistical analyses to determine whether mothers who participated in the intervention ($n = 127$) differed on study variables from mothers who were interested in the intervention but did not participate ($n = 14$). These analyses indicated no significant differences between the two groups of mothers on pretest measures of coparenting confidence, perceptions of father–child contact, or coparenting alliance. However, participating mothers were significantly more likely to report disagreements with fathers at pretest ($p = .02$) and undermining the father at pretest ($p < .01$). These findings suggest that mothers who participated in the intervention had more coparenting challenges than mothers who did not participate.

Effects of the Intervention

Pretest to Post-Test

Repeated measure ANOVAs showed significant change for mothers' reports of coparenting confidence and disagreements, but not for mothers' perceptions of coparenting alliance, undermining, or father-child contact. Mothers' confidence increased significantly from pretest to post-test. We calculated effect sizes using the *partial eta squared* ($\acute{\eta}^2$) statistic for all outcomes. An effect size of .01 to .06 is considered a small effect, .06 to .14 is considered medium, and greater than .14 is considered large. The effect size for coparenting confidence was medium ($\acute{\eta}^2 = .07$). Mothers' perceived disagreements with the father decreased significantly from pretest to post-test, with a medium effect size ($\acute{\eta}^2 = .08$).

There was one moderation effect for mothers: dosage moderated mothers' reports of disagreements from pretest to post-test. Pairwise comparisons revealed that low-dose mothers reported significantly fewer disagreements at post-test than at pretest, with a large effect size, $\acute{\eta}^2 = .17$. High–dose mothers showed no significant decrease in disagreements, $\acute{\eta}^2 = .00$. There were no significant moderation effects for mother-father co-residence, mother race/ethnicity, or recruitment of mother before or after the father was recruited.

Pretest and Post-Test to Follow-Up

Compared with data from pretest to post-test, the repeated measure ANOVA with data that included pre-, post-, and follow-up assessments was based on a smaller sample size due to researchers not being able to contact parents three months following the intervention. The sample went from 105 to 81 for mothers (29% reduction). Repeated measure ANOVAs showed significant change over time for mothers' reports of coparenting confidence, disagreements, and undermining, but not for mothers' perceptions of coparenting alliance or father-child contact. Across the three time periods, mothers reported higher levels of coparenting confidence and lower levels of disagreements and undermining. The effect sizes were large for these outcomes ($\acute{\eta}^2 = .23$, $\acute{\eta}^2 = .23$, $\acute{\eta}^2 = .17$, respectively). Pairwise comparisons showed that mothers' coparenting confidence increased significantly from pretest to follow-up ($p < .001$), and from post-test to follow-up ($p < .001$); mothers' perceptions of disagreements with the father decreased significantly from pretest to follow-up ($p < .001$), and from post-test to follow-up ($p < .001$); and mothers' perception of their undermining the father decreased from pretest to follow-up ($p < .001$), and from post-test to follow-up ($p < .001$). There were no moderation effects for dose, recruitment of mother before or after father was recruited, co-residence, or race/ethnicity.

Qualitative Component

For the qualitative interviews, we compiled a list of phone numbers for the mothers who participated in the intervention and the fathers of their children and called at random times to schedule the qualitative interviews. Those who agreed to participate in the interviews were compensated an additional $30 for their time. Upon obtaining consent from participants, individual interviews took place over the phone with one researcher administering the interview guide while another researcher listened silently and took detailed notes, which permitted verbatim transcription. The focus group occurred in person at the New Jersey site and was audio-recorded and later transcribed. Both phone interviews and the focus group focused on the issues of self-awareness, likes and dislikes about the intervention, and any noticeable change in the coparenting relationship since participation.

Interviewed mothers were asked a variety of open-ended questions: why had they been interested in the coparenting class, did they find the class useful, program likes and dislikes, coparenting experiences prior to and following class participation, feelings about self and the father as parents, levels of conflict with the other parent, and ways of dealing with disagreements. Interviewed fathers were asked whether coparenting, conflict, and communication with the other parent had changed following class participation. Once all of the interviews were completed, the focus group transcripts and interview notes were reviewed and coded using an iterative approach. Four codes emerged for mothers and were defined and entered in a codebook: *Salient curriculum components, Change in coparenting relationship, Self-reflection, and Empathy for father*. The same four codes were used for father interviews with the substitution of *Empathy for father*, with *Empathy for mother*. Two researchers separately referenced the codebook while analyzing the interview notes and transcripts and coded quotes and notes that aligned with the specific code definitions. Once all of the interviews were coded, the researchers conducted an inter-rater reliability check to test the level of agreement across the two coders. The researchers found more than 80% agreement across the coded segments, thus demonstrating reliability. Interviewed mothers and fathers resembled their counterparts in the full sample who participated in the coparenting intervention, with the exception of income level for fathers where qualitative interview subjects were better earners ($p = .001$).

Qualitative Results

Interviews and focus groups with 17 mothers and 12 fathers revealed a variety of reactions and perceived changes that are consistent with the quantitative results. Mothers reported learning some emotional and practical tools in the coparenting program including: being more aware of their own behavior, holding fewer unrealistic expectations about the other parent, interacting with reduced levels of emotion, considering the father's perspective, and feeling more empathy for his situation. As one mother put it, "I don't jump the gun or bust at him anymore." Another mother explained,

> Biggest thing I got from class is unrealistic expectations. I try to think from his point of view. In the past, I would expect him to see things the way I do. For example, if he doesn't show up, I would expect he would know how that makes me feel. I am learning to let that go. I am interacting with him differently. I try to take emotion out of it. I try to be very clear and concise about what I expect from him. It has made a difference in that it doesn't make me feel as crazy and upset. But it has not changed his behavior.

A mother from California credited the class with helping her "not to get mad about things." Another maintained that she no longer "stops texting or hangs up the phone on him ... and actually listens to what he says." And one mother said she was trying not to "ruminate on situations or bring (them) back up to get control over it." Consistent with the significant reductions in conflict and disagreement observed in the quantitative component, mothers described improved communication, fewer arguments, and lower levels of conflict. For example, a mother from South Carolina stated,

> We wouldn't talk at all. We wouldn't get along. Every time he came there was an argument. Now I've learned to be quiet and listen. I've been learning stuff [in class]. I try to be understanding and hear his point of view. I praise him when he does something good. I think he likes that I'm now not mean. We don't fight. We respect each other now.

Another mother from South Carolina described, "Now we are quick to see we are saying the same things. Sometimes we don't realize we are saying the same thing. Now we listen to the whole thing that another person is saying, and that helps to realize we are saying the same thing. Reduces conflict."

Some mothers reported that the other parent had demonstrated some parenting improvements as a result of participating in a fatherhood program, although this was not substantiated in the quantitative study. The qualitative interviews with fathers reinforced mothers' observations of improved communication and reduced levels of conflict. Fathers felt as though mothers were more understanding and empathetic, which aligns with the quantitative findings of reduced undermining.

As one father exclaimed, "It's amazing that I don't have to really worry about the arguments." Another observed that the intervention had made it easier for him to be close to the mother, "Before the classes we were a little more distant. When we were around each other we were not getting along so well.... The changes are just more and less us being around each other more without an argument and being able to understand each other's sides." Still another father credited the mother's participation in the coparenting intervention to reduced levels of conflict: "There was negative communication and now it is positive communications ... the classes avoid a bunch of fights.... From then to now, I'm guessing after the class, it's gotten a lot healthier; there is less bickering, fighting over the little things." In a similar vein, a father noted, "She was always willing to work but our opinion on things, our perception on things was different. Now, it's less stressful. The collaboration is easier."

TEXT BOX 8.2

"Before the classes we were a little more distant, when we were around each other we were not getting along so well... The changes are just more and less us being around each other more without an argument and being able to understand each other's sides."

Fathers attributed the mothers' reduced level of hostility to her becoming more empathetic and understanding of the father's perspective. When asked whether the mother of his child was better able to see his side of a disagreement after taking the class, a father replied, "Yes, most definitely. Just easier to get along and to work out things between each other. She's able to understand my perspective." Another father made a similar statement, "Since the classes she doesn't look at things one way, like her way. She says 'OK' you made some good points but here is how I see it and we come to mutual agreement. Sometimes I let her go her way and sometimes she lets me go my way and now we just compromise since the classes."

Discussion

The current mixed-methods study was conducted because of growing interest among programs serving low-income, predominantly nonresident fathers to recruit mothers for coparenting interventions. Researchers and practitioners have suggested that coparenting relationships are more likely to improve if both fathers and mothers receive coparenting services (Cowan & Cowan, 1995); however, engaging mothers in coparenting interventions is difficult to do. Only about 50%

of targeted mothers appear to be willing to participate, despite the use of attractive incentives and strong outreach efforts. Once engaged, however, mothers (and the fathers of their children) find the program to be valuable. Pretest and post-test evaluation of the 105 mothers who participated in the six-session *Understanding Dads*™ curriculum found that mothers reported significant improvements in conflict, that is fewer disagreements with the father, and increased confidence in their ability to coparent with the father. Follow-up data three months following completion of the intervention showed continued improvement in conflict and coparenting confidence as well as decreased maternal undermining of fathers. Interviews and focus groups with 17 and 12 of these mothers and fathers, respectively, revealed perceived changes that are consistent with the quantitative results.

The study findings suggest that brief, mother-only interventions have the potential to improve coparenting among low-income, nonresident parents in striking ways. Both the quantitative and qualitative findings suggest that mother-only interventions can have a positive impact on coparenting outcomes. While the "gold standard" for coparenting interventions may well be couple-based with both parents participating together (Pilkington et al., 2019), our findings suggest that a mother-only approach can achieve some important goals such as improved communication, reduced conflict, and mother's understanding of the father's point of view. This is an important finding given the limited and/or negative relationships of many unmarried, nonresident parents.

Although some mothers would have liked to continue meeting and a few suggested the value of including fathers in the group, most mothers appreciated the support they received from other mother participants and a trained facilitator. The mix of discussion, activities, and reflections was also appealing. Finally, the findings lend support for interventions that try to teach both behavioral strategies like communication and conflict resolution as well as skills in support, empathy, and acceptance (Bradbury & Lavner, 2012).

Overall, several aspects of the *Understanding Dads*™ curriculum appear to do a good job of fostering empathy and self-reflection and might be considered for replication in other coparenting interventions. These include attention to a mother's experience with her own father, the use of metaphors such as an "emotional bank" to promote understanding of communication patterns, the introduction of animal analogies to describe and highlight different conflict styles, and a focus on realistic and unrealistic relationship expectations. The current study suggests that coparenting and relationship studies that have focused exclusively on communication and conflict outcomes may be overlooking outcomes that are not typically assessed such as empathy, self-awareness, and realistic relationship expectations. Researchers should develop and validate measures of these types of outcomes.

Caution should be exercised in concluding that the mothers' intervention caused improvements in coparenting. Without the inclusion of a no-treatment control group we cannot say that the intervention caused coparenting changes. It is possible that the positive changes in coparenting were the result of passage of time. It is also difficult to state that the mothers' intervention was responsible for improved coparenting because many fathers were also involved in a coparenting intervention at about the same time as mothers. Conceivably, mothers' perceptions of improved coparenting resulted from fathers' changed behavior rather than their own. Future research will need to closely examine fathers' simultaneous participation in coparenting programs to determine what is affecting change. We also need studies that compare coparenting outcomes for mothers and fathers who participate in interventions together and separately. The goal of these studies would be to determine whether there is greater similarity in their ratings of their coparenting relationships following program treatments as compared with before.

Finally, the study has implications for fatherhood program practice. If improving child outcomes tracks with positive father engagement, and mother-father relationship quality is a key predictor of father engagement, fatherhood programs may need to make coparenting and maternal engagement more of a priority. This may necessitate the adoption of new curricula that promote realistic relationship expectations and empathy, and new program structures and collaborations that may enhance mother engagement.

Conclusions

We learned several important lessons about recruiting mothers to attend coparenting classes in this study. The study coordinators had greater success at recruitment when the incentive was increased from $15 per class to $35–$45 per class. The incentive was increased in order to pay for mothers' childcare rather than providing childcare in the fatherhood program. Many community programs do not have the resources to pay mothers an incentive of this size and therefore may have difficulty starting *Understanding Dads*™ classes. We also learned that it was considerably easier to recruit mothers first rather than through fathers already attending fatherhood programs. Previous studies have shown that low-income nonresident mothers often mistrust that fatherhood programs will have their best interests in mind (Whitton & Sperber, 2018). Programs and policy makers may need to rethink how services are marketed to parents in order to ensure that mothers, who are most frequently the primary caregivers of children in low-income families, receive the support they need to effectively coparent with fathers.

In conclusion, the findings of this study indicate that low-income mothers can benefit from a short group-based coparenting program (*Understanding Dads*™) that is for mothers only. Moreover, mothers benefit regardless of their residential status, race/ethnicity, or timing when they are recruited for the intervention. The benefits appear to be both attitudinal and behavioral. That is, the mothers expressed improved attitudes such as greater confidence in coparenting, but they also expressed reduced coparenting conflict in interactions with fathers. Finally, the effects of the intervention on mothers' coparenting ranged from medium to large. These findings provide preliminary evidence to suggest *Understanding Dads*™ as an evidence-based intervention. It will be important, however, to conduct a randomized control trial of the intervention to confirm the value of this program.

References

Adamsons, K., & Johnson, S. K. (2013). An updated and expanded meta-analysis of nonresident fathering and child well-being. *Journal of Family Psychology, 27*(4), 589–599.

Avellar, S., Covington, R., Moore, Q., Patnaik, A., & Wu, A. (2018). *Parents and children together: Effects of four responsible fatherhood programs for low-income fathers* (OPRE Report #2018-50). Administration for Children and Families, Office of Planning, Research and Evaluation, U.S. Department of Health and Human Services. https://www.acf.hhs.gov/sites/default/files/opre/pact_rf_impacts_to_opre_508.pdf.

Bradbury, T. N., & Lavner, J. (2012). How can we improve preventive and educational interventions for intimate relationships? *Behavior Therapy, 43*(1), 113–122.

Cowan, C. P., & Cowan, P. A. (1995). Interventions to ease the transition to parenthood: Why they are needed and what they can do. *Family Relations: Journal of Applied Family & Child Studies, 44*, 412–423.

Cowan, P. A., Cowan, C. P., & Know, V. (2010). Marriage and fatherhood programs. *The Future of Children, 20*(2), 205–230.

Cox, R. B., Jr. & Shirer, K. A. (2009). Caring for my family: A pilot study of a relationship and marriage education program for low-income unmarried parents. *Journal of Couple & Relationship Therapy, 8*(4), 343–364.

Dion, M. R., Zaveri, H., & Holcomb, P. (2015). Responsible fatherhood programs in the parents and children together (PACT) evaluation. *Family Court Review, 53*(2), 292–303.

Fagan, J. (2008). Randomized study of a prebirth coparenting intervention with adolescent and young fathers. *Family Relations, 57*, 309–323.

Fagan, J., Cherson, M., Brown, C.A., & Vecere, E. J. (2015). Pilot study of a program to increase mothers' understanding of dads. *Family Process, 54*, 581–589.

Froehle, M. (2008). *Lessons from responsible fatherhood initiatives* (InfoSheet 14). Minnesota Fathers & Families Network. http://www.mnfathers.org/wp-content/uploads/2013/06/InfoSheetResponsibleFatherhoodInitiatives-COLOR.pdf.

Kim, Y.-I., & Jang, S. J. (2018). FRPN grantee report: A randomized controlled trial of the effectiveness of a Responsible Fatherhood Program: The case of Tyro Dads. Fatherhood Research and Practice Network. www.frpn.org.

Pilkington, P., Rominov, H., Brown, H. K., & Dennis, C.-L. (2019). Systematic review of the impact of coparenting interventions on paternal coparenting behavior. *Journal of Advanced Nursing, 75*, 17–29.

Sobolewski, J. M., & King, V. (2005). The importance of the coparental relationship for nonresident fathers' ties to children. *Journal of Marriage and Family, 67*(5), 1196–1212.

Whitton, S., & Sperber, K. (2018) *Final evaluation report: Evaluating mother and nonresidential father engagement in coparenting services in a fatherhood program*. Fatherhood Research and Practice Network. https://www.frpn.org/asset/frpn-grantee-report-evaluating-mother-and-nonresidential-father-engagement-in-coparenting.

9

FATHERHOOD AND COPARENTING

A Study of Engaging Mothers in Paternal Involvement Interventions

Armon R. Perry, Aaron C. Rollins Jr., Ebony O'Rea, and Abby F. Perez

Introduction

Demographic shifts, including decreasing marriage rates and higher rates of nonmarital childbearing, have led to an increased interest in the roles that fathers play in their children's lives. Much of the extant research indicates that the quality of the coparenting relationship between mothers and fathers plays a major role in shaping paternal involvement (Pudasainee-Kapri & Razza, 2015; Varga & Gee, 2017). Therefore, many programs for unmarried fathers target the coparenting relationship as a part of their intervention. Despite the emphasis placed on them, most of what is known about coparenting relationships focuses on the conflict and difficulties that are characteristic of many of these relationships (Petren et al., 2017; Russell et al., 2016). Coparenting challenges are associated with issues pertaining to child support orders and payments (Goldberg, 2015), mothers' new partners, and fathers' multiple partner fertility (Goldberg & Carlson, 2015).

However, to move the field forward, practitioners need to know more about what works in fatherhood and coparenting interventions. Fortunately, there is a growing body of literature on the factors associated with functional coparenting relationships and the results of interventions aimed at reducing coparenting conflict (Owen & Rhoades, 2012). For example, Fagan et al. (2015) examined the effects of 34 mothers participating in the *Understanding Dads*™ curriculum on their attitudes towards fathers, knowledge of healthy pro-relationship skills, and relationship self-efficacy. After the eight-week intervention, mothers increased their knowledge and reported improved attitudes and self-efficacy. In Marczak et al.'s (2015) experimental evaluation of a Coparent Court project, parents in the treatment group received 12 hours of coparenting education, case management, and referrals to community-based social service agencies, whereas control group parents received the typical family court experience. The results revealed that treatment group mothers reported higher quality coparenting relationships and more father involvement. Most recently, Stolz et al. (2017) evaluated Parenting Together, a nine-hour coparenting intervention for never-married parents who were in court for a child-related dispute. The study included a racially diverse sample of 55 participants, including 29 fathers and 26 mothers. At the conclusion of the intervention's three sessions, the results revealed positive changes in coparenting knowledge, attitudes, and teamwork behavior.

Despite what we have learned from previous research, a gap remains as it relates to how to effectively engage mothers in fatherhood programming. Moreover, much of the existing intervention literature is limited by studies with small samples (Fagan et al., 2015), homogenous samples (Bonach, 2005, 2009), and studies without control groups (Owen & Rhoades, 2012). In response, the purposes of this study were to 1) investigate the feasibility of recruiting custodial mothers whose coparents were participating in a fatherhood program into a brief coparenting intervention, 2) understand the reasons why they were willing or unwilling to be engaged in the intervention, and 3) employ an experimental design to test the effectiveness of the intervention on mothers' reports of conflict resolution skills, coparenting relationship quality, and fathers' involvement with children.

Program Description

Funded by the U.S. Department of Health and Human Services, Administration for Children and Families, Office of Family Assistance, the *4 Your Child* program is a responsible fatherhood intervention for nonresident fathers ages 16 and up. *4 Your Child* aims to help fathers increase their capacity for taking more active roles in their children's lives by providing 28 hours of parent education and up to 6 months of case management services. The parent education component of the program contains fatherhood, parenting, and healthy relationship training delivered via group workshops featuring content from the National Fatherhood Initiative's *24/7 Dad® A.M.* curriculum (National Fatherhood Initiative, 2015). Given that a large proportion of *4 Your Child's* participants are involved in high-conflict relationships with the child's mother over custody, visitation, and/or child support, program participants also receive additional coparenting modules featuring content from the *Together We Can* curriculum. The *4 Your Child* program's 28 hours of parent education are delivered in 7 four-hour group-based workshops.

In addition to the group-based training workshops, *4 Your Child* participants are also eligible to receive solution-focused case management services. These case management services are led by Parent Resource Coordinators (PRCs) who conduct an initial intake assessment to determine the participants' strengths and needs. This initial assessment is followed by a goal-setting meeting in which the PRCs work with the participants to identify their parenting goals and objectives, ultimately leading to the development of individualized service plans. For the remainder of the participants' time in *4 Your Child*, the PRCs provide referrals to community resources and monitor participants' progress toward their goals.

Through its Continuous Quality Improvement (CQI) process, data analysis revealed improvements in *4 Your Child* participants' parenting knowledge and reports of consumer satisfaction. However, fathers also reported that in many cases, they had trouble applying what they learned in *4 Your Child* because after graduating, they had to negotiate access to their child with a coparent with whom they had a tenuous or conflictual relationship. Therefore, there was interest in developing and pilot-testing a coparenting intervention aimed at increasing custodial mothers' receptivity to coparenting. The intervention consisted of two phases. The first phase involved a two-hour parent education workshop. The workshop included selected content and activities from modules in the National Fatherhood Initiative's *24/7 Dad® A.M.3rd edition* and the *Together We Can* curriculum developed by the Michigan State University Extension Office. In addition to presenting the content to mothers, facilitators brought anonymous comments and questions that fathers raised in the *4 Your Child* workshops to the mothers' sessions, where they were discussed so that mothers could acquire more insight into typical father reactions. Subsequent to completing the parent education workshop, mothers were invited to participate in the second phase of the intervention, which was a coparenting session led by a court-approved mediator. The purpose of these sessions was to bring mothers and fathers together to work on developing mutually agreed-upon parenting plans.

TEXT BOX 9.1 COPARENTING INTERVENTION CONTENT AND ACTIVITIES

24/7 Dad AM
- What It Means to be a Man
- Family History
- Showing and Handling Feelings
- Grief and Loss
- Communication
- Getting Involved and Parenting Time
- Working With Mom

Together We Can
- The Balloon Activity
- Family Wheel
- My Hopes and Dreams

Methods

The following section describes the study methods. This description includes the study design, participants, procedures, measures, and data analysis.

Study Design

The study employed a mixed-methods design. The quantitative methods included an experimental design featuring mothers being randomly assigned to either an intervention group or a control group. The qualitative methods included post-workshop focus groups and six-month follow-up interviews related to the participants' coparenting experiences and perspectives, as well as their feedback on the intervention's strengths and weaknesses.

Study Participants

To recruit mothers, we made announcements during *4 Your Child's* fathers' workshops about the possibility of referring their coparent to a brief intervention. As part of the announcement, we queried fathers regarding their interest in having their coparent exposed to a sampling of the content that they had received. Fathers expressing interest provided the name and a contact number for their coparent. After receiving names and contact information for mothers from fathers, we made attempts to reach mothers by telephone and text message.

We collected data for this study from a sample of 153 custodial mothers. Seventy-two (48.0%) of the mothers self-identified as Black, 67 (44.6%) self-identified as White, eight (5.3%) self-identified as biracial, and two (1.3%) reported as "other." Seventy (46.7%) of the mothers were not married or dating anyone, 42 (28.0%) were married to or were dating the father enrolled in *4 Your Child*, and 34 (22.7%) were married to or were dating someone other than the father enrolled in *4 Your Child*. On average, the mothers were 34.75 (SD = 8.09) years old, earned \$23,303.94 per year (SD = \$17,500.17), and had 2.61 (SD = 1.28) children with 1.83 (SD = .94) childbearing partners (Figure 9.1).

Procedures

Mothers assigned to the control group did not receive any services. Instead, they were simply mailed coparenting brochures developed by NFI that provided tips on effective coparenting. Mothers assigned to the intervention group were invited to participate in a one-time parent education workshop that lasted approximately two hours. Immediately following each of the workshops, mothers were invited to participate in a focus group. These focus groups were facilitated by the same person who conducted the workshop (either the first or second

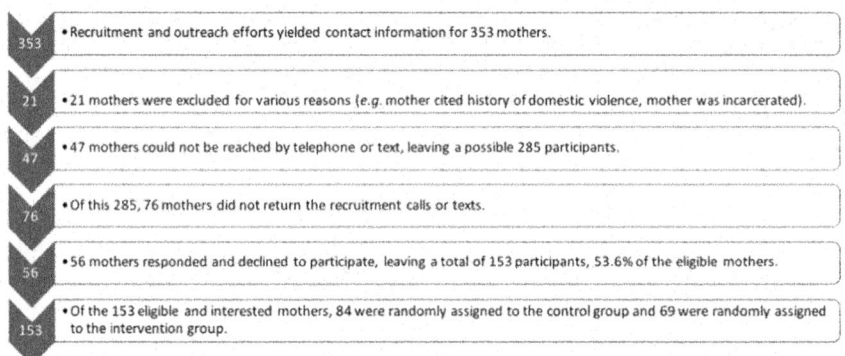

FIGURE 9.1 Recruitment, Exclusion, and Enrollment Flow Chart

author) and followed a semi-structured format. The proceedings were audio-recorded to ensure accuracy during transcription. Subsequent to the focus groups, mothers were offered a free coparenting session with fathers that was facilitated by the second author, a court-approved mediator. The intent of these sessions was to bring mothers and fathers together to discuss and negotiate mutually agreed-on coparenting plans. Intervention group mothers were also invited to participate in telephone interviews as a part of the six-month follow-up data collection.

Measures

The primary outcomes under examination in this study were measured in three data-collection waves, including pre-intervention, three months post intervention, and six months post intervention. These outcomes included mothers' reports of conflict resolution skills, coparenting relationship quality, and fathers' parenting behavior. Conflict resolution skills were measured using the Relationship Dynamics Scale (Renick et al., 1992). This measure has 12 items focused on the frequency with which respondents used various styles (e.g., launching personal attacks, tuning the other person out, throwing insults and digs) to deal with arguments and disagreements. Because the wording of the items reflected negative conflict resolution styles (e.g., launching personal attacks), aggregated scores ranged from 12 to 60, with lower scores indicating better conflict resolution skills.

Mothers' reports of coparenting relationship quality was measured using the Coparenting Questionnaire (Margolin et al., 2001). This measure has 14 items focused on the amount of conflict between parents, the extent of cooperation between mothers and fathers, and the extent to which parents distort boundaries by attempting to form a coalition with the child that undermines or excludes the other parent. Aggregated scores ranged from 14 to 70, with high scores indicating positive coparenting relationships.

Mothers' reports of fathers' parenting behavior were measured using the Index of Father Involvement (Hawkins et al., 2002). This measure has 26 items that focused on the extent to which fathers participate in various parenting activities (e.g., spending time with child, reading to child, attending events in which the child participates). Aggregated scores ranged from 26 to 156, with high scores indicating more-involved fathers. See Perry et al. (2020) for a full description of the study measures.

Data Analysis

Data analyses involved repeated measures mixed ANOVAs that were used to determine the differences in various outcome measures by study condition across the three data-collection waves. There was one repeated-measures mixed ANOVA for each primary outcome, including mothers' conflict resolution skills, mothers' reports of fathers' involvement, and coparenting relationship quality. Of the 153 (69 intervention group, 84 control group) mothers completing baseline surveys, 146 completed (67 intervention group, 79 control group) three-month follow-up surveys, and 141 (64 intervention group, 77 control group) completed six-month follow-up surveys. Missing data were omitted from final analyses.

Qualitative data analysis focused on transcripts from the six-month follow-up interviews. Analysis followed the phenomenological tradition, which focuses on the commonality of a lived experience within a particular group. Following a round of initial open coding by members of the research team, the team identified the most salient themes while placing an emphasis on finding significant, illustrative statements within the text of the transcripts (Creswell, 1998). These statements were then grouped into meaning units that led to an overall description of the participants' coparenting experiences and their feedback regarding the services that they received, as well as those that should be added to the program.

Results

Objective 1: Recruiting Mothers Into a Coparenting and Fatherhood Intervention

The first objective of this study was to investigate the circumstances under which mothers would be willing to coparent and to recruit them into a coparenting intervention based on the child's father's enrollment in a fatherhood program. Therefore, we presented mothers with an a priori list of reasons to coparent and asked them to identify all that applied to them. Table 9.1 displays the frequency of responses to a question about the 153 participating mothers' willingness to coparent. The most frequently identified ($n = 119$, 50.0%) reason was that children need to have a relationship with both parents. This was followed by the father being nominated as a good dad who positively impacted the child's life ($n = 55$, 23.1%), the father being identified as a good provider ($n = 28$, 11.8%), and the mother reporting that she was romantically involved with the father ($n = 22$, 9.2%). Finally, 14 (5.9%) of the mothers' responses indicated "other" reasons for their willingness to coparent. Some of these included "We communicate very well with the raising of our children," "He deserves the chance to be a dad. I know he loves our daughter," "I always try to coparent with him. But his girlfriend will not allow him to coparent with me," and "I am not the sole caretaker of our son. We both have a past. However I think he should be able to be in a relationship with him when it's established that he's actually trying to do something different with his life."

We also examined mothers' reasons for being unwilling to coparent. Table 9.2 displays the frequency of responses from the 56 mothers who declined to participate in the intervention and the reasons for their unwillingness to coparent. The most frequently identified ($n = 35$, 50.0%) reason was mothers reporting that the child's father was not a good dad. This was followed by 25 (35.7%) of the mothers' responses indicating an "other" reason for their unwillingness to coparent. Some of these responses included "I can't tolerate the disrespect," "He doesn't have a stable home," "My child doesn't feel safe with his dad," and "No contact orders, domestic violence convictions, including strangulation, and child abuse charge. They cannot be around him, because he cannot or will not be able

TABLE 9.1 Reasons Given by Mothers Explaining Their Willingness to Coparent

Response	n	%
Children having a relationship with both parents is best for them.	119	50.0
My child's father is a good dad and positively impacts my child's life.	55	23.1
My child's father is a good provider.	28	11.8
I am romantically involved with my child's father.	22	9.2
Other	14	5.9
Total	238	100.0

Note: We instructed mothers to respond with all that applied.

TABLE 9.2 Reasons Given by Mothers Explaining Their Unwillingness to Coparent

Response	n	%
My child's father is not a good dad.	35	50.0
I can play the roles of mother and father to my child.	10	14.3
My child's father is not a good financial provider.	0	0.0
I am romantically involved with someone other than my child's father.	0	0.0
Other	25	35.7
Total	70	100.0

Note: We instructed mothers to respond with all that applied.

to keep them safe." Finally, 10 (14.3%) mothers reported that they could play the roles of both the mother and the father.

Objective 2: Test the Effectiveness of the Coparenting Intervention

The second major objective of this study was to test the effectiveness of the coparenting intervention on mothers' reports of conflict resolution skills, fathers' involvement, and coparenting relationship quality. Quantitative data analysis revealed that control group mothers' reports of conflict resolution skills stayed relatively stable across the three data collection waves (see Table 9.3). However, intervention group mothers reported improved conflict resolution skills at each data collection wave. As a result, there were increasingly larger differences in the control group and intervention group mothers' reports of conflict resolution skills across the three data collection waves. The largest of these differences occurred at the six-month follow-up. These differences were also statistically significant, $F(2,141) = 4.66\ p < .01$.

With respect to father involvement, control group mothers reported less father involvement at each data collection wave with the largest drop off occurring between the three- and six-month data collection waves. Conversely, intervention group mothers reported higher levels of fathers' involvement at each data collection wave with the largest increase occurring between the pre-intervention and three-month data collection waves. The largest differences in the intervention and control groups' reports of fathers' involvement occurred at the six-month data collection wave. However, these differences were not statistically significant, $F(2, 141) = 1.68, p = .51$.

TABLE 9.3 Control and Intervention Group Mothers' Reports of Outcomes

Variable	Study Group	Pretest		3-Month		6-Month	
		M	SD	M	SD	M	SD
Conflict Resolution							
	Control	30.05	7.51	28.53	5.76	29.34	4.31
	Intervention	27.82	6.98	26.82	6.51	24.90**	6.67
Fathers' Involvement							
	Control	82.41	43.38	81.04	35.61	76.89	29.02
	Intervention	78.65	47.72	81.88	40.59	81.93	35.30
Coparenting Relationship Quality							
	Control	48.47	12.23	48.71	8.98	48.27	7.15
	Intervention	50.19	12.25	51.67	9.81	53.56*	9.68

Note: Lower conflict resolution scores indicate better skills.
*$p < .05$, **$p < .01$.

For coparenting relationship quality, control group mothers reported relatively stable ratings across all three data collection waves. However, intervention group mothers reported progressively better coparenting relationship quality ratings at each data collection wave. As a result, there were increasingly larger differences in the control group and intervention group mothers' reports of coparenting relationship quality across the three data collection waves. The largest of these differences occurred at the six-months follow up data collection wave. These differences were also statistically significant, $F(2, 141) = 3.74$, $p < .05$.

Interviews With Mothers

> **TEXT BOX 9.2 ABRIDGED PARTICIPANT QUOTE ON THE INTERVENTION'S IMPACT ON FATHERS' INVOLVEMENT**
>
> ... He's really helped me get her back on track as far as discipline and listening to mommy. She was having a little trouble and he got on the phone with her one night and I kind of overheard, he was really cool about it, just letting her know that mommy loves her and that mommy was just doing what she has to do. He had my back and that was great.—30-year-old single mother of three

We conducted telephone interviews with mothers who participated in the coparenting intervention six months after its conclusion to inquire about their experiences and solicit their feedback. The emergent themes revolved around the study outcomes and the participants' recommendations for future coparenting interventions. The data from the qualitative analyses about coparenting experiences corroborated the quantitative analyses. Many of the participants discussed the ways in which their conflict resolutions skills, reports of fathers' involvement, and coparenting relationship quality increased as a result of their participation in the coparenting intervention. They also provided recommendations for improving the intervention. These recommendations included increasing the dosage or extending the duration of the intervention, making the intervention available online, and offering combined sessions for mothers and fathers. Table 9.4 displays the emergent themes for the qualitative interview data along with illustrative quotes.

Parenting Plan/Mediation Services

Phase two of the intervention provided an opportunity for participants to receive a free coparenting session from a court-approved mediator. The intent of these sessions was to bring mothers and fathers together to establish mutually agreed-upon

TABLE 9.4 Qualitative Themes and Illustrative Quotes From Participants' Follow-Up Interviews

Theme	Illustrative Quote
Conflict Resolution	Well after the session, he pointed out something, where I was … he said that I could have been more open. I tend to … instead of arguing, I'll just shut myself off and not deal with the situation. I have to make myself open so that I can hear what he's saying and then try to get my point across. But I have a tendency to ignore him and shut him out. So yeah, it [the workshop] was effective. It even surprised him, just because I haven't been ignoring him. He's used to me ignoring him.—40-year-old never-married mother of one
Fathers' Involvement	I guess from before, I didn't feel like he had my back as much and that might have been due to resentment or other things. I've actually noticed a real change recently and I don't know what it's about. I don't know if it's because of the classes he was in. I think it is because of the classes, so it's really awesome what you're doing… He has really helped me with [child's name], that's our daughter's name that we share. He's really helped me get her back on track as far as discipline and listening to mommy. She was having a little trouble and he got on the phone with her one night and I kind of overheard, he was really cool about it, just letting her know that mommy loves her and that mommy was just doing what she has to do. He had my back and that was great.—30-year-old single mother of three
Coparenting Relationship Quality	Just based on the workshop, I kind of feel like, like you said, one of the first things was the respect thing. And I kind of gave pushback a little bit in the beginning. At first, it was just like why are you… not necessarily why are you being so nice, but why is it that I'm throwing this at you and you're not responding to it… I was kind of giving that pushback, like what's the angle on this? Then, after I had the workshop, you know, that's when I saw that he was doing it to try to help better our friendship, our overall relationship that we have for the sake of our kid.—31-year-old married mother [not to *4 Your Child* participant] of two
Increased Dosage	Basically, like taking the data to reevaluate and come up with some new workshops. I mean like maybe

TABLE 9.4 (continued)

Theme	Illustrative Quote
	have brainstorming session, one for mothers and one for fathers. Then integrate or try to do more workshops revisiting the ideas from the brainstorming session over the next few months. You know, it would be like a refresher 'cause there will always be bumps in the road. I would definitely be interested in that to receive some extra support.—33-year-old single mother of two
Online Format	I would truly recommend it for anybody, even young parents, really for any parents no matter the age. But I have to say, I'm lucky. I had someone to watch my kids on the day of the program. If I didn't, I wouldn't have made it. Maybe y'all could do it online. I know a lot of moms have trouble finding people to watch their kids, so doing it on the computer or even on the phone would be a good way to reach more people.—29-year-old single mother of one
Combined Sessions	I know the program is really, really important. I just wish that maybe we [participant and child's father] could've gotten more involved as a unit, you know, like as a family. If we could have came together, we could make sure we left on the same page. You know what I'm saying?—30-year-old romantically involved mother of three

parenting plans that reflected both parents' values and desires. Of the 69 mothers participating in the parent education workshop, only 4 (5.7%) agreed to participate in the parenting plan session. When providing a rationale for declining the offer for mediation services, some mothers expressed a concern about the potential decrease in their decision-making authority, while others were apprehensive about what they perceived as the formality and potentially legally binding nature of mediation. Due to the small number of mothers participating in the coparenting sessions with the mediator, no further analyses were conducted on their impact.

Discussion

The purposes of this study were to explore the feasibility of recruiting custodial mothers into a coparenting intervention based on their child's father's enrollment in a fatherhood program, their reasons for agreeing or declining to participate, as well as testing the effectiveness of that intervention on mothers' reports of conflict resolution, fathers' involvement, and coparenting relationship quality. With regard to the first aim, 153 of a possible 285 mothers were successfully recruited into the study. This means that 53.6% of the mothers who were contacted agreed to participate. It is noteworthy that the study sample was comprised largely of never-married mothers. This is important because, unlike their divorced counterparts, never-married mothers' relationships are not covered by family law, and issues like custody and parenting time are not automatically adjudicated by the court as they are in divorce proceedings. Moreover, this also means that never-married parents are less likely to be court ordered or referred into mediation or parent education services (Pearson, 2015). That about half of the mothers enrolled voluntarily may also have particular importance because although many of the parents had contentious coparenting relationships, their willingness to participate in the intervention without being mandated suggests that the mothers held out some hope that the coparenting relationship could be improved. Finally, the feasibility of recruiting diverse samples of mothers into a coparenting intervention through their coparents' participation in a fatherhood program can help to move the field forward in ways that are consistent with recent calls to engage both parents in services to families (Pruett et al., 2017) and to adopt a triangular framework that treats both mothers and fathers as coparenting partners and allies who can better serve children (McHale & Negrini, 2018).

As it relates to the second study aim, data analysis revealed that the intervention mothers reported greater improvements in their perceptions of conflict resolution, fathers' involvement, and coparenting relationship quality than control group mothers with statistically significant improvements in conflict resolution and coparenting relationship quality at the six-month follow up. These results are consistent with previous research indicating that brief, low-dosage interventions can produce positive outcomes (Braver et al., 2016). The fact that these small, but positive, gains can be made with custodial mothers is important in light of previous research pointing to the central role of mothers as children's primary caregivers who are critical in their ability to serve as gateways to fathers' involvement (Perry et al., 2016) and decrease competitive coparenting (Murphy et al., 2017).

Although the study's results indicate that mothers can be recruited into coparenting interventions that can produce positive outcomes, the study had some limitations that should be considered. Included in these limitations are that the intervention was a single, low-dosage workshop and the primary outcomes were all based on self-report survey measurement instruments. To address these limitations, future studies should examine whether longer, more sustained interventions produce better outcomes that are measured using data that are less vulnerable to socially desirable responses.

Recommendations

The results from this study indicate that not only can many custodial mothers (most of whom are unmarried) be recruited into a coparenting intervention through their child's fathers' participation in a fatherhood program, but also that exposing mothers to content that fathers are learning in a fatherhood program can have a positive impact on their perceptions of the coparenting relationship and their reports of father involvement with their children. To build on this work, we offer several recommendations. First, we recommend that the intervention be extended and its dosage increased. In the current study, mothers participated in a single workshop that was two hours in duration. Despite the popularity and cost effectiveness of brief interventions, much of the feedback that mothers provided indicated that they were curious to learn more about what the fathers were receiving in their program than could reasonably fit into a single workshop.

Second, we recommend exploring alternate delivery options, including online workshops through webinars or web conferencing. Not only did several mothers indicate that they would have been willing to participate in virtual workshops, but many also stated that it would have been their preference. Having this option available would have the potential to increase recruitment and retention as it would remove several barriers for custodial mothers related to transportation or childcare.

The third recommendation that was offered by several participants was to explore the feasibility of bringing mothers and fathers together into the same coparenting sessions after each parent completed the workshops independently. Unlike the mediation sessions that the mothers rejected as being too formal and legalistic, group workshops were viewed as informal opportunities for coparents to apply what they learned in their separate interventions. Perhaps bringing mothers and fathers together to develop coparenting plans could be streamlined if, as Shrage (2018) suggests, policy makers worked with practitioners and clinicians to explore the feasibility of creating basic rules about custody, caregiving, and financial support to serve as guidelines to never-married parents who had to negotiate the terms of their coparenting arrangements. In the meantime, the findings from the current study indicate that although recruiting mothers into coparenting programs is challenging, brief interventions can produce positive effects on mothers' perspectives on coparenting.

Acknowledgments

- Funding for the Fatherhood and Coparenting project was provided by the Fatherhood Research and Practice Network (FRPN) under grant #90PR0006 from the U.S. Department of Health and Human Services, Office of Planning Research and Evaluation (OPRE) to Temple University and the Center for Policy Research. The points of view expressed in this document are those of the author and do not represent the official views of OPRE.
- Funding for the *4 Your Child* project was provided by the U.S. Department of Health and Human Services, Administration for Children and Families, grant number 90FK0074-01-00. Any opinions, findings, and conclusions or recommendations expressed in this material are those of the author(s) and do

not necessarily reflect the views of the U.S. Department of Health and Human Services, Administration for Children and Families, Office of Family Assistance or the Office of Planning, Research, and Evaluation.

References

Bonach, K. (2005). Factors contributing to quality coparenting: Implications for family policy. *Journal of Divorce & Remarriage, 43*(3/4), 79–103.

Bonach, K. (2009). Empirical support for the application of the forgiveness intervention model to postdivorce coparenting. *Journal of Divorce & Remarriage, 50*(1), 38–54.

Braver, S. L., Sandler, I. N., Cohen Hita, L., & Wheeler, L. A. (2016). A randomized comparative effectiveness trial of two court-connected programs for high-conflict families. *Family Court Review, 54*(3), 349–363.

Creswell, J. W. (1998). *Qualitative inquiry and research design: Choosing among five traditions.* SAGE.

Fagan, J., Cherson, M., Brown, C., & Vecere, E. (2015). Pilot study of a program to increase mothers' understanding of dads. *Family Process, 54*(4), 581–589.

Goldberg, J. S. (2015). Coparenting and nonresident fathers' monetary contributions to their children. *Journal of Marriage & Family, 77*(3), 612–627.

Goldberg, J. S., & Carlson, M. J. (2015). Patterns and predictors of coparenting after unmarried parents part. *Journal of Family Psychology, 29*(3), 416–426.

Hawkins, A., Bradford, K., Palkowitz, R., Christensen, S., Day, R., & Call, V. (2002). The inventory of father involvement: A pilot study of a new measure of father Involvement. *Journal of Men's Studies, 10*, 183–197.

Marczak, M. S., Becher, E. H., Hardman, A. M., Galos, D. L., & Ruhland, E. (2015). Strengthening the role of unmarried fathers: Findings from the co-parent court project. *Family Process, 54*(4), 630–638.

Margolin, G., Gordis, E. B., & John, R. S. (2001). Coparenting: A link between marital conflict and parenting in two-parent families. *Journal of Family Psychology, 15*(1), 3.

McHale, J. P., & Negrini, L. S. (2018). How the assumption of a coparenting frame will transform social work practice with men and fathers. *Social Work Research, 42*(1), 9–21.

Murphy, S. E., Gallegos, M. I., Jacobvitz, D. B., & Hazen, N. L. (2017). Coparenting dynamics: Mothers' and fathers' differential support and involvement. *Personal Relationships, 24*(4), 917–932.

National Fatherhood Initiative. (2015). *24/7 Dad® A.M.* (3rd ed.). Author.

Owen, J., & Rhoades, G. K. (2012). Reducing interparental conflict among parents in contentious child custody disputes: An initial investigation of the working together program. *Journal of Marital & Family Therapy, 38*(3), 542–555.

Pearson, J. (2015). Parenting time and coparenting for unmarried parents. *Family Court Review, 53*(2), 217–220.

Perry, A., Rollins, A., & Perez, A. (2020). *Fatherhood & coparenting.* Fatherhood Research and Practice Network. https://www.frpn.org/asset/frpn-grantee-report-fatherhood-coparenting.

Perry, A., Rollins, A., Sambree, R., & Grooms, W. (2016). Promoting paternal participation in maternal and child health services. *Human Service Organizations: Management, Leadership & Governance, 40*(2), 170–186.

Petren, R. E., Ferraro, A. J., Davis, T. R., & Pasley, K. (2017). Factors linked with coparenting support and conflict after divorce. *Journal of Divorce & Remarriage, 58*(3), 145–160.

Pruett, M. K., Pruett, K. D., Cowan, C. P., & Cowan, P. A. (2017). Enhancing paternal engagement in a coparenting paradigm. *Child Development Perspectives*, *11*(4), 245–250.

Pudasainee-Kapri, S., & Razza, R. (2015). Associations among supportive coparenting, father engagement and attachment: The role of race/ethnicity. *Journal of Child & Family Studies*, *24*(12), 3793–3804.

Renick, M. J., Blumberg, S. L., & Markman, H. J. (1992). The prevention and relationship enhancement program (PREP): An empirically based preventive intervention program for couples. *Family Relations*, *41*(2), 141–147.

Russell, L. T., Beckmeyer, J. J., Coleman, M., & Ganong, L. (2016). Perceived barriers to postdivorce coparenting: Differences between men and women and associations with coparenting behaviors. *Family Relations*, *65*(3), 450–461.

Shrage, L. (2018). Decoupling marriage and parenting. *Journal of Applied Philosophy*, *35*(3), 496–512.

Stolz, H. E., Sizemore, K. M., Shideler, M. J., LaGraff, M. R., & Moran, H. B. (2017). Parenting together: Evaluation of a parenting program for never-married parents. *Journal of Divorce & Remarriage*, *58*(5), 358–370.

Varga, C. M., & Gee, C. B. (2017). Coparenting, relationship quality, and father involvement in African American and Latino adolescents. *Merrill-Palmer Quarterly*, *63*(2), 210–236.

10
ENGAGING MOTHERS IN COPARENTING SERVICES WITH THE NONRESIDENT FATHERS OF THEIR CHILDREN VIA FATHERHOOD PROGRAMS

Insights Into Barriers and Solutions

Kimberly Gentry Sperber and Sarah W. Whitton

Introduction

Current Population Survey data in March 2019 show that 22% of U.S. children live in single-parent households (Payne, 2019). Of the children living in single-parent households, 86% reside with a single mother, with only 14% residing with a single father. Family structure also varies significantly by race/ethnicity. For example, 84% of Asian children and 71% of White children live with two biological parents, while only 36% of Black children live with two biological parents. Children living apart from their fathers are at risk for poverty, delinquency, lower academic achievement, school dropout, and substance use (Adamson & Johnson, 2013; McLanahan et al., 2013). Efforts to improve these children's outcomes are clearly needed. Fatherhood programs designed to improve involvement of noncustodial fathers with their children may be valid approaches toward this aim, given that relationships with engaged and competent fathers are associated with children's self-concept, attachment security, cognitive ability, emotional regulation, school performance, social skills, and mental health (Amato & Gilbreth, 1999; Cabrera et al., 2007; King & Sobolewski, 2006; Nelson, 2004). Such fatherhood programs are particularly needed for low-income, never-married, minority fathers, who are not only more likely to live apart from their child, but often face greater challenges to becoming or staying involved with their child (Nelson, 2004).

One common barrier to effective father involvement is that many low-income, nonresident fathers were never married to the mother and often do not have access to their children because they do not have legally established visitation or parenting time rights that typically require navigating complex and costly legal processes to establish (Pearson, 2015). A second common barrier to effective father involvement is a poor coparenting relationship with the child's mother. Children benefit from high-quality coparenting, in which the two parents communicate respectfully and effectively with each other about the child, share control, support each other's parenting, and protect the child from exposure to their conflict with each other (Cabrera et al., 2012). Unfortunately, there are many obstacles to such quality coparenting for nonresident fathers. Many low-income, nonresident fathers desire to be good fathers but face significant barriers stemming from a weak or highly conflicted relationship with the child's mother. Many of the mothers have significant pain surrounding their relationship with the father, do not trust him or his parenting abilities, and have new partners who do not want them to be in contact with the father. All of these factors can lead to high levels of maternal gatekeeping, which has shown a significant, negative relationship with father involvement (e.g., Fagan & Barnett, 2003). In addition, many mothers and fathers have poor affect regulation and communication skills, which significantly impede coparenting and can negatively impact their child through exposure to destructive parental conflict. These barriers to effective coparenting are especially problematic for nonresident fathers as there is empirical evidence that the quality of the coparenting relationship has a stronger impact on the father–child relationship for nonresident parents than for resident parents (Fagan & Palkovitz, 2011).

TEXT BOX 10.1

The Talbert House Fatherhood Project assists men in their efforts to become responsible, committed, and nurturing fathers. Since 1998, the Fatherhood Project has helped fathers strengthen their connection and involvement in the lives of their children by providing classes, coparenting and individual coaching, and fellowship support meetings. Additional services include legal, employment, and housing assistance (Talbert House, n.d.).

Improving coparenting between low-income, nonresident fathers and the mothers of their children, therefore, is an important step toward increasing father involvement and thereby improving child outcomes (Martinson & Nightingale, 2008). However, little is known about how to improve coparenting in this population. Further, there is a lack of knowledge about how to increase accessibility and attractiveness of coparenting programs, particularly in regard to engaging mothers. Consequently, this chapter (1) outlines the attempts of a fatherhood program to recruit and engage nonresident fathers and mothers into coparenting services; (2) discusses ongoing challenges to recruit sufficient numbers of nonresident parents, particularly mothers, into these services; and (3) presents findings from qualitative interviews from both mothers and nonresident fathers about barriers to participation and ways to increase the appeal of coparenting services offered to mothers by fatherhood programs.

The Talbert House Fatherhood Project

Talbert House is a community-wide nonprofit network of services focusing on prevention, assessment, treatment, and reintegration provided across five service lines at multiple sites throughout Southwest Ohio. These five services lines are addictions, community corrections, mental health, housing, and community care. Talbert House's Fatherhood Project ("Fatherhood Project") has served low-income, noncustodial, and custodial fathers seeking to improve parenting skills and access to their children for 19 years. Nearly all the fathers served by the program face a host of internal and external barriers to fathering well. Consequently, the program offers an array of services that include case management, legal services, employment services, and attendance at a Nurturing Father Class (Perlman, 1998). The Nurturing Father Class is a 10-week/25-hour class focused on nurturing children and selves, effective discipline, anger management and conflict resolution, teamwork with spouse or partner, communication and problem solving, balancing work and fathering responsibilities, and dealing with feelings. The program also employs a fatherhood coach who offers individual coaching sessions for fathers who cannot attend the weekly group classes.

Evolution of Coparenting Services at Talbert House

In 2013, Talbert House began offering services to the mothers of children whose fathers were involved in the Fatherhood Project. The impetus for these mother-directed services came from staff observations that mothers commonly experienced pain surrounding their relationships with fathers, which led to distrust of fathers and restrictions on their access to children. Staff also perceived that mothers would often use the family court system and denial of access to Perlman, 1998 children as a way to get back at fathers for past transgressions.

To address these issues, the Fatherhood Project began offering coparenting services to both mothers and fathers. However, fewer than 15% of mothers agreed to participate in these services between 2013 and 2015. To address the low participation rate, Talbert House applied for and received funding from the Fatherhood Research and Practice Network to conduct a study testing the efficacy of providing enhanced coparenting services that were believed to be more appealing to mothers. The enhanced program aimed to (1) convey an understanding of the mother's concerns about fathers and the issue of coparenting; (2) communicate staff intentions to help the mother and her child rather than forcing her to allow father involvement; (3) attend to common maternal issues such as lingering relationship pain and emotional dysregulation; and (4) offer mothers-only individual and group services.

Unlike earlier programs, outreach to the mother to participate in coparenting services was conducted by a female staff member known as a "coach." To improve mother recruitment outcomes, this female coach was trained to emphasize that she understood the mother's position and potential concerns about engagement, to convey that Talbert House was not "on the father's side," and to highlight the potential benefits to the mother of participating in mother-focused individual and group services. Second, the enhanced services included a three-session support group for mothers to allow them to gain support from other women in similar circumstances. The support group was to be co-led by a female and a male coparenting coach using materials from *Mom as Gateway* (National Fatherhood Initiative, 2008) and PREP's unpublished father-focused program, *On My Shoulders*. The focus of these sessions was on identifying and meeting the mother's individual needs, addressing relationship pain, minimizing excessive gatekeeping, and learning communication skills.

Third, the enhanced services increased the number of joint coparenting sessions available to interested mothers and fathers to six sessions to permit mediation and instruction on new skills drawn from *PREP* (Markman et al., 2010) and *On My Shoulders*. PREP is an evidence-based relationship education program that has demonstrated efficacy in improving couple communication, conflict management, and relationship quality in numerous longitudinal studies (see Markman & Rhoades, 2012). *On My Shoulders* is a research-based curriculum adapted for use with fathers, particularly low-income, nonresident fathers, which heavily emphasizes skill building for effective coparenting. It is modeled upon *Within My Reach* (Stanley et al., 2005), another adaptation of PREP that has been shown to be effective in improving relationship skills and conflict resolution in low-income, high-risk individuals (Antle et al., 2011). Session topics included healthy communication, stress management, personality and parenting, strategies for effective coparenting relationships, and human feelings and needs.

Studying Mother Engagement in Coparenting Services at Talbert House

In October 2016, we began inviting nonresident fathers of minor children who were participating in the Talbert House Fatherhood Project to participate in a study of the enhanced coparenting services. While we enrolled 97 fathers into the study between October 2016 and September 2017, we experienced dramatically less success with mother enrollment, enrolling only five. This low enrollment was due to several factors. First, only 45 of the interested 97 fathers were able or willing to provide the name and contact information for his child's mother, with five of the fathers providing name and contact information for two mothers each. This yielded a total of 50 women whom the coparenting coach attempted to contact. Second, we experienced a high rate of nonresponse and refusals from mothers: 22 refused, 17 did not respond to multiple phone calls and messages, and six had phone numbers that were disconnected or no longer in service. Third, our outreach efforts were hindered by staff turnover and inconsistent follow-through on plans to contact and recontact potential program participants, to track outreach efforts, and to deliver the central elements of the recruiting messages (e.g., conveying concern for and intentions to help the mother, not just the father). It was also difficult to continuously monitor the quality of outreach efforts and hold staff accountable for these activities without a more robust internal infrastructure to support the new coparenting services. In the end, only five mothers were successfully enrolled in the study, with four of the five mothers attending at least one coparenting session.

Engagement of fathers in coparenting services during the study was also low, with only 23 of the 97 enrolled fathers attending at least one coparenting session. Father attrition was due to incorrect contact information (18 fathers) and refusals to participate either with or without the mother (37 fathers). While 38 fathers did attend an orientation to discuss coparenting, only 23 of these agreed to attend one or more coparenting sessions. Because the program demonstrated little success with engaging mothers and fathers into coparenting services during the course of the study, we elected to conduct qualitative interviews with both mothers and fathers to examine perceived barriers to participation in coparenting services and to gather information about what factors might increase interest in such services.

Interview Measures and Methods

We conducted semi-structured interviews with mothers and fathers who participated in coparenting services, as well as those who did not. We interviewed mothers and fathers separately, and most interviews were conducted via telephone. We used an interview guide that included both open-ended and forced-choice items related to barriers to participation, suggestions for improvements in both outreach methods and services offered, and relationship status with the other parent. We asked participants to rate a series of items about barriers to participation in coparenting services, the demands placed on individuals participating in services, and the relationship with program staff using items adapted from the Barriers to Treatment Participation Scale (Kazdin et al., 1997). We also used open-ended interview questions that explored the following domains:

- Barriers to participation in coparenting services—this included structural barriers like time and transportation as well as relational barriers due to lingering pain from the breakup and/or concerns about protecting the child from harms related to violence and substance abuse.

- Factors that make participation more attractive or feasible—these included ways to improve outreach and services, structural supports, gender of outreach staff, and perceptions about staff understanding of the mother perspective.
- Perceptions of the value and impact of services—this included satisfaction with services received for those who had participated in services, perceived changes in the coparenting relationship, and changes in father involvement with the child.

Interview Participants

A total of 16 mothers and 30 fathers participated in interviews during the study. The research team started with a pool of 50 mothers for whom we had contact information. Of these 50 women, eight women refused to participate, 17 did not respond to multiple outreach attempts, and nine had invalid phone numbers. Of the 16 women interviewed, 14 had not participated in any coparenting services. Due to the small number of women who participated in services, we combined the responses from all the women when coding themes, except in instances where not applicable.

From the original sample of 97 fathers enrolled into the study, eight fathers declined to participate in an interview and 27 fathers did not respond to multiple attempts to contact them for participation. Twenty-eight fathers were deemed ineligible for the interview due to reasons such as death, incarceration, becoming the custodial parent during the study timeframe, and length of time between admission into the program and the time of the interview being too great for accurate recall. Of the 30 fathers interviewed, 18 had not participated in any coparenting services while 12 had participated in at least one coparenting session.

Of the mothers interviewed, 75% had two or more children, with 68.8% reporting that they shared only one child with the father in the study. Slightly less than a third of the mothers (31.3%) had been married to the father in the past, with the same percentage reporting that they had never lived with the father. Fewer than half of the mothers reported that their relationship with the fathers was friendly (37.5%), while the remainder described their relationship as neutral (25%), nonexistent (18.8%), or hostile (18.8%). Sixty-eight percent of the mothers reported that the father was seeing their child on at least a monthly basis, while only two mothers reported that the father did not see the child at all. All but one mother interviewed had at least a high school education, with three quarters of the mothers reporting that they had completed at least some college. The average age of the mothers interviewed was 33 years of age.

Of the fathers interviewed, 58.3% had two or more children, with two-thirds of the fathers reporting that they shared one child with the mother identified as a potential coparticipant in the coparenting services. Three-quarters of the fathers had never been married to the mother, and only 16.7% of the fathers described their relationship with the mother as friendly. The remainder of the fathers described the relationship as neutral (33.3%), nonexistent (33.3%), or hostile

(16.7%). All fathers interviewed had at least a high school education, with 58.3% reporting that they had finished at least some college. The average age of fathers interviewed was 35 years of age.

Interview Coding Methods

We used the two-phase process described by Charmaz (2014) to identify themes from the interview responses. During the initial phase, two research staff independently reviewed transcribed interview responses and named or coded them according to content. In the focused phase, the same research staff jointly reviewed the initial set of codes to identify commonalities and to simplify the original list into a smaller, more focused set of agreed-upon thematic codes. Once these thematic codes were established, the two research staff again independently coded the interview responses using the subset of focused codes. We then statistically examined the agreement between raters and found excellent/very good agreement for mother codes and substantial/good agreement for father codes. Nearly all disagreements related to father codes were resolved by consensus, with only one father code needing to be removed. Once this code was removed, we achieved excellent/very good agreement for the father codes[1].

Interview Themes

Here we present the salient themes identified through the qualitative interviews. They are perceived value of coparenting services, barriers to engagement in coparenting services, and recommendations related to engaging more mothers into coparenting services. Because this chapter focuses on engaging mothers into coparenting services, we only present findings from father interviews that were specific to engaging mothers into coparenting or to illustrate important differences in mother and father responses.

Perceived Value of Coparenting Services

All interviewees were asked whether there is a need for a program to help mothers and fathers who do not live together to do a better job working together to raise their children. This interview question resulted in a near universal positive response with all of the mothers and all but one father providing a "yes" response. One mother did qualify her response to indicate that the need for such services at the individual family level would depend on each family's specific circumstances.

Barriers to Engagement in Coparenting Services

Interview responses from mothers and fathers revealed three primary types of barriers to engagement in coparenting services; these were logistical barriers, limited contact between coparents, and mothers' lived experiences and perceptions.

Logistical

Logistical barriers to participation was a theme that was shared by both mothers and fathers; however, the types of logistical barriers experienced by mothers and fathers differed in ways important to fatherhood programs attempting to recruit mothers into coparenting programs. Large proportions of both mothers (71.4%) and fathers (53.3%) indicated that they were too busy to participate in coparenting services. The two primary logistical barriers identified by mothers were the inconvenient location of the Fatherhood Project, which required traveling a long distance to attend services, and other family responsibilities such as caring for children, the elderly, or sick relatives. Few fathers, on the other hand, reported these types of logistical barriers: only two fathers indicated childcare was a barrier, and three fathers indicated location was a barrier. Rather, fathers were more likely to describe logistical barriers to program participation based on characteristics of their employment status, such as working two jobs, working long shifts, working overtime, dedicating time to job seeking, and a desire to secure a job and income prior to engaging in coparenting services.

Contact Status

Contact status between the mother and father was a common barrier to participation. For example, 42.9% of mothers indicated that they did not have contact with the father, and 56.1% reported that they did not want contact with the father. Similarly, 40% of the fathers endorsed lack of contact with the mother as a barrier to participation in coparenting services. Recall also that fewer than half of all 97 fathers enrolled into the study were able and/or willing to provide contact information for the mother of his child.

Mothers' Lived Experiences and Perceptions

Three thematic barriers emerged that were specific to the lived experiences of the mothers. These were labeled as mistrust of the fatherhood program, frustration with father behaviors, and safety concerns. A number of the women expressed distrust of either the Talbert House Fatherhood Project specifically or father-serving programs generally as a barrier to engagement. To illustrate, more than one mother expressed skepticism that a program that has had a tradition of only serving fathers could be trusted to represent her point of view. As one mother pointed out when asked why she declined to participate in coparenting services:

> There were a couple of reasons. First being that the program had already been working with my child's father and in my and my attorney's opinion, he already had a relationship with program staff and I didn't...He [the coparenting coach] also wanted to do what was in my family's best interest rather than my child's best interest. I found that to be alarming. My son is on the visitation schedule he is on for a reason.

This skepticism that staff might not adequately represent the interest of the mother was validated for one mother who did attend joint coparenting sessions with the father. This mother shared that she had stated to the coparenting coaches that she "had no interest in discussing child support" and that the topic of her child support case against the father was "completely off the table." According to the mother, one of the coparenting coaches brought up the topic anyway during a subsequent session. She shared that this was the reason that she discontinued her participation in services as she felt that her wishes had been disregarded in favor of the father's wishes.

> **TEXT BOX 10.2**
>
> There were a couple of reasons. First being that the program had already been working with my child's father and in my and my attorney's opinion, he already had a relationship with program staff and I didn't...He [the coparenting coach] also wanted to do what was in my family's best interest rather than my child's best interest. I found that to be alarming. My son is on the visitation schedule he is on for a reason.

About three-fourths of the women interviewed also expressed frustration with father behaviors. The majority of examples provided by the women were related to inconsistent parenting and perceptions that the father was unlikely to change his behaviors; however, a couple of mothers also cited past violence or anger management issues as concerns that informed their decisions to decline participation. The following quotes from three mothers illustrate frustrations with inconsistent parenting practices of the father:

> "My situation's not too bad. We just don't see eye to eye. He's not an absent father, so can't really say that's an issue...I've known him over half my life. I know how closed minded he is and don't see that changing. He's the fun time dad. But if she's sick and needs medicine and I can't afford it, then he doesn't want to help. I can count on one hand how many times I ask him for help with something like that and then he doesn't want to do that or understand why he should have to help with that. He doesn't have parents, so he lacks understanding of what it means to be a parent." Later in the interview she reiterated these sentiments by stating: "he's very difficult, stuck in his ways. We have very different views on what it means to raise a child. We have different priorities."

"Mainly because we were not really coparenting. It's really just me; he just visits. Like he hasn't seen him in two months. He's not consistent. He's often not available…physically, financially, emotionally."

"I don't believe it would help. I don't know what his deal is. He's with his daughter every other week (from another woman) but not sure what the deal is with his son. Not sure if it's his feelings toward me. I see him making an effort with his daughter, but not with our son."

> **TEXT BOX 10.3**
>
> Mainly because we were not really coparenting. It's really just me; he just visits. Like he hasn't seen him in two months. He's not consistent. He's often not available…physically, financially, emotionally.

Finally, 60% of the women cited being angry at the father for things he had done to her in the past as reasons for declining to participate in coparenting services. Also of note is that three of the 16 women (18.8%) interviewed shared that they had current or past protection orders against the father and that concerns related to safety accounted for a great deal of their apprehension in participating in services. For example, when asked about the primary reason for declining to participate in coparenting services, one mother responded: "concern for me and my son's safety at the time." She also provided the following contextual information:

> We are divorced now. It just became final two weeks ago. He's a very abusive person. He was in a standoff with the SWAT team, 16 hours in [city].[2] He pulled a gun on me and the police officer.

Recommendations

During the interviews, we also solicited feedback from both mothers and fathers about how to make coparenting services more appealing to mothers. Of interest here is that fathers recommended providing groups for mothers only, having mothers and fathers attend individualized services separately prior to participating in joint services, and using a female staff person to reach out to mothers—all features of the enhanced coparenting services under scrutiny in the study. A number of fathers recommended that the program should improve how staff communicate with them about coparenting services. These fathers commented that they sometimes had difficulty reaching staff, that staff did not always follow up with them about their attempts to reach and engage mothers, and that staff did not always provide detailed information early in the recruitment process about the benefits and requirements of participating in coparenting services. They also suggested using more aggressive and persistent outreach efforts to engage mothers. Finally, they frequently cited the use of social media as a way of letting mothers know that they are not alone and that there are services available to help with coparenting.

Mothers, on the other hand, most commonly provided recommendations that reflected concepts of service equity, premised on perceptions that current services available through the Fatherhood Project were primarily for the benefit of the fathers and did not equally represent the interests of mothers. Women also recommended providing mothers additional services that would reduce barriers to participation, including assistance with food, legal services, childcare, activities for the children, gift cards, and assistance with household supplies.

Lessons Learned and Practical Implications

The Fatherhood Project, like many fatherhood programs, has evolved in an organic fashion at the intersection of needs and shifting resources in a particular community. The program's efforts to engage mothers in coparenting services represented an attempt to more effectively improve father involvement by addressing issues observed by clinical staff (e.g., relationship pain and poor communication between parents interfering with father involvement) and using evidence-based approaches (e.g., *Moms as Gateway; PREP*). The program's lack of success in recruiting mothers and fathers to participate in these coparenting services prohibited evaluation of them. However, it did allow for collection of rich qualitative data describing the parents' perceived barriers to participation, which translate into practical tips for fatherhood practitioners wishing to engage mothers into coparenting services and provide guidance for future research efforts:

1. Programs that have historically served fathers only will need to work to overcome mother distrust to increase their participation in coparenting services. This distrust was at least partially due to the program's primary mission of serving fathers. Another perceived inequity was the fact that mothers were only offered coparenting services while fathers were offered an array of services and practical assistance with issues, including employment, mental health, housing, and so forth. Understandably, this disparity led at least some mothers to feel as though their involvement was sought only to further the best interest of fathers. If fatherhood programs choose to include mothers, they may need to re-engineer their services and provide a more

balanced and family-focused approach. Altering the focus of existing fatherhood programs to be more inclusive of the whole family (while not losing the father-specific services that originally prompted the need for fatherhood programs) may provide women with their own reasons to come to the program other than only to supplement the father's programming. Additionally, if women already had a reason to be involved with the program, staff would have independent access to mothers and could recruit them for coparenting services without having to rely on the father as the conduit to mothers.

2. Programs that have primarily served fathers will need to provide comprehensive and ongoing training to staff about the differences in working with mothers and families rather than fathers only if they seek to offer coparenting services. Staff will likely need training and ongoing consultation to help them view parenting issues through a lens that is not exclusively father-focused and incorporate perspectives of all participants.

3. Fatherhood programs would benefit from anticipating that existing staff may struggle with the type of active efforts it may take to recruit both mothers and fathers into new, dyadic coparenting services. Often, fatherhood program staff are trained in providing client-centered services and are highly motivated to respond to the needs of clients in the moment. In contrast, they may lack experience or find it less rewarding to focus on tracking down people who are difficult to contact, persisting in efforts to reach people who may seem like they do not wish to be reached, or following set protocols in outreach or service delivery. Perhaps programs would benefit from hiring new staff with different skill sets and priorities for outreach and retention efforts, separate from the service-focused staff who provide the services. Alternately, it might help to provide training to clinically focused staff in outreach and retention activities and set up systems of accountability for their completion. Our experiences also point to a need for structured communication/outreach protocols for staff to use when engaging clients in coparenting services. Such protocols will need to acknowledge and accommodate the fragile nature of the relationships between many of the mothers and fathers, however, so as to avoid further harm to the coparenting relationship.

4. Exploration and testing of effective marketing strategies may be warranted for fatherhood programs wishing to engage mothers in coparenting services; however, a review of existing literature in marketing of social services should be consulted prior to acting on specific ideas. For example, Hayward et al. (2019) found that providing cell phones along with twice weekly text messages within a randomized controlled trial did not result in increased engagement or retention of fathers in a fatherhood program, even though a number of fathers had expressed satisfaction with the texting intervention and reported finding it helpful.

5. Both mother and father responses during the qualitative interviews revealed significant inter-parental relationship challenges. These include differing parenting philosophies, weakened parental alliance, and a lack of contact between parents. Lack of contact between parents was a primary barrier to the recruitment of mothers into coparenting services as fathers often did not have contact information for the mother or had contact information that was out of date.
6. Common among many community-based programs is the need to assist participants with practical barriers to participation, which differ for mothers and fathers in fundamental ways. To address the barriers mothers experienced, future programs should explore expanding location options for housing coparenting services; working with parents to minimize the time required to participate, perhaps by investigating the use of technology-based delivery of services (e.g., via apps or virtual environments); providing transportation vouchers; and providing on-site childcare or assistance with elder care. Prior fatherhood program research has demonstrated the positive impact on participant retention when support such as transportation assistance, stipends, and gift cards are provided (e.g., Tannehill et al., 2009).

Conclusions

In the end, the findings from this study, along with our experiences in conducting it, suggest that fatherhood programs seeking to offer coparenting services that involve mothers are likely to face significant challenges in engaging them. While low and/or incomplete attendance by both mothers and fathers is not unusual in parenting programs and is not unique to the Talbert House Fatherhood Project (e.g., Baker et al., 2010; Gadsden et al., 2016), attempting to provide coparenting services through a long-established fatherhood program—compared to a general parenting program—made mother recruitment extremely challenging. This study also highlights the importance of gathering information from women directly about why they are reluctant to participate in coparenting services and the barriers they experienced rather than only relying on assumptions filtered through a father-centric lens.

To that end, our study is an important contribution to the field as there is no existing literature on the perceptions of women targeted by existing fatherhood programs to participate in coparenting services with nonresident fathers. Our study is the first to solicit, codify, and interpret mother perceptions of, and barriers to, voluntary participation in coparenting services with a nonresident father when such services are offered by a fatherhood program that is already providing services to the father. Overall, our findings indicate that existing fatherhood programs that are interested in engaging mothers in coparenting services may need to significantly change current operations, endorse a program mission that is less strictly focused on fathers and more inclusive of the mother's and child's interest, and create an environment that is more appealing to women by offering a wider array of services, thereby providing opportunities for mothers to form their own independent relationships with the program.

Notes

1 See Whitton et al. (2018) for more information about the statistical procedures used to assess rater agreement.
2 Name of city was withheld to protect identities of parties involved.

References

Adamson, K., & Johnson, S. K. (2013). An updated and expanded meta-analysis of nonresident fathering and child well-being. *Journal of Family Psychology*, 27(4), 589–599.

Amato, P. R., & Gilbreth, J. G. (1999). Nonresident fathers and children's well-being: A meta-analysis. *Journal of Marriage and Family*, 61(3), 557–573.

Antle, B. F., Karam, E., Christensen, D. N., Barbee, A. P., & Sar, B. K. (2011). An evaluation of healthy relationship education to reduce intimate partner violence. *Journal of Family Social Work*, 14(5), 387–406.

Baker, C. N., Arnold, D. H., & Meagher, S. (2010). Enrollment and attendance in a parent training prevention program for conduct problems. *Prevention Science*, 12(2), 1–13.

Cabrera, N. J., Shannon, J. D., & Tamis-LeMonda, C. (2007). Fathers' influence on their children's cognitive and emotional development: From toddlers to pre-K. *Developmental Science*, 11(4), 208–213.

Cabrera, N. J., Scott, M., Fagan, J., Steward-Streng, N., & Chien, N. (2012). Coparenting and children's school readiness: A mediational model. *Family Process*, 51(3), 307–324.

Charmaz, K. (2014). *Constructing grounded theory* (2nd ed.). SAGE.

Cohen, J. A. (1960). Coefficient of agreement for nominal scales. *Educational and Psychological Measurement*, 20, 37–46.

Fagan, J., & Barnett, M. (2003). The relationship between maternal gatekeeping, paternal competence, mothers' attitudes about the father role, and father involvement. *Journal of Family Issues*, 24(8), 1010–1043.

Fagan, J., & Palkovitz, R. (2011). Coparenting and relationship quality effects on father engagement: Variations by residence, romance. *Journal of Marriage and Family*, 73(2), 637–653.

Gadsden, V. L., Ford, M., & Breiner, H. (eds.) (2016). *Parenting matters: Supporting parents of children 0–8*. National Academies Press. https://www.ncbi.nlm.nih.gov/books/NBK402024/pdf/Bookshelf_NBK402024.pdf.

Hayward, R. A., McCue, R., Hou, W., McKillop, A. J., & Lee, S. J. (2019). *A randomized clinical trial to examine the impact of cell phone technology on engagement and retention of fathers in a fatherhood program*. Fatherhood Research and Practice Network. https://www.frpn.org/asset/frpn-grantee-report-randomized-controlled-trial-examine-the-impact-cell-phone-technology.

Kazdin, A. E., Holland, L., Crowley, M., & Breton, S. (1997). Barriers to treatment participation scale: Evaluation and validation in the context of child outpatient treatment. *The Journal of Child Psychology and Psychiatry*, 38(8), 1051–1062.

King, V., & Sobolewski, J. M. (2006). Nonresident fathers' contribution to adolescent well-being. *Journal of Marriage and Family, 68*(3), 537–557.

Markman, H. J., & Rhoades, G. K. (2012). Relationship education research: Current status and future directions. *Journal of Marital and Family Therapy, 38*(1), 169–200.

Markman, H. J., Stanley, S. M., & Blumberg, S. L. (2010). *Fighting for your marriage* (3rd edition). Jossey-Bass.

Martinson, K., & Nightingale, D. (2008). *Ten key findings from responsible fatherhood initiatives.* The Urban Institute. https://www.urban.org/sites/default/files/publication/31516/411623-Ten-Key-Findings-from-Responsible-Fatherhood-Initiatives.PDF.

McLanahan, S., Tach, L., & Schneider, D. (2013). The causal effects of father absence. *Annual Review of Sociology, 39*, 399–427.

National Fatherhood Initiative. (2008). *Mom as gateway: A module for 24/7 Dad and other fathering programs* [Curriculum]. https://www.fatherhood.gov/sites/default/files/resource_files/e000001792.pdf.

Nelson, T. J. (2004). Low-income fathers. *Annual Review of Sociology, 30*, 427–451.

Payne, K. K. (2019). *Children's family structure, 2019* (Family Profiles No. 25, 2019). National Center for Family & Marriage Research. https://www.bgsu.edu/content/dam/BGSU/college-of-arts-and-sciences/NCFMR/documents/FP/payne-children-family-structure-fp-19-25.pdf.

Pearson, J. (2015) Establishing parenting time in child support cases: New opportunities and challenges. *Family Court Review, 53*(9), 246–257.

Perlman, M. (1998). *The nurturing fathers program.* Center for Growth & Development, Inc.

Stanley, S. M., Pearson, M., & Kline, G. H. (2005, November 3–5). *The development of relationship education for low income individuals: Lessons from research and experience* [Conference presentation]. The Association for Public Policy Analysis and Management Fall Conference, Washington, D.C., United States.

Talbert House. (n.d.). *Community care.* https://www.talberthouse.org/help/community-care-3/.

Tannehill, T. G., O'Brien, C. T., & Sorensen, E. J. (2009). *Strengthening families through stronger fathers initiative: Process evaluation report.* New York State Office of Temporary and Disability Assistance. https://www.urban.org/sites/default/files/publication/28106/1001412-Strengthening-Families-Through-Stronger-Fathers-Initiative-Process-Evaluation-Report.PDF.

Whitton, S., Sperber, K. G., Ludwig, K., Vissman, A., & Howard, H. (2018). *Final evaluation report: Evaluating mother and nonresidential father engagement in coparenting services in a fatherhood program.* Fatherhood Research and Practice Network. https://www.frpn.org/asset/frpn-grantee-report-evaluating-mother-and-nonresidential-father-engagement-in-coparenting.

11

"YOU GOTTA MAKE THEM *FEEL*"

A Study of Evidence-Informed Strategies for Addressing Domestic Violence in Fatherhood Programs

Kristie A. Thomas and Fernando Mederos

Study Rationale

DV, or intimate partner violence, is a pervasive social problem that includes physical and sexual violence, stalking, psychological aggression, coercive control, and economic abuse by a current or former spouse, boyfriend, girlfriend, or sexual partner (Breiding et al., 2015). Approximately 25% of women and 11% of men have experienced at least one incident of severe abuse by a partner (Smith et al., 2017). In addition, children and adolescents often witness, hear, and absorb the aftermath of parental and caretaker DV (Davies & Lyon, 2014; Hamby et al., 2011). For low-income communities and communities of color, DV occurs within a larger context of structural oppression that serves to heighten risk, exacerbate impact, and limit opportunities for help-seeking (Al'Uqdah et al., 2016; Mehrotra et al., 2016; Richie, 2012). Research with low-income women of color underscores how they must juggle a range of competing needs in addition to safety from an abusive partner (Goodman et al., 2009; Ragavan et al., 2018; Richie, 2012). For low-income men of color, help-seeking options for DV victimization and perpetration are even scarcer (Boggess & Groblewski, 2011).

FGs are a rare exception to the general lack of programs and services for low-income men and men of color. Research demonstrates that FGs are an important resource for low-income fathers, providing them with a safe space to share their experiences and learn new skills such as self-reflection and emotion regulation (Anderson et al., 2002; Black et al., 2010; Holcomb et al., 2015). These very features are also essential components of DV education, indicating that FGs have considerable potential for DV intervention and prevention with low-income fathers (Hayward et al., 2018; Thoennes & Pearson, 2015; Thomas et al., 2019).

Although momentum to address DV in FGs has been building for quite some time, information on effective strategies and practices is scarce in both the practice and research literature. For example, although FGs receiving Office of Family Assistance (OFA) funding are required to address DV in some way (Roulet, 2009), little has been written on what these programs are doing to meet the OFA requirements. In addition, the majority of FGs are not federally funded; thus, they have neither the resources nor the obligation to address DV. Similarly, research provides little guidance on how to effectively integrate DV into FGs due to the lack of studies on the topic. In short, there is a need for more research on how DV is being addressed in FGs and practitioners' thoughts about what is helpful (or not helpful) and why.

The Current Study

The purpose of this chapter is to offer an evidence-informed framework for fatherhood programs (FPs)[1] on how to address DV in ways that support the needs of fathers and their families. The framework is based on findings from a rigorous research project that took a deep dive into the topic of FGs and DV, with specific attention to whether and how FGs are addressing DV in their formal curricula, current strategies and approaches for incorporating DV into the work of FGs, and the universe of factors that act as barriers and supports to addressing DV (see Thomas & Mederos, 2020). In this chapter, we distill the most salient of those findings into a user-friendly framework for practitioners who work with fathers attending FGs.

Method

This study used a qualitative design that involved a review of curricula used in FGs and interviews with staff who work with fathers in FGs. The study was also guided by a practice–research engagement approach, in which practitioners (co-author Mederos) and researchers (co-author Thomas) co-conduct scientifically rigorous research projects that are directly relevant and responsive to the needs of the community (Brown et al., 2003). The Simmons University Institutional Review Board approved the study.

Curricula Review

In consultation with leaders in the fatherhood field, we selected four core curricula used in FGs: *24/7 Dad: AM®* (National Fatherhood Initiative, 2015), the *Fatherhood Development Program* (National Partnership for Community Leadership, 1995), *Fatherhood Is Sacred® & Motherhood Is Sacred™* (Native American Fatherhood Families Association, 2016), and *Nurturing Fathers Program* (Perlman, 1998). In addition, we reviewed one DV-specific curriculum, *Understanding Domestic Violence™* (Mesa et al., 2009), which is used as a supplement to the *24/7 Dad: AM®* and other NFI curricula.

Interviews

We conducted phone interviews with a total of 40 people from three different stakeholder groups: 10 fatherhood "leaders," (i.e., fatherhood curricula developers or directors of a fatherhood program); 20 FG facilitators with at least five years of facilitation experience; and 10 DV "advocates" (i.e., staff at a DV-specific program) who have experience collaborating with a fatherhood program. On average, participants were in their mid-50s, and 60% identified as a person of color (i.e., African American, Latino, Multi-racial, and Native American). Regarding gender composition, fatherhood leaders and facilitators were comprised primarily of men (87%), and DV advocates were comprised mainly of women (90%). Participants worked in programs spanning five regions: Mid-Atlantic (35%), New England, (22.5%), Southwest (20%), Midwest (12.5%), and South (7.5%). Interviewees were asked open-ended questions related to addressing DV in FGs, including curricular content, activities and best practices, barriers, opportunities, and collaboration between fatherhood and DV programs. Participants were offered a $25 gift card as a thank you for their time.

Results

The curriculum reviews and stakeholder interviews produced rich insight into the many factors that FPs need to consider when addressing DV in FGs. In synthesizing these factors, two overarching categories emerged: 1) goals for FPs and 2) strategies and practices for facilitators. We describe each category separately but discuss how they are closely connected. When quoting study participants, we identify them with their number and stakeholder group (i.e., "L" for leader, "F" for FG facilitator, and "DV" for DV advocate).

TEXT BOX 11.1 GOALS FOR FPS

- Foster a program-wide commitment to DV
- Develop authentic collaborations with DV programs
- Incorporate DV content into existing core curricula
- Stay true to the purpose of FPs

Goals for FPs

We found that addressing DV with fathers in FGs requires attention from the program as a whole in order to be successful. Thus, FPs should strive to achieve the following goals.

Goal #1: Foster a Program-Wide Commitment to DV as a Core Concern of Fatherhood Work

Although the majority of DV-related education and skill-building typically occurs within the group sessions, the effectiveness of that work depends on a program-wide commitment to DV. When programs embrace DV as a core concern of fatherhood work, they are more likely to engage in the full scope of activities needed to support the needs of fathers *and* facilitators. This work includes training all staff to ensure they have a nuanced understanding of DV. This training should include attention to coercive control as a form of DV, fatality risk factors for female survivors, and men's experiences of being abused by their partners. This commitment also includes hiring social workers and psychologists with DV expertise to conduct DV screening and assessments, provide fathers with individual counseling and referrals, and support facilitators. Doing so is important because fathers often need more intensive support and resources beyond what facilitators can provide given their role and level of training.

Two factors appear to affect programs' willingness and ability to adopt such a holistic commitment. First, commitment at the founder/director level is particularly helpful, especially when motivated by personal experiences of DV or professional experience working with DV programs. Many of the leaders in this study described how those experiences had instilled a deep understanding of the importance of addressing DV in fatherhood work. As one leader explained, "the truth is I confronted myself with the reality, could this program really do what it says to do, unless issues of violence, family violence, domestic violence were really addressed?" These directors can then help their staff explore their own connections with and attitudes toward DV in order to facilitate similar "aha" moments.

Second, and not surprisingly, much of what programs can do regarding DV education and intervention depends on funding. We found that larger agencies, especially those with federal funding, had more comprehensive approaches to addressing DV. Smaller, less-resourced agencies rely, instead, on the dedication of one or two facilitators who choose to integrate DV education into their FGs—often on top of their other responsibilities. Although innovation and transformation certainly can happen at the facilitator level alone, it is not a sustainable approach because the work ends when the facilitator burns out or moves on.

Goal #2: Develop Authentic Collaborations With DV Programs

Authentic collaboration with DV programs is essential to ensuring that FPs have the capacity and ability to address DV. Successfully fostering an authentic collaboration requires being open and willing to overcome some of the enduring tensions that have divided the fatherhood and DV fields. (See Thomas &

Mederos, 2020, for an in-depth discussion of these tensions.) Participants described how overcoming those tensions is possible and offered three strategies that have worked for them in their collaborations: *find areas of common ground, build personal relationships, and engage in mutual education.*

In general, fatherhood and DV programs share several areas of common ground that can be used to facilitate authentic collaboration. First, DV advocates and fatherhood practitioners both see the importance of preventing DV. As one fatherhood leader (L6) said, "None of us, you know, want to have a situation where there's abuse going on, and if we can, you know, educate our dads in an effort to prevent it from happening, you know, we're gonna to do that." Likewise, DV advocates stressed that "working with men is the way to prevent domestic violence," otherwise, "you are only working with half of the problem." Second, both groups are deeply committed to helping children and ending the cycle of violence. According to one DV advocate (DV6), collaboration is "extremely important, because this is about creating a better future for the children." Finally, these programs serve the same population (i.e., very low-income families experiencing multiple forms of trauma). Once advocates and practitioners recognize that, it becomes abundantly clear that they need to collaborate with one another.

> We were working and serving clients from the same community. So it would make logical sense for us to come together to figure out how can we work together to support one another, while still maintaining our identity and integrity of who we were, but also being open to potential change that could be beneficial to the families we both serve. (L7)

In addition to finding common ground, developing relationships between DV advocates and fatherhood practitioners is another primary strategy for building authentic collaboration. For some participants, pre-existing friendships were the catalyst for their collaboration; in other cases, these friendships developed over time as they got to know one another. According to participants, this process must include exploring each other's motivations for the work and their understanding and awareness of DV, racism, and poverty. One DV advocate explained how getting to know her fatherhood partners beyond superficial acquaintance "allowed us to have conversations that were very different." Moreover, with true relationship-building, comes the mutual trust necessary for overcoming tensions and reluctance to collaborate. In other words, "I can learn from you because I don't have to protect my folks [staff and clients] from you" (DV5).

Finally, mutual education is essential for authentic collaboration between DV and FPs. This involves learning about each other's work and the challenges that their different clientele face. An advocate summed up the primary blind spots of each group:

Fatherhood programs need to get themselves taught about DV 101—the basics of domestic violence. But also learning about gender and gender roles and issues ... DV folks have to learn about poverty and how gender impacts low-income men in poverty, and how the child support system may negatively impact families, and what street violence is about and what's going on in people's lives and unemployment and racial discrimination. (DV5)

Goal #3: Incorporate DV Content Into Existing Core Curricula

Among the four core curricula we reviewed, none addressed DV explicitly. There were, however, many openings in each curriculum that could lead to a discussion of DV, especially the sessions that explore the men's own childhoods, discipline of children, and healthy relationships. The Nurturing Fathers Program (NFP) gets most closely at DV—specifically coercive control—with its emphasis on "power to" versus "power over." Three of the core curricula offer supplemental content on DV ranging from discrete activities to entire modules that can be added (e.g., NFI's *Understanding Domestic Violence*^{TM} [Mesa et al., 2009]). Many of FG facilitators we spoke with, however, did not know about these supplements.

Although not universal, the general sentiment among facilitators was that they wanted to have deeper discussions about DV with fathers, but they needed more guidance and structure for how to do so. According to one facilitator (F20), "I don't think there's enough, frankly, focused activities that can be used by facilitators to get to the real discussions that need to happen." To fill this gap, some facilitators created their own activities:

> I've added an extra week, a 14th week, to specifically talk about the effects of trauma, the effects of domestic violence, and how that relates to families and nurturing. Been doing that now I would say probably four to five years. (F1)

These findings indicate that FPs should require integration of DV-specific content and activities into whatever core curricula their FGs use, rather than relying on optional supplements and facilitator discretion. Doing so has the potential to ensure more consistent implementation and increase facilitators' feelings of support and preparedness.

Goal #4: Stay True to the Purpose of FPs

FPs should be careful to not stray from the original purpose of FGs when incorporating attention to DV. Study participants were emphatic that FPs are not

Batterer Intervention Programs (BIPs); therefore, they should not be used as a treatment for fathers who are currently perpetrating DV or have an extensive DV history that has not been addressed. Instead, FGs should be used to promote DV education, awareness, and prevention. Participants were in overwhelming agreement that FGs have the power and "platform" to achieve these goals. According to a DV advocate (DV1), the varied group composition is one reason for this potential. That is, unlike batterer intervention programs, which consist entirely of men who have been abusive, FGs include men who think violence is appropriate with those who do not: "You've got this mixture of people ... men with really different experiences, including those who would strenuously argue that violence is never helpful or appropriate."

In addition to inadvertently turning FGs in BIPs, another risk is letting attention to DV eclipse other necessary FG content areas. Although many participants endorsed the importance of addressing DV within fatherhood work, they stressed it is not the primary issue for the fathers who participate in FGs; thus, they do not want "the lens of domestic violence to be larger than the lens of fatherhood." In other words, DV should not overshadow the other areas and skills that need to be addressed. As one leader (L3) stressed: "Domestic violence is not the central issue. It is a very important issue, but the central issue is an economic issue."

Given that FGs should focus on education (vs. treatment), programs need to develop policies regarding whether to include fathers with current or recent DV perpetration in FGs. The participants in this study identified two approaches. One approach involves requiring prior attendance at a BIP before attending a FG; another approach involves allowing concurrent participation in the FG and the BIP. Regardless of which approach is adopted, it is essential to engage in careful screening to exclude what some participants called "hardcore batterers," as these men were seen as not being ready to participate in or benefit from an FG. In addition, programs might need to develop their own "in-house" groups for fathers with active DV given the scarcity of BIPs in some communities as well as fathers' resistance to attend them.

Strategies and Practices for Facilitators

The interviews with leaders, facilitators, and DV advocates uncovered a range of creative and thoughtful practices that are being used to address DV with fathers in FGs. Moreover, it was clear that these practices were heavily informed by participants' deep understanding of fathers' experiences and needs. In this section, we describe each of the six categories of strategies that emerged and connect them to practitioners' reasons for why they are important for this particular population of fathers.

> **TEXT BOX 11.2 STRATEGIES AND PRACTICES FOR FACILITATORS**
>
> - Harness men's desire to be a good father
> - Keep children at the center of DV education
> - Combine cognitive and emotional strategies in DV education
> - Embrace a framework of empathy *and* accountability
> - Provide a safe space for DV discussion and self-reflection
> - Engage in reflective and appropriate use of self

Strategy #1: Harness Men's Desire to Be a Good Father

According to participants, an important asset for men in FGs is their deep commitment to be a good father. It is the primary motivating force behind their willingness to participate in an FG and engage in self-transformation. Also, because it is a relatively universal feeling, it can be used to highlight similarities and build connections among fathers. As one facilitator (F11) explained, "they're motivated for many factors. But the one commonality is they want a better relationship with their children, number one. Number two, they don't want their children to make the same mistakes that they made."

Thus, an important strategy to addressing the topic of DV with men in FGs is to connect it to their desire to be a good father. Doing so cultivates buy-in by acknowledging fathers' strengths and appealing to their self-interest. One way to do this is for facilitators to stress to fathers that learning about and reflecting on DV is ultimately in the best interest of their children. This involves making sure that DV-related discussions and activities focus on the negative impact of DV exposure on children's physical and emotional health, educational outcomes, and future relationships. Study participants stressed that fathers' strong desire to protect their children from harm and prevent them from experiencing abuse by a partner (or abusing a partner) makes them eager to learn about nonviolent behaviors and communication skills.

An especially important benefit of focusing the conversation on children's well-being is that it can open the door to conversations in which fathers reflect on their own unhealthy and abusive behaviors and how those behaviors directly impact their own children. It is critical to make this connection because fathers often understand abstractly that DV exposure is harmful to children but struggle to see the harm in their own violent or emotionally abusive behavior:

> By and large, my feeling is that these men, as I said before, want to be good fathers and want to learn how to be good fathers. And of course as we

know, there's a disconnect sometimes between their use of violence and their desire to be good fathers. (DV4)

One participant (F9) described the impact of making these connections on fathers: "They're crying more about [the fact] that they lived that life [of violence] before, okay? And they don't want to pass that to the children … They wanna do better."

Strategy #2: Keep Children at the Center of DV Education

Introducing DV content works best when children are the focus of discussions and activities. According to participants, fathers often feel resistant to the topic and reluctant to share openly, partly because they fear being judged and possibly even being arrested. Rooting the conversation in children's well-being can help to ease some of that fear because fathers can see that the purpose is to help them enhance their parenting—not some covert attempt to judge them or get them in trouble. As one participant (F20) described, fathers are hesitant to talk openly about conflict in their intimate relationships but "you can get into a very deeper place with the guys when you can relate it [DV] back to the well-being and the development of their children."

It is also important to convince fathers that learning about DV and reflecting on their own behaviors is in *their* own best interest too. For example, one of the leaders connects DV education with fathers' strong desire to spend more time with their children.

> So I thought if we could provide a service to help men to understand how not to move towards a direction that might involve domestic violence, that we would enhance the likelihood of him being able to put together a parenting agreement, or a coparenting agreement with the mother of his children so that he can then have interaction with his child. Fathers love their children … but they must have an opportunity to be involved and interact with their child in order for their love to nurture and grow. (L3)

Another way to engage fathers' self-interest is skill-building for when the mother of their children is abusive to their children or is involved with a new partner who is abusive. One of the DV advocates in this study described how she had originally used more of a knowledge-building approach when presenting on DV in FGs, but altered her approach in response to feedback from fathers who wanted more skill-building activities that they could apply in their own lives:

> So, I shifted the focus to be a bit more about "here's the dynamics of abuse," and then on how can we remain safe in a relationship when our partners are choosing violence as a way to parent or partner and how to navigate that landscape. (DV9)

Strategy #3: Combine Cognitive and Emotional Strategies in DV Education

Another key strategy in DV education is to blend cognitive and emotional learning activities to address the specific needs of fathers in FGs and increase their engagement. For example, cognitive learning was seen as important because fathers' knowledge about DV is limited in scope (e.g., they often equate DV with physical violence only). Emotional or affective learning was also seen as critically important, given fathers' tendency to minimize, deflect, and sometimes resist conversations about DV. In fact, many study participants argued that emotional learning is even more important than knowledge-building activities. As one leader (L5) stressed, "You just can't say don't do this. Don't hit, don't hit. They all know that. They all know that. So I said, knowledge does not change people. You gotta make them *feel*." The next few paragraphs offer examples of cognitive and emotional learning activities to use with fathers in FGs.

Cognitive Learning. Among study participants, the main way to engage fathers cognitively is through interactive psychoeducation. This involves developing sessions in which fathers are exposed to essential content through a didactic presentation but also given opportunities for reflection, discussion, and skill development. For example, a common activity is to review and discuss the Duluth Power and Control Wheel (Pence & Paymar, 1993), a seminal DV education tool that outlines the different forms of DV, with an emphasis on the role of coercive and controlling tactics—a common blind spot for fathers in FGs. An important part of the discussion is to help fathers brainstorm strategies they can take to avoid engaging in these behaviors and recognizing when they are the victim of these behaviors from their partners.

The majority of study participants endorsed the importance of giving men practical tools and techniques that they can implement, especially related to anger management and conflict resolution. As one facilitator (F11) explained, "there are so many different dynamics where a man's emotional intelligence may not have developed to be able to face conflict effectively." Similarly, another participant (L3) focuses on helping fathers "understand what is domestic violence, how to recognize their anger as it is escalating, how to deescalate their own anger … We put it straight on the men that they are responsible to prevent domestic violence." One specific strategy is to have the men share moments when they used violence or abusive behaviors toward a partner and then reflect with the group "what would I do again if I were faced with this situation tomorrow" in order to "prevent the past relation of conflict in such a way that could lead to domestic violence." Another participant described teaching the men grounding exercises such as meditation and deep breathing to help them regulate their emotions.

Emotional Learning. Two primary ways to facilitate emotional learning with fathers in FGs are to *personalize DV victimization* (i.e., "adding a face" to the issue) and *engage in "deep work"* (i.e., helping fathers explore their traumatic experiences and connect them with their attitudes and behaviors about DV). In terms of *personalizing DV victimization*, participants described how it is difficult for some fathers to empathize with female survivors due to deeply entrenched victim-blaming attitudes and beliefs about traditional gender roles—both of which stem from living in neighborhoods of hypermasculinity and normalized interpersonal violence. According to one facilitator (F4), "I think it takes a conscious effort to educate men and to enlighten them about these unconscious attitudes that we carry as males, you know, that kind of destroy our relationships because we're so heavy-handed and quote-unquote 'manly.'"

One particularly effective strategy for promoting empathy and understanding involves having the men engage directly with female survivors—either speakers from the community or staff willing to disclose their experiences. One leader (L8) explained how sharing her story had a profound impact on fathers' conceptualization of DV and who experiences it: "They're like, 'What, *you*? Like, you're the person that's in charge, that's not supposed to happen to the strong woman that we perceive is in charge,' right?" She and others stressed that it is especially important to allow the men an opportunity to ask the speakers candid questions about their experiences (e.g., "why did you stay?") in order to debunk some of the stereotypes that they hold about survivors and foster "some empathy for women who were going through this."

Another strategy to elicit emotional responses is to have the men think about DV in the context of their female relatives. As one participant (F5) explained, "Then we flipped the script: would you believe your mother if she told you? Would you believe your sister if she told you? And it automatically, the room got all, 'wait a minute, wait a minute!'" This participant said that he feels strongly that this exercise has the potential to "change some perspectives" and "open up some kind of consciousness of what you're doing and who you're doing it to."

Engaging in "deep work" was identified as another essential strategy, given the various forms of trauma that fathers in FGs have endured. *"Deep work"* involves engaging fathers in activities that elicit their traumatic memories, especially their own childhood DV exposure. These activities help men unpack the source of their own aggressive or abusive behaviors and begin to take ownership of the impact their behaviors have on their children. One participant provided a helpful summary of what "deep work" entails:

> We're trying make them better parents, and the only way you can do that is through this kind of self-examination, Socratic way of looking at, at your past and looking at you and not blaming other people, but seeing if there are systemic things in your family—in your family's history. Mom got beat, you did nothing, how did you that feel about that? You got beat, mom did nothing, how did you feel about that? And for them to see the link and that's, that is the, the point of the whole lesson is to personalize to the point

> that you can see, that you can see yourself here and how does that relate to you going forward. (F14)

"Deep work" activities help to override or unfreeze fathers' cognitive-level resistance to sharing and reflecting on their experiences. Examples of activities include presenting detailed scenarios in which children of various ages witness abuse, listening to 911 calls from children witnessing DV, showing drawings by children who had been exposed to DV, having the men draw how their children might see them, and showing movies and documentaries about DV.

> In one film, the child says he's tired of the monster that keeps hurtin' his mother. And he says he wants to kill the monster that keeps hurtin' his mother. Blows all our minds, because the monster was the child's father. You should see, you can hear a pin drop in the room. (F5)

These activities often result in intense "aha moments" and insight into DV and its impact on themselves and their children.

> They see the link between their past and the trouble and the violence that was either visited on them or that they observed, witnessed as children ... And it sometimes can be a very difficult bridge for them. Some of them will actually leave the room and come back later and say, you know, I was just having a moment where I was recognizing what happened in my own life. (DV6)

In addition to unpacking father's childhood DV exposure, participants also worked with fathers to explore their internalized hypermasculinity and historical trauma. For example, the Native American facilitators in our study often use culturally specific activities to promote healing and identity restoration (e.g., sweat lodges, healing circles, and mirrors to help reflect on how fathers' ancestors would see them).

It is critical that facilitators who use these "deep work" activities have the support they need to handle fathers' potentially intense reactions, both during and after the group session. Indeed, several facilitators reported being hesitant to dive too deeply into men's trauma for fear of "opening wounds" they "can't close." This concern is warranted given that most FG facilitators are not trained clinicians; rather, they are fathers from the community who serve as teachers and role models. We found that facilitators in programs without any trained clinicians on staff were more likely to express worry about engaging in "deep work." This trend highlights how FPs interested in effectively integrating DV content into FGs (i.e., change the attitudes and norms that drive behavior) must invest in a workforce that possesses the lived experience and professional training necessary to support fathers' varying needs.

Strategy #4: Embrace a Framework That Balances Empathy and Accountability

Participants were emphatic that anyone who delivers DV content in FGs must approach fathers with an equal amount of empathy and accountability. To apply one without the other risks either condoning fathers' harmful behaviors or shutting fathers down—neither of which will lead to growth and change. Participants explained that adopting an empathic stance is important because the majority of fathers they serve are struggling with what one participant called "low-income living." Essentially, fathers in FGs face substantial stress and trauma because they have few prospects for living wage jobs, endure racism and discrimination by systems and society that are "stacked against them," and live in neighborhoods where interpersonal violence is often normalized and sometimes expected of them. And yet, they are rarely taught how to identify their trauma triggers or express their anger and frustration in healthy ways.

Thus, an empathic approach involves recognizing the individual and structural-level factors that have influenced men's attitudes and behaviors. Similar to a trauma-informed approach, it replaces the question of "what is wrong with you" to "what has happened to you." Participants discussed the importance of seeing fathers as inherently good, capable of growth and transformation, and worthy of forgiveness. Facilitators and guest speakers must convey genuine care, concern, and respect for fathers, especially when focusing on DV. One participant stressed (L5): "You must first of all truly love the people whom you serve. That is critical, because they can tell within a matter of minutes if you can care for them or not. That applies to anybody."

Showing fathers empathy and care, however, should not equate to "condoning" men's violent, harmful, or unhealthy behaviors. Study participants stressed that programs and staff should clearly convey the message that fathers are responsible and accountable for their behaviors. One participant described his program's supportive but firm approach:

> So we don't say "well, you've engaged in this behavior in the past; get out of our program, out of our building." We said, "well, that's not acceptable. And you have to make changes so that you can continue to grow and be a part of our program." (L7)

In terms of specific practices, several facilitators in this study use activities that foster fathers' internal sense of agency, empowerment, and control over their own reactions. One facilitator (F1) uses the term, "self-personal power" with fathers when talking about DV and trauma. He explains to them that it is a power only they own: "Doesn't belong to anybody else. This is something that you can choose to give it away. You can choose to keep it. This is your own self being. And once you learn to control it, life will seem a lot easier."

Strategy #5: Provide a Safe Space for DV Discussion and Self-Reflection

Effective integration of DV content into FGs depends heavily on fathers feeling emotionally safe enough to discuss their thoughts and experiences of DV candidly. One way to cultivate a safe space is for facilitators and DV advocates to avoid using terms such as "batterer," "perpetrator," and "abuser," because fathers see these terms as one of the many negative labels that systems and society places on them. As one advocate (DV10) explained, "it's hard to go into a space and say, you know, you're all a batterer, let me tell you why you're a bad person." Even the term "domestic violence" must be used carefully given the connotations it carries among low-income men. According to one facilitator (F10), the term "is literally an acronym for really bad men." As a result, "there's a fear factor in even talking about it" (F8) because fathers worry that doing so will result in them being blamed unfairly, labeled, and possibly even arrested.

To avoid labeling, one advocate (DV10) described how "we always just try to use person-first language when possible and really focus on the behaviors because I think that builds some trust and understanding." Building trust increases fathers' willingness to share with one another as well as have conversations about DV with their own families and seek out other supportive services. One facilitator (F1) explained that many of the fathers he works with are transformed by the "relief of having a safe place to talk about these things" (i.e., DV and trauma) to the extent that they come back to tell him, "I called the phone number you told me, or I reached a therapist or I'm on medication."

In addition to focusing on behaviors, it is important to convey a balanced view of DV victimization and perpetration. As one of the leaders explained,

> There were often times when I came in to a training or a conference, and right away, what was put out there is "women are the victims, men are the perpetrators." And that kind of dynamic wasn't gonna work in our nurturing fathers program. It had to be "we are here together, men and women, to solve the problem." (L10)

Avoiding a gendered lens is necessary because the fathers in FGs who experience DV often do not see themselves as victims: "I think it's that they don't see that they're actually going through what women go through." Moreover, the few who do recognize it as abuse are reluctant to share given the stigma and shame that surrounds male DV victimization, especially among low-income men. And yet, FGs are often the only place where fathers can discuss their experiences. Thus, it is essential to cultivate a safe space where fathers' experiences of DV are normalized and heard.

Strategy #6: Engage in Reflective and Appropriate Use of Self

Not surprisingly, FG facilitators play an enormous role in whether conversations and activities regarding DV are effective with fathers. Participants described how the most successful facilitators are those who share their own experiences of DV (victimization and perpetration) as a way to connect and educate fathers. However, facilitators must engage in deep reflection and self-transformation, *first* to ensure that what they share is appropriate and helpful for conveying a nuanced understanding of DV. As one facilitator explained, "I always try to use myself as an example ... I don't try to say, 'Oh, I know somebody,' or anything, or try to call anybody out in the group, you know, because I was an abuser before I knew what abusing even was." In addition to fostering connection with fathers, sharing personal accounts provides fathers with examples of vulnerability, transformation, and self-forgiveness to which they can aspire.

Facilitators' use of self also includes connecting based on shared aspects of identity such as race, ethnicity, and class. As one facilitator (F8) explained, "the men need to see success in themselves," meaning that "the facilitator needs to reflect the community that they're facilitating in ... that's a natural and a very organic connector." Participants stressed that facilitators' identity and lived experience often mattered more than academic credentials or advanced teaching skills. The same is often true for the DV advocates who serve as guest speakers:

> The ones that came in like the college professor kind of thing, knew all the information and had a Master's degree in women's studies didn't do as well as the woman working at the [DV] center who ... could talk to the men on a level from having had experiences living in similar situations to where they were living. (L10)

The critical role of conveying a common bond with fathers highlights a point made earlier in this chapter about the need for a program-level commitment to addressing DV. Facilitators who reflect the community have struggled, and often continue to struggle, with the same challenges of "low-income living" that fathers who attend FGs do (e.g., barriers to education, interpersonal trauma, hypermasculine culture). Thus, they need support, training, and an investment in their professional development to ensure their success. Although it is essential to have staff on site with the advanced clinical training necessary to work with fathers who are engaging in DV or experiencing it, these staff should support, not replace, facilitators from the communities they serve. As one participant captured so well, "Here's the other thing. You also don't want to make the job so clinically based that you change the makeup of who the fatherhood practitioner population is. You follow me?"

Discussion

This chapter presents a framework for how FPs can address the topic of DV in ways that resonate with low-income fathers' needs and lived experiences. The framework was informed by immense practitioner wisdom; the 40 people we interviewed had been working with FG fathers for years—often decades—and reflected a range of roles, geographic locations, and social locations (i.e., gender, race, ethnicity, and age). Their insight coalesced into a two-tiered, interrelated approach to addressing DV that involves attention at the program level as well as the facilitator level.

First, it is essential to foster a commitment to DV that permeates the entire program. Superficial commitment can result in the use of practices and activities that are ineffective and possibly even harmful for fathers and their families. A program-wide commitment includes recruiting directors and administrators with a passion for addressing DV; ensuring that all staff receive DV education and training; hiring staff with clinical training to support fathers and facilitators; and advocating for funding to pay for these activities. It also requires developing authentic collaborations with DV programs. Authenticity is necessary to ensure that both sets of programs are willing to work together to develop activities, materials, and policies that resonate with fathers and protect DV survivors (Boggess et al., 2007). These strategies align with organizational development theory, particularly its emphasis on targeting program culture, climate, and capacity to achieve sustainable change (Butterfoss et al., 2009).

It is also essential that programs practice consistency in *how* DV education is incorporated into FG curricula and the *purpose* behind it. We recommend that programs work with curricula developers and DV advocates to incorporate DV content *into* the core curriculum (rather than rely on optional supplements) and expand the curriculum by at least one session to ensure the topic is given adequate attention. Relatedly, as programs decide what DV content and activities to include, it is important to remember that the purpose of doing so is to educate fathers, raise awareness, and provide them with referrals when necessary. In meeting these goals, programs will need to think creatively and intentionally about what DV content should be covered as well as how to best serve fathers with current or recent DV perpetration. Given the wealth of innovative work that is already happening on these fronts, FPs would benefit from an increase in cross-pollination of ideas, practices, and policies.

At the facilitator level, the six strategies that emerged in this study share an important common denominator: the need for a deep understanding of fathers' lived experiences and how those experiences have a profound influence on fathers' willingness to discuss DV, as well as which activities are most helpful for them. Thus, a primary strategy to overcome fathers' resistance is to connect DV-related conversations and activities with their parenting goals and desire to protect their children. As others have noted, the desire to be a good father is an enormous motivating factor for engagement and change among men in both FGs and batterer programs (Dion et al., 2018; Poole & Murphy, 2019; Scott & Mederos, 2012).

The strategy of combining psychoeducation and emotional engagement highlights the importance of using affective learning practices with fathers in FGs. This finding aligns with the theories of Transformative Learning (Mezirow, 1997) and Dual Process (Epstein & Pacini, 1999), which assert that people process information through two different systems: a rational system that operates at a conscious level and an experiential system that operates at an unconscious level. Both systems must be engaged to truly change attitude and behaviors. To that end, the practice of "deep work" engages fathers' unconscious system, which can help to rewire some of their automatic thinking and responses. Part of what makes this strategy effective with fathers in FGs in particular is that it invites them to explore their own traumatic experiences, possibly for the very first time. Prior research supports that fathers in FGs have substantial trauma histories (Holcomb et al., 2015; Thomas et al., 2019), and there is increasing evidence that helping them reflect on those experiences is an important first step in changing DV-related attitudes, norms, and behaviors (Hayward et al., 2018; Webermann et al., 2020).

The third and fourth strategies underscore how is not only essential but also possible to foster a sense of accountability for DV prevention among fathers in FGs without shaming or blaming them. A review of studies on the mechanisms of change for men attending abuse intervention groups found that self-reflexive processes and differentiating between shame (being a bad person) and responsibility (acknowledging harmful behaviors) increases empathy and acceptance of responsibility (Velonis et al., 2018). It is especially important for DV advocates who implement DV education in FGs to understand and embrace this approach, given how it differs from traditional batterer intervention programs.

Finally, FG facilitators play many roles in the lives of the fathers they serve. An obvious one is that of educator and discussion facilitator; however, they also act as positive role models and examples of success that fathers aspire to achieve. Given this powerful influence, it is critical for facilitators to reflect deeply on their own experiences of and attitudes toward DV before engaging fathers in conversations about the topic. And, as has been mentioned, FG facilitators need a range of supports from the program and other staff in order to be equipped with the knowledge, skills, and emotional stamina that it takes to deliver successful DV education in FGs.

Conclusion

The evidence-informed framework presented in this chapter offers practical and much-needed guidance for FPs and facilitators on how to effectively address DV with fathers in FGs. However, the extent to which programs can achieve the recommended goals and facilitators can implement the recommended strategies depends largely on financial resources and human capital. Thus, there is a need for an increase in dedicated funding to support FPs in their efforts to engage in holistic DV education and prevention.

Note

1 Please note that throughout this chapter we use the term "fatherhood programs" (FPs) broadly to refer to fatherhood agencies that are funded by the Office of Family Assistance (i.e., Healthy Marriage and Responsible Fatherhood Grantees) as well as fatherhood-focused programs, often housed within social services agencies that address multiple social problems, which are funded in other ways.

References

Al'Uqdah, S. N., Maxwell, C., & Hill, N. (2016). Intimate partner violence in the African American community: Risk, theory, and interventions. *Journal of Family Violence, 31*, 877–884.

Anderson, E. A., Kohler, J. K., & Letiecq, B. L. (2002). Low-income fathers and "responsible fatherhood" programs: A qualitative investigation of participants' experiences. *Family Relations, 51*, 148–155.

Black, T., Walker, M. S., & Keyes, S. (2010). *Nurturing families network father involvement study: Final report.* Center for Social Research.

Boggess, J., & Groblewski, J. (2011). *Women of color speak about their communities.* Center for Family Policy and Practice. https://cffpp.org/wp-content/uploads/Safety_and_Services.pdf.

Boggess, J., May, R., & Roulet, M. (2007). *Collaboration and partnership: Fatherhood practitioners and advocates working together to serve women, men, and families.* Center for Family Policy and Practice.

Breiding, M. J., Basile, K. C., Smith, S. G., Black, M. C., & Mahendra, R. (2015). *Intimate partner violence surveillance: Uniform definitions and recommended data elements* (Version 2.0). National Center for Injury Prevention and Control, Centers for Disease Control and Prevention. https://www.cdc.gov/violenceprevention/pdf/intimatepartnerviolence.pdf.

Brown, L. D., Bammer, G., Batliwala, S., & Kunreuther, F. (2003). Framing practice-research engagement for democratizing knowledge. *Action Research, 1*, 81–102.

Butterfoss, F. D., Kegler, M. C., & Francisco, V. T. (2009). Mobilizing organizations for health promotion: Theories of organizational change. In K. Glanz, B. K. Rimer, & K. Viswanath (Eds.), *Health behavior and health education: Theory, research, and practice* (4 ed., pp. 335–360). Jossey-Bass.

Davies, J., & Lyon, E. (2014). *Domestic violence advocacy: Complex lives/difficult choices.* SAGE.

Dion, R., Holcomb, P., Zaveri, H., DAngelo, A. V., Clary, E., Friend, D., & Baumgartner, S. (2018). *Parents and children together: The complex needs of low-income men and how responsible fatherhood programs address them* (OPRE Report #2018-18). U.S. Department of Health and Human Services, Office of Planning, Research, and Evaluation. https://www.acf.hhs.gov/sites/default/files/opre/pact_fatherhood_programs_022618_b508.pdf.

Epstein, S., & Pacini, R. (1999). Some basic issues regarding dual-process theories from the perspective of cognitive-experiential self-theory. In S. Chaiken & Y. Trope (Eds.), *Dual process theories in social psychology* (pp. 462–503). Guilford Press.

Goodman, L. A., Smyth, K. F., Borges, A. M., & Singer, R. (2009). When crises collide: How intimate partner violence and poverty intersect to shape women's mental health and coping? *Trauma, Violence & Abuse, 10*, 306–329.

Hamby, S. L., Finkelhor, D., & Turner, H. (2011). *Children's exposure to intimate partner violence and other family violence* (No. NCJ 232272). U.S. Department of Justice, Office of Juvenile Justice and Delinquency Prevention. https://www.ncjrs.gov/pdffiles1/ojjdp/232272.pdf.

Hayward, R. A., Honegger, L., & Hammock, A. C. (2018). Risk and protective factors for family violence among low-income fathers: Implications for violence prevention and fatherhood programs. *Social Work, 63*, 57–66.

Holcomb, P., Edin, K., Max, J., Young, A., DAngelo, A. V., Friend, D., Clary, E. & Johnson, W. E. (2015). *In their own voices: The hopes and struggles of responsible fatherhood program participants in the parents and children together evaluation* (OPRE Report #2015-67). U.S. Department of Health and Human Services, Administration for Children and Families, Office of Planning, Research and Evaluation. https://www.acf.hhs.gov/sites/default/files/opre/pact_qualitative_report_6_17_2015_b508_3.pdf.

Mehrotra, G. R., Kimball, E., & Wahab, S. (2016). The braid that binds us: The impact of neoliberalism, criminalization, and professionalization on domestic violence work. *Affilia, 31*, 153–163.

Mesa, L. E., Vecere, E., & Brown, C. (2009). *Understanding Domestic Violence*^{TM}. National Fatherhood Initiative.

Mezirow, J. (1997). Transformative learning: Theory to practice. *New Directions for Adult and Continuing Education, 74*, 5–12.

National Fatherhood Initiative. (2015). *24/7 Dad: AM*® *curriculum* (3rd ed.). Author.

National Partnership for Community Leadership. (1995). *Fatherhood development curriculum*. Author.

Native American Fatherhood Families Association. (2016). *Fatherhood Is Sacred® & Motherhood Is Sacred*™ (6th ed.). Author.

Pence, E., & Paymar, M. (1993). *Education groups for men who batter: The Duluth Model*. Springer.

Perlman, M. (1998). *The nurturing fathers program: Developing attitudes and skills for male nurturance* (Facilitator manual). Center for Growth & Development.

Poole, G. M., & Murphy, C. M. (2019). Fatherhood status as a predictor of intimate partner violence (IPV) treatment engagement. *Psychology of Violence, 9*, 340–349.

Ragavan, M. I., Thomas, K. A., Fulambarker, A., Zaricor, J., Goodman, L. A., & Bair-Merritt, M. H. (2018). Exploring the needs and lived experiences of racial and ethnic minority domestic violence survivors through community-based participatory research: A systematic review. *Trauma, Violence, & Abuse, 21*(5). https://doi.org/10.1177/1524838018813204.

Richie, B. (2012). *Arrested justice: Black women, violence, and America's prison nation*. New York University Press.

Roulet, M. (2009). *Fatherhood programs and healthy marriage funding*. Center for Family Policy & Practice. https://cffpp.org/wp-content/uploads/policy_marriage.pdf.

Scott, K., & Mederos, F. (2012). *Parenting interventions for men who batter*. National Resource Center on Domestic Violence, VAWnet: The National Online Resource

Center on Violence Against Women. https://vawnet.org/sites/default/files/materials/files/2016-09/AR_ParentingInterventions.pdf.

Smith, S. G., Basile, K. C., Gilbert, L. K., Merrick, M. T., Patel, N., Walling, M., & Jain, A. (2017). *National intimate partner and sexual violence survey (NISVS): 2010–2012 state report*. Centers for Disease Control and Prevention, National Center for Injury Prevention and Control. https://www.cdc.gov/violenceprevention/pdf/NISVS-StateReportBook.pdf.

Thoennes, N., & Pearson, J. (2015). *Fatherhood programs and intimate partner violence*. Fatherhood Research and Practice Network. https://www.frpn.org/asset/frpn-research-brief-fatherhood-programs-and-intimate-partner-violence.

Thomas, K. A., & Mederos, F. (2020, January). *Responsible fatherhood groups and domestic violence education: An exploratory study of current practices, barriers, and opportunities*. Fatherhood Research and Practice Network. https://www.frpn.org/asset/frpn-grantee-report-responsible-fatherhood-groups-and-domestic-violence-education-exploratory.

Thomas, K. A., Mederos, F., & Rodriguez, G. (2019). "It shakes you for the rest of your life": Low-income fathers' understanding of domestic violence and its impact on children. *Psychology of Violence, 9,* 564–573.

Velonis, A. J., Mahabir, D. F., Maddox, R., & O'Campo, P. (2018). Still looking for mechanisms: A realist review of batterer intervention programs. *Trauma, Violence, & Abuse, 21*(5), 946–963.

Webermann, A. R., Maldonado, A., Singh, R., Torres, S., Bushee, S., & Murphy, C. M. (2020). Centrality of traumatic events and men's intimate partner violence perpetration. *Psychological Trauma: Theory, Research, Practice, and Policy, 12,* 200–206.

12
JOURNEY OF A POLICY CHANGE TO INCLUDE FATHERS IN HOMELESS SHELTERS

Karin M. Eyrich-Garg and Karen M. Hudson

Families Experiencing Homelessness

According to the Philadelphia Office of Homeless Services (OHS) (2019), 5,735 people in Philadelphia experienced homelessness on one night in January 2019. This number includes 1,983 people who compose 663 families with children. The majority (64%) of these families were in emergency shelters, and the balance were in transitional shelters. Like other cities, Philadelphia has a growing homeless population. In 2018, Philadelphia ranked 13th in the number of people (5,788) who were homeless across all Continua of Care (bodies that coordinate housing and services funding for people who are homeless) in the nation, and it ranked 14th with its per-capita rate (37 per 10,000) of homelessness (National Alliance to End Homelessness, 2019).

The term "family homelessness" usually brings to mind mothers and their children; fathers are typically unintentionally overlooked or intentionally excluded. Indeed, fathers often are not permitted to stay in family shelters (Barrett-Rivera et al., 2013). In two-parent households with one mother and one father, the mother and children can reside together in the family shelter, and the father can stay in a single men's shelter. In single-parent households with one father and in two-parent households with two fathers, the family cannot stay together in a shelter. Families can choose to remain together (on the streets, in automobiles, in hotels/motels, or doubled-up with another family), or families can choose to separate (often with fathers staying in a single men's shelter and children living with kin or in an emergency foster care placement).

Keeping fathers in their children's lives is beneficial to child health and well-being. Children whose fathers (or father figures) are involved with them in positive ways score higher than others on measures of social, emotional, and cognitive growth (Lamb, 2004; Revell, 2015). And, they are less likely than others to drop out of school, use drugs, take risks, become involved in the criminal-justice system, and become young parents themselves (Allen & Daly, 2007). As a general rule, the entire family benefits when fathers are involved in their children's lives.

Context for the Study

In Philadelphia, Pennsylvania, families enter the homeless services system through a centralized intake process. They are then directed to one of ten publicly funded family emergency shelters that operate in Philadelphia. Three of these shelters have a long (15 + year) history of admitting fathers as residents. In the seven other shelters, families that included an adolescent or adult man faced a difficult choice: remain together outside of the shelter system or separate and enter the shelter system.

Philadelphia has been a national leader in providing services to people experiencing homelessness. Three developments gave rise to the father inclusion efforts within the OHS. The first was a grass-roots movement of local leaders focusing on fathers experiencing homelessness. The second was support for greater father inclusion in shelter services by OHS staff. The third was the U.S. Department of Housing and Urban Development's new 2016 grant requirement to demonstrate nondiscrimination across several protected classes, including sexual orientation and gender identity.

In 2016 and 2017, the Philadelphia OHS began developing a "Nondiscrimination Policy." In November 2017, the Philadelphia Continuum of Care Board adopted the new policy, planning for it to be effective on January 23, 2018 (Philadelphia Office of Homeless Services, 2017).

TEXT BOX 12.1

This new policy (Philadelphia Office of Homeless Services (2017)) *prohibits discrimination against persons requiring shelter based on 15 protected classes: race, ethnicity, color, sex, sexual orientation,* **gender identity***, religion, national origin, ancestry, disability, marital status, age, source of income, familial status, and domestic or sexual violence victim status.*

The new policy ensures that all people are afforded equal opportunities, as stipulated in the Fair Housing Act, the Civil Rights Act, the Americans with Disabilities Act, HUD's Equal Access Rule, and Philadelphia's Fair Practices

Ordinance. The policy states that "providers may not exclude potential participants based on their sex" (Philadelphia Office of Homeless Services, 2017, p. 1). In other words, each family emergency shelter is required to admit fathers as residents. The Philadelphia OHS started encouraging the seven family shelters that did not admit fathers as residents to alter their policies to admit them.

Research Questions

The purpose of this study was to explore why and how this system change occurred and to identify the benefits and challenges of shifting policy from father exclusion to father inclusion in family emergency shelters. This study explored the motivation for the system change, preparation for the system change, short- and long-term consequences of the system change, and the commitment to the system change through the voices of multiple stakeholder groups.

The research team used the Diffusion of Innovations theory to guide the study because it explains how new ideas spread among groups of people. Rogers and Shoemaker (1971) classifies people by how they adopt a new idea and explores the role of communication in spreading new ideas among groups. The team adopted this approach and identified shelters as falling into one of three groups that reflected the timing of their adoption of the OHS policy. Thus, shelters in this study are classified as Early Adopters, Late Adopters, and Laggard shelters.

Methods

Recruitment and Procedure

The voices of a total of 127 study participants were included in this qualitative study. Interviews were completed with 13 OHS staff. Three focus groups (one each with Early Adopter, Late Adopter, and Laggard Shelters—see Text Box 12.2) were facilitated with a total of 20 shelter staff who worked at nine out of the ten family emergency shelters. Ten focus groups were facilitated with 94 parents (mothers and fathers) who resided in the ten Philadelphia family emergency shelters.

All interviews and focus groups were audiotaped and transcribed. All names were replaced with participant-selected pseudonyms. Family participants were paid $35 in cash for focus group participation. The City Institutional Review Board disallowed any payment for OHS Staff interviews or shelter staff focus groups. Focus groups were facilitated by two members of the research team. Because racial dynamics could affect the data collected, the research team for each focus group consisted of two facilitators—one African American and one Caucasian. This model was employed to ensure that families felt free to share openly on all topics, including topics related to race during the focus groups.

Measurement

Shelters were classified into one of three groups (Early Adopters, Late Adopters, or Laggards) based on the timing of their inclusion of fathers as residents.

TEXT BOX 12.2

Early Adopter Shelters—shelters that admitted fathers prior to the policy change
Late Adopter Shelters—shelters that admitted fathers within eight months of the policy change
Laggard Shelters—shelters that admitted fathers more than eight months after the policy change or still did not admit fathers

---

Early Adopter shelters ($n = 3$) permitted fathers to reside in their shelters prior to the OHS policy requiring all family emergency shelters to admit fathers as shelter residents. Two of the three "Early Adopter" shelters were represented in the focus group. This included six shelter staff, most of whom were people of color (five African American and one Caucasian), but with an even gender distribution (three male and three female). The research team conducted an individual interview with the Director of the third Early Adopter shelter (an African American male) because a last-minute emergency prevented him from attending the focus group. Late Adopter shelters ($n = 5$) changed their policy from excluding fathers to including fathers as residents within eight months of the OHS policy change. Four of the five "Late Adopter" shelters were represented in the focus group. Eight shelter staff participated. Most were people of color (five African American and three Caucasian) and female (six female and two male). Laggard shelters ($n = 2$) had not yet or were very late in enacting a policy change to include fathers as residents in their shelters. The two "Laggard" shelters were represented in the focus group. This included five shelter staff who were primarily of color (three African American and two Caucasian) and all female.

Each stakeholder group was asked a slightly different set of questions. OHS staff were queried about the origins of and motivations for the policy change; how they developed, prepared for, and disseminated the policy change; how they supported shelters through the change process; and any challenges they had seen during the transition. Shelter staff in the Early Adopter group were asked when and why they decided to include fathers, how they prepared for the transition, how intended and unintended consequences played out, how they included fathers in their current work, and recommendations for shelters embarking on this transition. Shelter staff in the Late Adopter and Laggard groups were asked when they first learned about the policy change, how it was communicated, and any training or support they received. They were also asked questions regarding their original rationale for excluding fathers, how they prepared for the transition, any challenges that occurred during the transition, and any benefits they have seen from the inclusion of fathers in their shelters. Parents residing in the shelters were queried about how much they want fathers involved in their lives, the ways in which fathers are involved in their lives, how shelter policies facilitate or inhibit father involvement, and any communal benefits or drawbacks they see from having fathers in (or out of) the shelter.

Data Analysis

Qualitative data were analyzed using the constant comparison method. This approach begins with basic descriptive coding within and then across interviews/focus groups. Descriptive coding becomes the basis for analytical coding from which core themes are identified. As the core themes become more robust, more in-depth categorical and theoretical explanations are developed. The Principal Investigator and Co-Investigator read all 27 transcripts (13 OHS, three Staff Focus Groups, one Shelter Staff Interview, and ten Parent Focus Groups), and at least one of the Research Assistants read each of the 27 transcripts. In other words, at least three of the four research team members read each of the 27 transcripts. Each of the four research team members (diverse in terms of race, age, and life experience) developed themes independently. Subsequently, the research team met to discuss and reach a consensus on the primary themes that are presented in this chapter.

Results

Motivation for System Change

In 2016, HUD adjusted the scoring system for the national competition for Continuum of Care dollars to strongly reward applicants who could provide evidence that they complied with HUD's nondiscrimination policy. Simultaneously, multiple complaints that focused on fathers having difficulty accessing the family shelter system were filed through the OHS Complaint Hotline. Two OHS staff (who were male and African American) were involved in reviewing these complaints. Their review of these complaints led them to conclude that the family emergency shelter system was systematically discriminating against fathers, most of whom were African American. These two OHS staff began to communicate about and advocate for father inclusion in the family emergency shelter system. OHS then invited one of these staff to draft and develop the "Nondiscrimination Policy." OHS leadership decided to require that every family emergency shelter admit fathers as residents. The following quotes from OHS staff highlight some motivations for the new requirements:

> So overall, we want to make our whole system ready to embrace anybody who needs help, who is homeless or housing insecure. No matter who and

what you are, we need to be a system that is ready and equipped to serve you. (OHS Staff)

Is someone having a housing crisis? That should be really what's guiding us to assist people, because that's what we're here for. Secondly, the equal access rule from HUD has given the compliance teeth that lets us push, that lets us write the policy, that lets us say, "HUD said we have to do it, and all that." (OHS Staff)

So, that's how I started to become interested in what was happening with our system discrimination wise. I feel like the motivation comes from injustice. If you feel like something is unjust, then you can act. And you can act however you may, maybe you quietly act. Maybe you write a policy. (OHS Staff)

They mostly were accepting intact families, and on a limited basis. So it was still biased there toward the fathers, and they were still being discriminated against. (OHS Staff)

It's been fraught, because at the end of the day it's not only about gender, it's also about race, because of who we serve in our system. That has been really serious for all of us to grapple with, and to wear, and acknowledge that we've been a part of that, for a long time. (OHS Staff)

Preparation for System Change

OHS informed providers of the policy change through emails, memoranda, and presentations at monthly provider meetings. They problem-solved with shelters through smaller shelter team meetings at OHS, phone calls, and visits to individual family emergency shelters. OHS provided small amounts of funding to some shelters to hire additional male staff. OHS developed a training on the "Nondiscrimination Policy," but they have not yet rolled it out completely. Some Late Adopter shelters sought guidance from Early Adopter shelters regarding how to integrate fathers smoothly. Shelter administrators held discussion forums with shelter staff and parents residing in shelters to prepare them for the change. Shelter administrators revised their paperwork to be more gender neutral. OHS trained intake staff to inform families entering the homeless shelter system that they may be placed at a shelter where a father resides. Quotes from OHS staff and shelter staff are below:

> I always strongly felt that OHS had a strong responsibility to be supportive of when we make a major change like this. So what we did is certain shelters requested extra staff or security to help diffuse situations where violence may occur, whether it's domestic or towards staff or other residents. We've supported requests for extra security or even at times, extra staffing, so they can be more accommodating to families of any composition. (OHS Staff)

> ... we had some shelters come and meet with us to find out how we do things. A lot of the concerns were around the bathrooms... And some of the fear was having men on the grounds... A lot of times we have women fleeing domestic violence... And then we have you bringing men in here, not saying that men are the abusers, but it might be perceived as a safer environment if it was just all women. (Staff at Early Adopter Shelter)
>
> We had a meeting with our staff because I needed their input, because they're the ones who have to deal with these situations. So I wanted number one, everyone to feel secure and confident in their position. (Staff at Late Adopter Shelter)

Short-Term System Change

Over a period of 24 months, nine out of ten family emergency shelters had begun to admit fathers as residents. The transition was easier for shelters that had a private room for each family, segregated bathrooms, and a philosophical belief or value in the importance of fathers being involved with their families. This was the case for all Early Adopters. On some occasions, families would be transferred from one shelter to another. Families who moved from a shelter where fathers were included to a shelter where fathers were excluded (or were recently included) appeared to have a greater appreciation for having fathers in the shelters and eagerly shared this viewpoint with other families. OHS staff, shelter staff, and parents were asked about the challenges of including fathers as residents in family emergency shelters. Many participants in all stakeholder groups (OHS staff, shelter staff, and parents living in shelters) reported fears that the introduction of fathers would generate violence/safety issues within shelters (for both families and staff), raise concerns about privacy (especially in sleeping quarters and bathrooms), increase the risk of retraumatization of mothers and children who have experienced or been exposed to domestic violence, generate conflicts of interest in service provision, and make it challenging to be respectful of various parenting styles within the shelter setting. Illustrative quotes from shelter staff and parents residing in shelters are presented below.

> I had to walk my kids to the bathroom because I have girls. They're older, they have bodies. (Mother at Late Adopter Shelter)
>
> I know I supervise different shifts, and they've come to me with their concerns, and they have voiced that they're fearful. The men come in, what they're going to do. And I've had to share with them, okay, well, let's break this down. Okay. Have you had this situation this woman had? Yes. Okay. Well, what's the difference? Male or female, they're both going to respond the same way. (Staff at Late Adopter Shelter)

My main concern was, looking at the violence that's happening in the city. Most of the families are young. And my concern was about, the probability of weapons coming on site. Maybe that's a stereotype, but that was a concern, a genuine concern. (Staff at Late Adopter Shelter)

OHS staff, shelter staff, and parents were asked about the benefits of including fathers as residents in family emergency shelters. Those citing benefits noted that fathers serve as role models for children, fewer families are separated (and further traumatized), fathers learn and grow through shelter programming and by seeing mothers and other fathers interacting with their families, and increased income from both parents working or combining their public income benefits at time of discharge from shelter. Quotes from OHS staff, shelter staff, and parents residing in shelters are below:

> I told the shelters, "You're going to love the men more than you love the women." I always found that they add... Some of them [mothers] kind of act a little bit better when there is a man walking around, whether that's staff or a resident. I always enjoy them. The men really don't get into verbal altercations or physical altercations really. I would say non-existent. (Staff at Early Adopter Shelter)
>
> It's also diversified staffing, which I think is a positive thing as well. (OHS Staff)
>
> So, I think it's real beneficial to have both. Because you learn to be a man from your father, and you learn the sensitivity and caring from your mom. If you don't have both sides equally, you're just not... I feel like it's a little imbalance. That's how I feel. (Father at Late Adopter Shelter)

Unintended Consequences

Some policies had unintended negative consequences. For instance, a common practice is for mothers to be automatically assigned as Head of Household upon entry into the shelter system. This practice can undermine the father's voice, power, or privilege. Additionally, shelters vary in the way they handle premature discharges (e.g., when a family member violates key shelter policies). For instance, some shelters automatically discharge the entire family unit. This practice negatively affects parents' ability to secure future housing for the family because families who reside in shelters are prioritized on housing assistance rolls. Other shelters automatically discharge the father (regardless of who was "at fault") and permit the mother and children to stay at the shelter. This negatively affects father–child relationships. Still other shelters use their discretion and discharge one parent and permit the other parent and children to stay at the shelter. This inconsistency in shelter policy sometimes left families to struggle more. It appeared that staff attitudes also impacted decisions around how much assistance families received. Addressing these unintended consequences and challenges may offer the possibility of long-term system change over time. Quotes from two parents residing in shelters are below:

> When an intact family enters the shelter it kind of looks like it's a good thing. My experience was horrible. It's a good thing because you're keeping the families together, and when the families are together you can move forward better. That's my opinion, and my kids' dad wanted to leave the shelter for his own personal reasons, and when he left the shelter we had to leave also because we came in as an intact family, and they told me if I wanted to receive services I'd have to do it all over again. I had just got picked up from Friends Transitional housing, so I lost my housing and I waited a whole nother year to re-enter the system, the shelters. That's why I'm here now. (Mother at Late Adopter Shelter)
>
> They don't know our circumstances or what's going on or what's the circumstances with the dad. The dad might got laid off. He might need a little assistance for temporarily. And for them to just single out, well, there's a man in the household, we're not going to help you get no housing, that's not right. (Mother at Late Adopter Shelter)

Impacts on Families

Staff and parents reported how shelter living can affect (both positively and negatively) family dynamics. For instance, parental dyads are able to help and support each other with childcare and family responsibilities while in shelter. One parent residing in a shelter describes this support:

> The dad is over there feeding the baby and the mom is getting a break. I don't get a break because there is no dad here. He was here, then maybe I could be like take them kids and go to the park. I would have a break. It's just the ah, I can breathe for a minute. Because I can only ah once they're all asleep. (Mother at Late Adopter Shelter)

Conversely, some parents experience additional tension in their marital/partner relationship, some families have difficulty de-escalating after an argument due to little "personal space," families have limited privacy, many parents feel demeaned by staff in front of their spouse/partner/child(ren), and families may perceive some staff as having negative attitudes towards people experiencing homelessness, fathers, and/or African Americans. Quotes from shelter staff and parents residing in shelters are below:

> And the mother and the father, they'll get into arguments. I mean, you're

living in a room this size, and you're calling this home. That's one thing I try to really instill in our staff. You got to remember, when you argue with your spouse, she goes one way and you go another way. Here, can't do that. You go get some air. Here, you can't do that. And that's the whole thing about being mindful, of that when they do have some arguments, we have areas that we call our sanctuary room and places. (Staff at Early Adopter Shelter)

This shelter will do one thing to a family. It'll do one or the other. It'll either make a couple strong, or it'll break you up. (Mother at Late Adopter Shelter)

Then you've got your kids like … even with your kids, people holler at you, do this, do that. Don't people understand kids get traumatized by stuff like that. What you think won't hurt them will hurt them. (Mother at Late Adopter Shelter)

Commitment to System Change

OHS, Early Adopter shelter staff and parents, and Late Adopter shelter staff and parents appeared to be committed to maintaining the integration of fathers in the family emergency shelter system. These groups reported that shelters should always serve "families," not only mothers with children. The two Laggard shelters agree with father-inclusion in theory. One Laggard shelter initially felt forced to admit fathers as residents despite the fact that they felt unprepared to do so. They felt challenged with this task but were finding ways to make it work. The other Laggard shelter was in the process of applying for an exemption/waiver from the father-inclusion policy. (This shelter viewed the blanket order of father inclusion as a barrier to their ability to provide trauma-sensitive services to women and children who live in a congregate living environment.) The mothers in the Laggard shelters expressed great compassion for fathers while also voicing concerns about safety and a desire to be open to finding ways to integrate fathers. Quotes from OHS staff and shelter staff are below:

> And the city's perspective has been, we've been 100% clear. We're not going back. We're not going to exclude people. (OHS Staff)
> It's all families. It should have always been all families. (Staff at Early Adopter Shelter)
> The benefits are huge. We just have to figure out how do you change a culture. And we all know that when you change a culture it takes time. (Staff at Laggard Shelter)

Discussion

All shelters—Early Adopter, Late Adopter, and Laggard—share a belief in the fact that fathers, in most cases, are important to their families. The Early Adopter shelters, which all have private rooms for families, have held this belief for years and, therefore, made a commitment to father inclusion decades ago. The Late Adopter shelters believe in father inclusion, too, and the two that had private rooms for families made the transition relatively easily. The three Late Adopter shelters that lacked private rooms and relied heavily on communal living space encountered more difficulty.

Two elements were important in making the transition for all Late Adopter shelters. First, the partnership between OHS and the Late Adopter shelters was critical. OHS staff have spent years cultivating relationships with shelter providers. Some OHS staff even used to be shelter providers. The respect and trust they have built over the years enabled this policy shift, albeit difficult, to happen. OHS listened to shelter concerns, problem-solved with shelter providers, and shared resources to assist in the transition (e.g., funding for hiring male shelter staff). Second, some Late Adopter shelters sought consultation from Early Adopter shelters regarding how they make things work.

Although the Laggard shelters appreciated the importance of fathers in the lives of children, they had more difficulty making the transition. According to one of the Laggard shelters, OHS "forced" the shelter to admit a father as a resident one night, and the shelter was completely unprepared for the admission. However, the shelter has since admitted fathers as residents. The other Laggard shelter has a staunch philosophical disagreement with the policy of requiring all family emergency shelters to admit fathers. They argue that the policy prevents mothers with children who want to avoid men (because of a history of abuse, rape, or trauma) from feeling safe in any family emergency shelter. They believe the policy creates systemic discrimination against these women and their children. This Laggard shelter has applied for a waiver/exception to the requirement of admitting fathers as residents in their shelter.

Additional themes raised through the study included the role of communication across channels (city employees, shelter staff, and families), the role of attitudes as they may have impacted how stakeholders accepted or denied the change in policy, the benefit of learning from Early Adopter shelters that can come from the decades of experience in serving families, and family dynamics that are impacted by shelter living. Additionally, the reality of racism and discrimination against African American men was presented by several study participants. It has impacted shelter access and experiences.

The Diffusion of Innovations theory is well suited for understanding this systems policy change. The theory seeks to understand the timing and rate of adoption of change innovation through communication. This theory explains how new ideas spread among groups of people. Rogers and Shoemaker (1971) classify people by how early they adopt a new idea. Identifying shelters by Early Adopters, Late Adopters, and Laggard shelters aided in the researchers' analysis of the study findings.

Since the conclusion of the study, more fathers have been admitted to the family shelters, increasing the need to foster ways to better support fathers and families in shelter settings. For any city considering a similar change, it would be important to assess the readiness of the system for such a change. The assessment should include reviewing the relationships between city agencies, reviewing relationships between shelters, and considering the entire system's openness to change.

Recommendations

This study's results lead to several practical recommendations for serving mothers, fathers, and children residing in shelters. Additional opportunities are offered for policy makers and researchers.

Direct Service

Shelters should consider acknowledging parents as stakeholders, possibly creating Parent Advisory Boards to solicit ongoing relevant input and recommendations. Both mothers and fathers expressed appreciation for the opportunity to participate in the focus groups and have their voices heard. At the end of the parent focus groups, parents requested future opportunities to share their thoughts and opinions. This speaks to a need for all family voices to be heard on a consistent basis.

As fathers are admitted to family emergency shelters, the shelters need to find ways to become more "family friendly." This includes hiring more male staff (particularly African American male staff) to reflect the demographics of the shelter residents. Staff need to be supported and trained to engage with fathers in ways that fathers experience as culturally appropriate, supportive, respectful, and productive. Shelters need to strategically prepare families for entry into family shelters by sharing common rules and emphasizing the need to focus on the family as a unit (or system) instead of each individual independently. Shelters should also adapt programming to be more inclusive of fathers to meet the total needs of the family and actively develop resources and build community partnerships with agencies that serve fathers and families.

Family shelters should consider shifting their thinking. Rather than focusing on each individual in the family (and their respective needs), we urge them to consider adopting a more family-oriented approach. This approach might involve focusing on services that address the following types of questions. What are two-parent couples doing to support one another and/or their children while at the shelter, and how can they be sustained following their exit? Are the family boundaries, roles, and power hierarchies that are being modeled for children at the shelter appropriate and positive, and how can they be optimized? While this shift in service provision at shelters would require staff training, it could be more holistic and supportive of families.

Shelter staff should be reminded of the resilience of women and children who have been traumatized. (Many of the mothers residing in shelters disclosed a personal history fraught with neglect, abuse, interpersonal violence, and other traumas. And the primary reason the two Laggard shelters did not want to include fathers as residents in their shelters was to protect women from further trauma.) The focus group facilitators saw great "movement" in the mothers' thinking and attitudes during the focus groups at the two Laggard shelters. Within the (approximately) 90-minute focus group sessions, both groups moved from wanting to exclude fathers entirely from the family shelters to considering what would need to happen for mothers to feel safe with fathers living in the family shelters. Continuing a series of, admittedly difficult, conversations with mothers at the Laggard shelters could lead toward sustained inclusive thinking as well as providing staff with concrete guidance about what the mothers desire and need and which strategies are working/not working for them.

Advocacy/Training

Shelter staff across all shelters (Early Adopter, Late Adopter, and Laggard shelters) should be encouraged to support one another, exchange information, improve problem solving, and enhance advocacy. Early Adopter shelters have experience and knowledge to share with Late Adopter and Laggard shelters. Late Adopter shelters that are structured with community living spaces have experience and knowledge to share with each other and with Laggard shelters. Some sharing of information occurred organically, but a more formalized system could be more inclusive and have greater impact.

OHS and shelter administrators should seek opportunities to build partnerships between city government, institutions, and community nonprofits to find solutions for problems encountered in implementing the nondiscrimination policy. This might include considerations of exploring possible partnerships with agencies (e.g., Habitat for Humanity) that could possibly conduct building renovations that would make them more family friendly.

Because fathers have been recently integrated into six family emergency shelters that have historically served women and children only, OHS and shelter staff would likely benefit from regular and ongoing training dealing with a host of issues. These issues include, but are not limited to, decreasing staff biases and increasing knowledge and comfort with serving fathers from diverse racial and ethnic backgrounds, exploring how fathers and mothers parent differently, increasing knowledge about the benefits to children of father inclusion, and the unique service needs of fathers and the community services that might be available to support them (e.g., employment, criminal record expungement, child support) as they reside in family emergency shelters. Training around being trauma-informed would also benefit OHS and shelter staff. Trauma-informed care is an approach that acknowledges an awareness, understanding, and responsiveness to the creation of environments that ensure safety, choice, control, and empowerment of survivors (Guarino, 2014). This trauma could include childhood abuse, domestic violence, community violence, substance abuse, incarceration, and even homelessness. The National Health Care for the Homeless Council is a national organization that advocates for the health care, human rights, well-being, and social justice of those experiencing homelessness (https://nhchc.org). This organization considers homelessness to be a traumatic experience.

Research

Future research areas could include studying this inclusion/integration process over time, exploring the similarities and differences in shelter experiences of married/partnered shelter residents and single-parent residents in family shelter settings, exploring the children's perceptions and experiences of having their fathers included in the shelters, and exploring the types of services and methods of service delivery that best address the needs of men (in addition to women) in shelter.

Policy

OHS should consider monitoring the integration of other protected classes of individuals in shelter settings. Participants raised concerns about the integration of people with disabilities, people of non-Christian faiths, and people who identify as LGBTQIA+. Additionally, policy leaders should consider the role of race in the experience of homelessness. For example, leaders should consider the policies that cause homelessness, such as poverty, unemployment, and disparities in educational opportunities.

Conclusions

This study explored the process of making system change in Philadelphia with respect to the adoption and implementation of a bold, new nondiscrimination policy requiring the inclusion of primarily African American fathers as residents in family emergency shelters. OHS and all family shelters—Early Adopters, Late Adopters, and Laggards—acknowledged being part of a service system that is inherently biased against fathers; yet, they simultaneously believed in the positive value fathers can contribute to their families during this housing crisis. Shelters that had building set-ups that allowed for private rooms for individual families were quicker to adopt this policy of father inclusion, while shelters in buildings with congregate living spaces encountered more difficulty in adopting this policy change. The most substantial concerns around implementing this policy change focused on safety and privacy issues. Despite some challenges in communicating the new policy, change occurred quickly. In a period of approximately 24 months, the Philadelphia OHS moved from having three to nine of its ten family shelters admitting fathers as shelter residents. All stakeholders plan to continue to work to make the shelters more father inclusive and "family centric" beyond just fathers living in the shelters. The ultimate goal is to decrease system biases and barriers that hinder advancing the overall quality of families' experiences in the homeless shelter system.

References

Allen, S., & Daly, K. (2007). *The effects of father involvement: An updated research summary of the evidence*. Father Involvement Research Alliance. https://library.parenthelp.eu/wp-content/uploads/2017/05/Effects_of_Father_Involvement.pdf.

Barrett-Rivera, B., Lindstrom, L., & Kerewsky, S. (2013). Parenting in poverty: The experiences of fathers who are homeless. *Journal of Human Services, 33*(1), 73–84.

Guarino, K. (2014). Trauma-informed care for families experiencing homelessness. In M. E. Haskett, S. Perlman, & B. A. Cowan (Eds.), *Supporting families experiencing homelessness* (pp. 57–77). Springer.

Lamb, M. E. (2004). *The role of the father in child development*. John Wiley & Sons.

National Alliance to End Homelessness. (2019). *Data visualization: Homeless population representation by location*. https://endhomelessness.org/resource/data-visualization-homeless-population-representation-by-location/.

Philadelphia Office of Homeless Services. (2017). *Philadelphia continuum of care: Nondiscrimination policy*. http://www.philadelphiaofficeofhomelessservices.org/wp-content/uploads/2017/12/scanned-signed-board-approved-nondiscrimination-policy.pdf.

Philadelphia Office of Homeless Services. (2019). *Point in time count*. http://philadelphiaofficeofhomelessservices.org/knowhomelessness/point-in-time-count/.

Revell, M. (2015). The African American father does matter in parenting. *International Journal of Childbirth Education, 30*(1), 25–28.

Rogers, E. M., & Shoemaker, F. F. (1971). *Communication of innovation*. The Free Press.

U.S. Department of Housing and Urban Development (2016). Equal access in accordance with an individual's gender identity in community planning and development programs. *Federal Register, 81*(183), 64763–64782.

13
ESTIMATING THE MONETARY VALUE OF FATHERHOOD PROGRAMS

Richard A. Chase

Introduction

For more than a decade, fatherhood programs, funded by the federal Administration for Children and Families and state and local governments have served low-income, primarily nonresident fathers to enhance their employment, parenting abilities, and healthy coparenting relationships so that they can contribute to their children's financial and emotional well-being, as well as their own well-being, and be positively involved with their children (Osborne et al., 2016).

Fatherhood programs typically provide services in three areas: the development of parenting skills, healthy relationships, and employment/economic stability development. They may also provide legal services or advice related to paternity, child support, and family law. In addition, a small number may also have connections with early learning programs that enhance child development and literacy skills.

Fatherhood programs have often measured their success based on child support payment compliance, although surveys with fathers typically also collect information on the amount of time and quality of time they spend with their children before and after program participation. Financial stability is evidenced by improved employment and wage rates, number of hours worked, job retention rates, improved educational attainment, volunteerism, and lower criminal conviction rates. Indicators of parental responsibility and engagement include compliance with child support payments and improved parenting skills.

This chapter, based on *Potential Monetary Value of Responsible Fatherhood Program Outcomes for Fathers and Children* (a report prepared for the Fatherhood Research and Practice Network; Chase, 2019), shows how to monetize the economic returns and avoided costs of these typical outcomes plus other potential two-generation, long-term child development and family well-being outcomes of father engagement. Its goal is to be a catalyst for fatherhood researchers and programs to make an economic case to policy makers about the monetary value of investing in fatherhood programs and broader father engagement.

Report Purposes, Methods, and Assumptions

The above-mentioned report provides and applies a framework for estimating the potential monetary value of nonresident father engagement, which broadly includes participating in fatherhood programs, performing positive parenting behaviors and interactions with their children in activities that promote healthy child development, and enrolling their children in high-quality early childhood education.[1]

It builds on models and methods used in studies completed by Wilder Research of Goodwill-Easter Seals FATHER (Diaz & Chase, 2010) and of the monetary value of investing in early childhood education and development in Illinois, Michigan, Minnesota, Ohio, and Vermont (Chase et al., 2009; Chase & Diaz, 2015; Chase et al., 2011; Diaz, 2017; Diaz & Chase, 2016; Pina et al., 2013).

Its model is similar to the cost-benefit model from the Washington State Institute for Public Policy (Washington State Institute for Public Policy, 2018) and the model for estimating the annual aggregate costs of childhood poverty (McLaughlin & Rank, 2018).

We estimate the expected monetary value of the benefits of nonresident father engagement with their children based on a model of the value of expected future benefits for and from low-income families. The model draws from a body of research on fathers, responsible fatherhood, and parenting programs.

The model is based on several assumptions and research findings about the potential benefits of participating in fatherhood programs for fathers, children, and society:

- Fatherhood program participation potentially improves education, employment, and wage rates of fathers, which is associated with increased lifetime employment, earnings, child support payments, and tax revenues and avoided or reduced costs of unemployment, welfare, food assistance, and arrests.
- Fatherhood program participation also potentially enhances positive father involvement in the lives of their children, which, in turn, improves their children's social-emotional and cognitive competence and academic achievement, which is associated with reduced special education and improved high school completion rates.
- When combined with high-quality early education for children, which is also associated with reduced special education and improved high school completion rates, the links potentially lead to increased lifetime earnings for children, which is linked with reduced costs of welfare, crime, substance abuse, and health care.

Sources of data include actual outcomes reported in evaluations of fatherhood programs, including details from the Goodwill-Easter Seals FATHER evaluation (Diaz & Chase, 2010); expenditure and incidence data from state agencies of education, health, and human services; and graduation rates, poverty rates, crime rates, and other demographic data from the U.S. Census American Community Survey. These data pertain to Minnesota and other states where noted.

The impact parameters used to compute the estimated monetary values of benefits and savings or avoided costs are drawn from the published research. See the full report mentioned above for the specific sources for each computation and parameter as noted throughout the report. Only potential benefits and cost savings with sufficient supporting evidence are included in this report. We combine the impact parameters or effect sizes identified in the research with data on the incidence rate of each outcome and demographic characteristics to estimate the actual or potential impact on the selected outcomes.

A dollar today is worth more than a dollar in the future. Accordingly, studies that look at benefits and savings that potentially are generated and accrue in the future commonly discount those monetary values of benefits and savings in future years to present values to reflect that time value of money. We report the monetary values as present values discounted at a rate of 3%, which is the standard currently used for a discount rate in similar studies.

The estimated value of each potential outcome of fatherhood programs is independent and applies to only fathers who could reasonably achieve the outcome through successful participation, such as fathers who enter a program with no high school diploma, or with no job, or not paying child support. Accordingly, the values for each outcome do not automatically add up to the total estimated value of all potential outcomes and could only reach the total level depending on the extent to which each father achieves each outcome.

Study Limitations

While this study calculates the present values of current benefits and savings in future years to account for the time value of money, it does not account for any potential changes in the incidence rate of each outcome and dollar value of social benefits over time. However, high school graduation rates and incarceration rates, for example, may improve or decline over time, thus changing the percentage of fathers and children with additional earnings and the value of the program outcomes. Therefore, the per-father and per-child present values throughout this report could overestimate or underestimate the present values of future benefits and savings.

Further, this study does not include all the potential cost savings associated with father programs, largely due to the lack of research that measures or monetizes many potential outcomes. Therefore, to the extent that savings might be realized in other areas, the estimates presented here understate the total potential savings.

Finally, this study is based mostly on data from Minnesota. However, benefits and monetary values will vary from state to state, depending on the quality and intensity of fatherhood, parenting, and early childhood programs; demographic characteristics of the population served; and local social and economic conditions.

For perspective, according to Minnesota Compass (2018), Minnesota's median household income, the 12th highest in the United States, is about $7,000 higher than the national average of $60,000, and its poverty rate of 9.5% is below the national rate of 13.4%. On the other hand, the high school graduation rate in Minnesota is 83%, below the national rate of 85%, and ranks 36th. For low-income students in Minnesota, the high school graduation rate is 70%. Finally, according to the U.S. Census Bureau (2018a), Minnesota spent $2,705 per capita on public welfare expenditures in 2016, ranking among the top five states.[2]

Monetary Value of Fatherhood Program Outcomes for Fathers

This section draws from a return-on-investment study completed in 2010 by Wilder Research of the Goodwill/Easter Seals of Minnesota's FATHER (Diaz & Chase, 2010), with the monetary values adjusted for inflation. We analyzed the results of that study to estimate the per-father value of the outcomes achieved by successful participants.

Fathers in that program ranged in age from 19 to 53, with an average age of 31. At the outset:

- Approximately 45% of 380 participants in the study reported not having a full-time or part-time job paying at or above minimum wages;
- 43% did not hold a high school diploma or a GED; and
- 36% had criminal convictions in the past.

These characteristics are similar to the over 10,000 fathers who were part of a noncustodial father child support and employment demonstration evaluation, with an average age of 35, nearly 70% with at most a high school education, 44% who were not employed, and 65% who had been incarcerated (Cancian et al., 2019). Similarly, an eight-state study of 1,674 fathers reported an average age of 33; low education levels, ranging from 13% to 71% with no high school degree or GED, and 45% of the fathers not employed (Pearson et al., 2003).

Increased Lifetime Earnings

Educational attainment is the main determinant of lifetime earnings. A primary outcome associated with father participation in fatherhood programs and engagement with their children is increased lifetime earnings for both father and child. This potential two-generational benefit is associated with the enhanced likelihood of completing a high school education or its equivalent.

Increased Lifetime Earnings of Fathers Due to Increased Educational Attainment

Fatherhood program participants receive services to help them obtain their GEDs, and education is a main determinant of lifetime earnings. In one estimation, GED holders earn nearly $9,500 more annually than non-GED holders (Diaz & Chase, 2010).

These calculations of increased lifetime earnings use present values based on the age when fathers attain a GED until age 65 and adjusted for inflation. The increase in the lifetime earnings per father due to attaining a GED reaches $124,000 (U.S. Census Bureau, 2018b).

Increased Lifetime Earnings of Fathers Due to Increased Wages

To assess the economic benefit of participation in a fatherhood program, we compared the changes in wages among fathers who received job placement services with changes in wages of the group of fathers who did not receive job placement services. The difference between these two groups, or the net gain in wages attributable to participating, is $3,130—a gain of more than 35% in annual income. The impact due to increased wages needs to be reduced by 20% to avoid double counting the educational impacts. After netting out the impact of educational attainment and assuming that employment impacts of the program would remain constant for the next ten years, and adjusting for inflation, the net present value of the long-term benefits due to increased wages of participants who received job placement services reaches approximately $25,000.

In all, the increased lifetime earnings associated with successful participation in a fatherhood program through attaining a GED and job placement services amounts to $149,000 per father.

Increased Child Support Payments

Complying with child support obligations is a central expected outcome of involvement in fatherhood programs. Based on a 2010 evaluation of the FATHER program in Minnesota, fathers were able to pay 51% of their child support obligation, averaging $1,222 per year, attributed to job placement services provided by the program. That rate is comparable to rates reported in other evaluations of fatherhood programs. For example, 41% of owed child support was paid by participants in Parents to Work! in Arapahoe County, Colorado, (Pearson et al., 2011), and fathers who participated in eight programs in eight states paid 36% to 72% of what was owed (Pearson et al., 2003).

Assuming that these fathers will pay at least the same amount for a minimum of eight years, based on their children's average age of ten, future child support payments that can be attributed to successful participation in a fatherhood program is nearly $10,000 per father. Discounted 3% per year and adjusting for inflation, present value amounts to $9,878 per father, not counting any potential changes in child support payments due to decreases or increases over time in parental earnings.

Benefits to Taxpayers of Increased Lifetime Earnings of Fathers

The benefits to taxpayers consist of additional sales and income tax revenues due to increased income of participants in a fatherhood program.[3] To estimate the additional revenues from taxes, we applied the marginal tax rate and sales tax incidence rate in Minnesota to the total additional lifetime income due to increased education of participants ($124,000) and increased wages ($25,000).

The estimated long-term additional tax revenues per successful FATHER participant is $8,002 in income tax and $3,129 in sales tax for a total of $11,131.

Value of Increased Community Involvement and Leadership of Fathers

Volunteer time spent working in the community by fathers has some monetary value. When this volunteerism can be reasonably attributed to or motivated by their involvement in a fatherhood program, part of the monetary value of this time can be estimated using a reasonable wage rate as a measure of the value of time. Another potential benefit, which is difficult to monetize, is the effect participating fathers may have on other fathers and potential fathers by being positive role models. Accordingly, we estimate only the value of the time allocated to community volunteerism and leadership work by fathers associated with the FATHER, and discount the resulting value using a conservative rate. If fathers volunteer 40 hours per year for five years at a value of $15/hour, and applying a discount rate of 50% to account for the assumed net impact of the fatherhood program, the value of a father's volunteer time reaches approximately $1,500.

Reduced Recidivism Per-Father Savings for Crime Victims and Taxpayers

Recidivism is commonly defined as a conviction in a court for any offense following release to the community. Benefits of reduced recidivism are assessed in terms of reduced costs to taxpayers for law enforcement, adjudication, and incarceration, and reduced costs to the victims of crime. The economics literature provides sufficient evidence of the magnitude of the economic costs that recidivism and incarceration impose on society (Aos et al., 2009). The benefits are usually estimated in terms of present value of crime-related costs avoided over the lifetime of an individual participant (Washington State Institute for Public Policy, 2007).

The relevant question is how many fathers who did commit crimes in the past or who might be at-risk for committing crimes without service intervention stayed out of the criminal justice system because of their involvement in the program.

A study by the Washington Institute for Public Policy (Aos et al., 2009) shows that interventions that seek to reduce recidivism produce reductions between 20% and 40%, with lifetime benefits of reduced recidivism ranging from $1,835 for minor crimes to $75,722 for victims of violent crimes and $1,069 to $28,713 for taxpayers, depending on the type of crime.

Based on national crime data that says 16% of crimes are property or violent crimes, we can use the upper amounts in the ranges to estimate the possible benefits for preventing 16% of repeat crimes and can use the mid-point amounts in the ranges for the rest (U.S. Department of Justice, 2008). About 36%, or 137 participants, had criminal convictions. Assuming a 65% rate of recidivism and that the project would reduce this rate by 20%, we can assume that about 27 participants would not commit new offenses due to the FATHER program. Four of these would probably be violent or property crimes.

Therefore, crime victims may receive estimated benefits of $1.2 million in terms of saved costs, and taxpayers would accrue savings in the order of $457,000 for these estimated 27 participants of the FATHER program that had a previous criminal conviction and did not commit a new offense because of the influence of the program, amounting to $1.66 million. Adjusted for inflation, the present value per-father savings associated with reduced recidivism is $3,637 for crime victims and $1,390 for savings to taxpayers.[4]

Per-Father Estimated Monetary Value of Successful Fatherhood Program Participation

Table 13.1 combines the estimated savings from all sources. It represents the potential lifetime savings per fatherhood program graduate.

TEXT BOX 13.1

Taken together, the total estimated value of all potential earnings, payments, and savings that would accrue for each successful participant in a fatherhood program like the FATHER program is about $177,000.

TABLE 13.1 Per-Father Estimated Monetary Value of Successful Participation in a Fatherhood Program

	Potential Lifetime Value for One Father
Increased lifetime earnings	$149,000
Increased child support payments	$9,878
Increased taxes paid	$11,131
Value of increased community involvement and leadership per father	$1,500
Crime victimization savings	$3,637
Recidivism savings to government	$1,390
Total estimated value of all potential outcomes[5]	**$176,536**

Potential Monetary Value of Fatherhood Program Outcomes for Children

Due to space limitations, this section on the potential lifetime monetary benefits and cost savings derived from outcomes per child summarizes the approach, research references, and findings reported in *Potential Monetary Value of Responsible Fatherhood Program Outcomes for Fathers and Children* (a report I prepared for the Fatherhood Research and Practice Network; Chase, 2019). It first describes the potential value of high-quality early education experiences and then the potential value of increased participation of fathers in low-income children's lives and of improved parenting skills. The estimates are based on actual government expenditure data, arrest rates, and other data for Minnesota as a whole and effect sizes and parameters from the existing research on effects of early childhood education and parenting programs, including fatherhood programs.

Effects and Potential Value of Early Childhood Education

Many studies show that high-quality early learning experiences pay off in the long run due to benefits related to increased education and earnings and reduced public costs associated with child welfare, public assistance, crime, and incarceration. Several studies focus specifically on measuring the effects of early childhood interventions and quality early care and education on school systems, time spent in K-12 special education, and special education spending. Other studies focus on the impact of early childhood education programs on specific areas of government spending, including criminal justice, public assistance, Medicaid, unemployment, child welfare, and health care. These studies provide assumptions and parameters to estimate the stream of expected future benefits outlined in Table 13.2 (Aos et al., 2004; Campbell et al., 2002; Friedman, 2004;

TABLE 13.2 Per-Child Estimated Potential Lifetime Monetary Values

	High-Quality Early Education $85,000 to $95,000	Fatherhood Programs $32,000 to $38,000
Benefits to individuals and the public		
Additional lifetime income due to education	$15,632 to $23,388	$20,000
Lifetime value of preventing child abuse on child's productivity	$5,768	$577 to $1,154
Value of improved health	$29,000	$2,900 to $5,800
Crime victimizations savings	$1,550	$155 to $310
Cost savings to K-12 education		
Savings in special education costs	$1,207	$121 to $241
Savings in fewer students repeating a grade	$117	$12 to $23
Cost savings to government and taxpayers		
Savings in reduced arrests and incarceration costs	$861	$99
Savings in Medicaid health care costs	$3,066	$307 to $613
Savings in MFIP cash and food assistance	$18,910	$1,891 to $3,782
Reduced costs of abuse, neglect, and out-of-home placements	$616	$62 to $123
Substance abuse savings	$4,427	$443 to $885
Unemployment insurance savings	$173	$17 to $35
Additional income tax and sales tax revenues	$3,899 to $5,833	$4,988

Note: Total estimated value and gains are rounded.

García et al., 2016; Lynch & Vaghul, 2015; McCoy et al., 2017; Reynolds et al., 2011; Rolnick & Grunewald, 2003; Schweinhart et al., 2012).

The estimates fall into three categories:

- Individuals and the public—through increased lifetime earnings and productivity, value of improved health, and reduced crime victimization
- K-12 schools—through reduced special education and grade repetition costs
- State government—through reduced costs of juvenile and adult crime; through lower welfare, Medicaid, substance abuse, and unemployment costs; and through higher tax revenues

The lifetime monetary value associated with early childhood education outcomes reaches an estimated $85,000 to $95,000 per child.

For information about this approach, the reader is referred to several studies of the cost savings of school readiness in Minnesota and other states completed by Wilder Research (available at https://www.wilder.org/wilder-research/research-library?).

Effects and Potential Value of Fathering and Parenting Programs

In an essay summarizing the economics literature on human development, James Heckman concludes that improving parenting and child skills is complementary and that parental engagement and positive parent–child interactions are the foundations of noncognitive (social-emotional) skill development that shape a child's later life education, health, earnings, and crime outcomes (Heckman & Mosso, 2014).

Interventions to increase parenting skills seek to improve knowledge, skills, attitudes, and behavior of fathers that are related to early childhood developmental outcomes that have potential lifelong consequences. The more stable economic conditions of the fathers and improvement in their parenting skills would likely have a positive impact on children's cognitive and social development that would contribute to their early learning success and to an ultimate path of future educational attainment and financial stability. That is especially the case when fatherhood programs include "play and learn" parent–child experiences with a focus on literacy and health—key skills to improve children's school success.

Studies have shown that fathering programs able to achieve high involvement of the participating fathers in a variety of interactive developmental activities with their children produce small to moderate effects on parenting and nurturing skills, children's prosocial skills, and children's early academic skills and achievement (Chacko et al., 2018; Fagan & Iglesias, 1999; Holmes et al., 2020). Similarly, consistent and positive father involvement, particularly for children in impoverished environments, has been linked to children's socioemotional and cognitive development (Adamson & Johnson, 2013; Coates & Phares, 2019; McWayne et al., 2013). Moreover, research on parenting programs shows that children in these programs are less likely to be arrested later in their life (Scott et al., 2014), and some studies have found that father involvement reduces their children's time in foster care and juvenile detention and their substance abuse behaviors (Coakley, 2013).

These studies provide assumptions and parameters linking positive parenting to children's social and academic skills and behaviors associated with increased likelihood of high school graduation and ultimately increased lifetime earnings, the associated taxes paid, and reduced probability of future arrests. However, other child outcomes that have potential benefits and cost savings have not been established in the research literature on father involvement and parenting programs. Accordingly, to provide an estimate of the potential full per-child monetary value of fatherhood programs, we draw on the early childhood education research literature described above, applying the effect sizes for father involvement and parenting programs to the full array of the other child outcomes data.

As listed in Table 13.2, the total estimated lifetime monetary value of the stream of expected future benefits of successful participation in a fatherhood program reaches about $32,000 to $38,000 per child.

Discussion

This study is the first attempt to monetize the economic returns and avoided costs of a broad set of potential two-generation, long-term child development and family well-being outcomes of responsible father engagement. While it is limited to available data pertaining to Minnesota and only to potential benefits and cost savings with sufficient supporting research evidence, this study makes a strong economic case for investing in fatherhood programs and provides a prototype for future research.

The study estimates the monetary value of successful participation in a fatherhood program could reach about $177,000 per father and about $32,000 to $38,000 per child. By adding high-quality early childhood education, the potential monetary value per child grows to an estimated $85,000 to $95,000.

Keep in mind these values do not include all the potential cost savings associated with father program and early education program outcomes. For example, this study does not include potentially reduced health care and unemployment costs for fathers, savings in incarceration costs for nonpayment of child support, and reductions in the use of public benefits following increases in child support payments to custodial parents.

In addition, the present study does not include potential per-child cost savings, for example, from reduced non-instructional and health costs related to special education and preventable health problems and from not providing education to students in juvenile detention. These potential savings were not included due to the lack of research that measures or monetizes these outcomes. Therefore, to the extent that savings might be realized in other areas, the estimates presented here understate the total potential savings.

Implications for Policies and Programs

This study shows the potential benefits of establishing and investing in comprehensive fatherhood programs. Comprehensive programs would include GED programming, job placement services, and diversion services as an alternative to incarceration. To promote positive father involvement associated with improved child development, fatherhood programs should consider strengthening content in program workshops dealing with child development and effective parenting techniques and adding hands-on activities like play and learn groups so fathers can acquire and practice new parenting skills. One example of this approach is the Building Bridges and Bonds (B3) Study, which incorporates skill-building videos and father–child play activities to strengthen father parenting skills (Manno et al., 2019). Strong links to early education programs would also boost child outcomes with lifelong positive value.

Finally, fatherhood programs should be aware of the potential monetary benefits they generate for fathers, their children, and the society as a whole and systematically collect appropriate data about their participants to generate accurate and robust outcome and return on investment studies.

Implications for Researchers

While this study calculates the present values of current benefits and savings in future years to account for the value of money over time, this study does not account for any potential changes in the incidence rate of each outcome and dollar value of social benefits over time. Future studies should consider methods for estimating those changes and ways to adjust the projected benefits and savings.

Future studies should also update the research literature to add new father and child outcomes with sufficient supporting research evidence to monetize them and consider comparative studies that account for variations from state to state in outcomes, demographic characteristics, and local social and economic conditions.

Further, this study describes the potential two-generation value of connecting fatherhood programs and early childhood education programs. Future studies could carry out a rigorous evaluation of the extent to which connecting or integrating those programs achieves the expected results relative to separate programs and the absence of any programs. Since that would require an experimental evaluation with a control group, that may be difficult to accomplish. Nevertheless, fatherhood programs could routinely collect and document data to enhance the scope of measuring their results pertaining to children. Such data would include, for example, before-, during-, and after-program participation data on child development–related parenting behaviors, behavioral indicators of the father–child bond, and the developmental status of their children.

Finally, while this study examines the potential monetary value of fatherhood program outcomes for fathers and children, it is not a cost-benefit study that compares the value of those benefits to the costs of the programs to produce those benefits. Future studies could also calculate the return on investment by documenting the total costs to deliver the programs.

Notes

1 Throughout this report, the impacts of fatherhood, parenting, and early education or early learning programs assume the programs are high quality.

2 Public welfare expenditures include cash assistance paid directly to needy persons, payments made directly to private health and welfare agencies for medical care and other services provided such as foster care, and payments to other governments for administration costs and support of private and private welfare agencies.
3 Not counted are potential savings due to reductions in the use of public benefits such as TANF, SNAP, and Medicaid by custodial parents following increases in child support payments. Also not counted are savings due to reductions in unemployment insurance claims. These additional potential benefits to taxpayers were found in an evaluation of the Texas Workforce Program known as NCP Choices (Schroeder & Doughty, 2009).
4 Not counted are the costs of bringing contempt actions against nonpaying fathers and incarcerating them, a practice that generates high public costs in some jurisdictions as reported, for example, by the South Carolina Center for Fathers and Families (see http://www.scfathersandfamilies.com/impact/2018_impact_report/).
5 To repeat, the estimated value of each potential outcome of fatherhood programs is independent and applies to only fathers who could reasonably achieve the outcome through successful participation, such as fathers who enter a program with no high school diploma, or no job, or not paying child support. Accordingly, the values for each outcome do not automatically add up to the total estimated value of all potential outcomes and could only reach the total level of $176,536, depending on the extent to which each father achieves each outcome.

References

Adamson, K., & Johnson, S. K. (2013). An updated and expanded meta-analysis of non-resident fathering and child well-being. *Journal of Family Psychology, 27*(4), 589–599.

Aos, S., Lieb, R., Mayfield, J., Miller, M., & Pennucci, A. (2004). *Benefits and costs of prevention and early intervention programs for youth.* Washington State Institute for Public Policy. http://www.wsipp.wa.gov/ReportFile/881/Wsipp_Benefits-and-Costs-of-Prevention-and-Early-Intervention-Programs-for-Youth_Summary-Report.pdf.

Aos, S., Miller, M., & Drake, E. (2009). Evidence-based public policy options to reduce crime and criminal justice costs: Implications in Washington State. *Victims and Offenders, 4,* 170–196.

Campbell, F. A., Ramey, C. T., Pungello, E., Sparling, J., & Miller-Johnson, S. (2002). Early childhood education: Young adult outcomes from the Abecedarian Project. *Applied developmental science, 6*(1), 42–57.

Cancian, M., Meyer, D., & Wood, R. (2019). *Final Impact Findings from the Child Support Noncustodial Parent Employment Demonstration (CSPED).* Institute for Research on Poverty. https://www.irp.wisc.edu/wp/wp-content/uploads/2019/07/CSPED-Final-Impact-Report-2019-Compliant.pdf.

Chacko, A., Fabiano, G. A., Doctoroff, G. L., & Fortson, B. (2018). Engaging fathers in effective parenting for preschool children using shared book reading: A randomized controlled trial. *Journal of Clinical Child and Adolescent Psychology, 53,* 47(1), 79–93.

Chase, R. (2019). *Potential monetary value of Responsible Fatherhood program outcomes for fathers and children: A framework for monetizing the future stream of two-generation benefits and avoided costs.* Fatherhood Research and Practice Network. https://www.frpn.org/asset/potential-monetary-value-responsible-fatherhood-program-outcomes-fathers-and-children.

Chase, R., Anton, P., Diaz, J., & Rausch, E. (2009). *Cost savings analysis of school readiness in Michigan.* Wilder Research. https://files.eric.ed.gov/fulltext/ED511595.pdf.

Chase, R., & Diaz, J. (2015). *Cost savings of school readiness per additional at-risk child in Detroit and Michigan.* Wilder Research. https://mmfisher.org/wp-content/uploads/2018/11/Wilder_2014014_FINAL-OneChild_Michigan_Detroit-02-05-2015.pdf.

Chase, R., Diaz, J., & Valorose, J. (2011). *Cost savings analysis of school readiness in Illinois.* Wilder Research. https://www.wilder.org/sites/default/files/imports/IlliniosEarlyChildhood_ROI_5-11.pdf.

Coakley, T. M. (2013). The influence of father involvement on child welfare permanency outcomes: A secondary data analysis. *Children and Youth Services Review, 35*(1), 174–182.

Coates, E. E., & Phares, V. (2019). Pathways linking nonresident father involvement and child outcomes. *Journal of Child and Family Studies, 28*(6), 1681–1694.

Diaz, J. (2017). *Vermont's early care & learning dividend.* Wilder Research. https://www.letsgrowkids.org/client_media/files/pdf/VermontECLDReport.pdf.

Diaz, J., & Chase, R. (2010). *Return on investment to the FATHER Project.* Wilder Research. https://www.wilder.org/sites/default/files/imports/Goodwill_FatherProject_ROI_10-10.pdf.

Diaz, J., & Chase, R. (2016). *Minnesota's one-child school readiness dividend.* Wilder Research. https://www.wilder.org/wilder-research/research-library/minnesotas-one-child-school-readiness-dividend.

Fagan, J., & Iglesias, A. (1999). Father and father figure involvement in Head Start: A quasi-experimental study. *Early Childhood Research Quarterly, 14,* 243–269.

Friedman, D. E. (2004). *The new economics of preschool: New findings, methods and strategies for increasing economic investments in early care and education.* Early Childhood Funders' Collaborative.

García, J. L., Heckman, J. J., Leaf, D. E., & Prados, M. J. (2016). *The life-cycle benefits of an influential early childhood program* (Working Paper No. 22993). National Bureau of Economic Research. https://www.nber.org/papers/w22993.

Heckman, J., & Mosso, S. (2014). *The economics of human development and social mobility.* https://heckmanequation.org/www/assets/2017/01/Econ-of-Hum-Dev-and-Soc-Mob_2014-05-20a_akc.pdf.

Holmes, E. K., Egginton, B. R., Hawkins, A. J., Robbins, N. L., & Shafer, K. (2020). Do Responsible Fatherhood programs work? A comprehensive meta-analytic study. *Family Relations.* Advanced online publication.

Lynch, R., & Vaghul, K. (2015). *The benefits and costs of investing in early childhood education.* Washington Center for Equitable Growth. https://equitablegrowth.org/research-paper/the-benefits-and-costs-of-investing-in-early-childhood-education/.

Manno, M.S., Mancini, P., & O'Herron, C. (2019). *Implementing an Innovative Parenting Program for Fathers: Findings from the B3 Study* (OPRE Report 2019-111). U.S. Department of Health and Human Services, Administration for Children and Families, Office of Planning, Research and Evaluation. https://www.acf.hhs.gov/sites/default/files/opre/innovative_parenting_b3_findings_dec_2019.pdf.

McCoy, D. C., Yoshikawa, H., Ziol-Guest, K. M., Duncan, G. J., Schindler, H. S., Magnuson, K., & Shonkoff, J. P. (2017). Impacts of early childhood education on medium- and long-term educational outcomes. *Educational Researcher, 46*(8), 474–487.

McLaughlin, M., & Rank, M. R. (2018). Estimating the economic cost of childhood poverty in the United States. *Social Work Research, 42*(2), 73–83.

McWayne, C., Downer, J. T., Campos, R., & Harris, R. D. (2013). Father involvement during early childhood and its association with children's early learning: A meta-analysis. *Early Education & Development, 24*(6), 898–922.

Minnesota Compass. (2018). *High school students graduating on time by income.* http://www.mncompass.org/education/high-school-graduation#7-6108-d.

Osborne, C., Dillon, D., Craver, J. W., & Hovey, I. (2016). *Making good on fatherhood: A review of the fatherhood research.* National Fatherhood Initiative. https://www.fatherhood.org/fatherhood/making-good-on-fatherhood.

Pearson, J., Davis, L., & Venohr, J. (2011). *Arapahoe—Parents to Work.* Center for Policy Research.

Pearson, J., Thoennes, N., Davis, L., Venohr, J., Price, D., & Griffith, T. (2003). *OCSE Responsible Fatherhood programs: Client characteristics and program outcomes.* Center for Policy Research and Policy Studies, Inc. https://www.frpn.org/asset/ocse-responsible-fatherhood-programs-client-characteristics-and-program-outcomes.

Pina, G., Diaz, J., & Chase, R. (2013). *Value of school readiness per additional at-risk child in Montgomery County, Ohio.* Wilder Research. https://www.wilder.org/sites/default/files/imports/MontgomeryCountyOneChildDividend_3-13.pdf.

Reynolds, A. J., Temple, J. A., White, B. A., Ou, S.-R., & Robertson, D. L. (2011). Age 26 cost-benefit analysis of the child-parent center early education program. *Child Development, 82*(1), 379–404.

Rolnick, A., & Grunewald, R. (2003). *Early childhood development: Economic development with a high public return.* Federal Reserve Bank of Minneapolis. https://www.minneapolisfed.org/article/2003/early-childhood-development-economic-development-with-a-high-public-return.

Schroeder, D., & Doughty, N. (2009). *Texas non-custodial parent choices program impact analysis.* Lyndon B. Johnson School of Public Affairs, University of Texas at Austin.

Schweinhart, L., Xiang, Z., Daniel-Echols, M., Browning, K., & Wakabayashi, T. (2012). *Michigan Great Start Readiness Program evaluation 2012: High school graduation and grade retention findings.* Michigan Department of Education. http://www.michigan.gov/documents/mde/GSRP_Evaluation_397470_7.pdf.

Scott, S., Briskman, J., & O'Connor, T. G. (2014). Early prevention of antisocial personality: Long-term follow-up of two randomized controlled trials comparing indicated and selective approaches. *The American Journal of Psychiatry, 171*(6), 649–657.

U.S. Census Bureau. (2018a). *Annual survey of state and local government finances, 2016.* https://www.census.gov/programs-surveys/gov-finances.html.

U.S. Census Bureau. (2018b). *U.S. Census American Community Survey five-year estimates—public use microdata sample, 2012–2016.* https://www.census.gov/programs-surveys/acs/technical-documentation/table-and-geography-changes/2016/5-year.html.

U.S. Department of Justice. (2008). *Crime in the United States: FBI Uniform Crime Reports 2008, Table 29.* https://ucr.fbi.gov/crime-in-the-u.s/2008.

Washington State Institute for Public Policy. (2007). *The Dangerous Mentally Ill Offender program: Cost effectiveness 2.5 years after participants' prison release.* http://www.wsipp.wa.gov/rptfiles/07-01-1902.pdf.

Washington State Institute for Public Policy. (2018). *Benefit-cost technical documentation.* http://www.wsipp.wa.gov/TechnicalDocumentation/WsippBenefitCostTechnicalDocumentation.pdf.

14

DEVELOPING FATHER INCLUSION POLICY AT THE STATE LEVEL

A Qualitative Assessment of Enablers and Barriers

Jessica Pearson

Introduction

Despite the growth in the number of children who live in father-absent homes, mounting research showing the benefits of father engagement for children, and the proliferation of father engagement programs for low-income, nonresident fathers (Tollestrup, 2018), the fatherhood field continues to struggle with sustaining long-term progress (Klempin & Mincy, 2011–2012). Even the expenditure of $50-$75 million per year on fatherhood programs from 2006 to 2020 by the Administration for Children and Families through the Healthy Marriage and Responsible Fatherhood (HMRF) grants program, has failed to build sustainability. This may reflect the scale of the father-absence problem, with more than a quarter (26.6%) of children under 21 living in single-parent households that suffer rates of poverty (31.2%) that are twice as high as the poverty rate of the total population (Grall, 2016). This may also be due to the structure of the HMRF grant program, which involves competitive, program-specific awards to a small number of grantees that amounted to only 39 programs in 19 states during 2015–2020 (Office of Family Assistance, 2016).

Although statewide fatherhood commissions and initiatives have the potential to enhance father engagement by bringing together multiple state agencies to focus on the issue, orchestrating braided funding strategies, promoting service integration, and advocating for father-friendly policies at a systemic level, they are rare. A recent national review found that only ten states have a fatherhood advocacy initiative with services in more than one jurisdiction, and only four states have a formal statewide fatherhood commission (of which only one is reliably funded and staffed) (Pearson & Fagan, 2019). This need not be the case. Notably, while TANF funding is permitted for Fatherhood and Two-Parent Family Programs, national spending on fatherhood programs accounts for less than 0.5% of total TANF spending (Office of Family Assistance, 2018). In FY 2017, 33 states had $3.3 billion in unobligated TANF balances, a portion of which could be utilized to support fatherhood services and initiatives to promote father inclusion in the lives of their children (Falk & Landers, 2019). Other funding sources that could be tapped include child support performance dollars (Office of Child Support Enforcement, 2018), child support program waivers to fund work activities for noncustodial parents (Office of Child Support Enforcement, 2019), and prevention activities associated with the Family First Legislation (Library of Congress, 2018).

As part of its six-year effort (2013–2019) to build research, practice, and policy in the fatherhood field, the Fatherhood Research and Practice Network (FRPN), co-created and operated by Temple University and the Center for Policy Research in Denver, Colorado, developed a statewide planning initiative to support states in developing long-term plans for enhancing father inclusion. This project had two layers: first, state planning teams developed and began to implement action plans to achieve systemic change aimed at father inclusion; second, FRPN researchers evaluated the policy development process that the planning teams engaged in to better understand what elements contributed to or detracted from their early efforts to engage fathers in programs and policies dealing with children and families. The latter goal is the focus of this chapter.

Overview of the Statewide Planning Project

In October 2019, FRPN released a Request for Proposal inviting states to apply for a small planning grant to develop long-term plans to promote systematic change aimed at enhancing father inclusion in state programs and policies. Eligible applicants included nonprofit father and/or children's advocacy and faith-based organizations, universities, and government agencies. To maximize policy outcomes, applicants were required to create a state planning team that included the State Child Support Director, a fatherhood or family-policy researcher, and at least one other high-level state leader such as a director of a state agency or program that serves fathers and families. Twenty states applied for an FRPN planning grant and in January 2019, FRPN made awards of $10,000 to 11 states: Colorado, Connecticut, Kentucky, Michigan, Minnesota, North Carolina, Pennsylvania, Rhode Island, South Carolina, Washington, and Wyoming. Grant funds were flexible and could be used on a variety of activities that the planning team determined to be relevant in developing and implementing an action plan. The activities that statewide teams conducted varied according to the needs and context of each state, but included focus groups with fathers and key stakeholders, surveys about the state of current fatherhood programming, statewide or regional fatherhood summits, cultivation of legislative champions, development of centralized information databases, conduct of strategic planning processes, and exploration of long-term funding strategies.

FRPN directors supported the nine-month planning processes in a variety of ways: preparing an initial logic model for each planning site highlighting their proposed goals and activities and revising them with each planning team; holding bi-monthly check-in calls with each planning team to monitor their progress and to provide feedback and suggestions; connecting team members with other planning teams and experts; and hosting webinars on fatherhood commissions, fatherhood summits, and engaging with state legislators. At the conclusion of the nine-month grant period, each team prepared an *action plan* that summarized their activities, accomplishments, and next steps. Subsequently, FRPN directors prepared a cross-site overview of the initiative that highlights similarities and differences in goals, activities, challenges, and accomplishments (Pearson, 2020). Tables 14.1 and 14.2 present key activities that the planning grant sites pursued and challenges that they experienced.

Literature Review

State-level advocacy and policy initiatives are among the most promising avenues to address fragmentation in family policy. Many programs and funding streams are siloed, and poor coordination across a multitude of services used by low-income families means that existing resources are not utilized to their full potential (Cowan & Cowan, 2018). Statewide policies have enormous potential to integrate diverse programming and streamline funding sources. They also can be instrumental in changing how nonresident fathers are viewed and treated as members of a family unit (Child and Family Research Partnership, 2018).

Despite the value of systems-level activism, we know little about the process and the elements that make them effective. Given the many influencing factors

TABLE 14.1 Main Activities Pursued by FRPN Planning Grant Teams

	Interviews & Focus Groups	Multi-Agency Coalition Building	Strategic Planning & State Policy Review	Fatherhood Summits & Conferences	Legislator Education & Cultivating Champions	Trying to Create a Fatherhood Commission & Funding
CO	+			+	+	+
CT	+	+		+	+	+
KY	+	+	+	+	+	+
MI	+	+	+			+
MN	+			+		
NC	+	+		+	+	
PA	+	+	+	+	+	+
RI			+	+	+	+
SC	+	+			+	
WA	+	+		+		
WY			+			

TABLE 14.2 Main Challenges That FRPN Planning Teams Encountered

	Political and Organizational Issues	Difficulty Engaging Fathers	Geographic Distance and Time Constraints	Lack of Data on Fatherhood
CO	+		+	
CT		+		+
KY	+		+	+
MI		+	+	+
MN		+		
NC	+		+	+
PA	+		+	
RI				+
SC	+			
WA	+	+	+	+
WY		+	+	

and organizations that are involved, it can be challenging to establish a causal relationship between a particular group's advocacy activities and any policy change that may occur (Jones, 2011). Additionally, since "total success" is rarely achieved and substantial gains tend to occur over long timeframes, evaluating advocacy efforts involves "an element of subjectivity in whether gains were significant, consistent with the wider goals of an organization or campaign" (Jones, 2011, p. 3). Finally, advocacy work is highly fluid, political, and context specific, making it difficult to replicate or compare in a controlled manner.

A number of different frameworks exist to evaluate the process of policy development. The Child and Family Research Partnership's model of "evidence-based systems-level change" involves using the knowledge and experience of community members with scientific research to identify the evidence-based drivers of change: "When communities decide upon their goals, they need to identify the known predictors of their goals and align their strategies and action steps accordingly" (Child and Family Research Partnership, 2018).

Another approach to measure the impact of advocacy efforts comes from Julia Coffman (2009) of the Center for Evaluation Innovation. She notes that "advocacy evaluations generally focus their data collection on three types of outcomes or results—advocacy capacity, progress toward policy goals, or an advocacy effort's impact." Using this framework, evaluators should document promising movement toward change through internal capacity development as well as positive changes that may have been indirect or unintended outcomes of an advocacy effort.

Still a third approach focuses on identifying the factors that support or impede effective coalitional work. Utilizing an "enablers and barriers" analysis to develop a deeper understanding of the determinants of successful legislative and other policy making to prevent childhood obesity (Dodson et al., 2009), researchers found that the top two enablers of successful policy change were the support or involvement of key stakeholders in the process of developing obesity prevention legislation, and national media exposure on the issue. The top two barriers were powerful lobbyists representing manufacturers of unhealthy foods and beverages, and misinformed constituents.

Since this study deals with an advocacy project in the early stages of change-making, Dodson et al.'s (2009) "facilitators and barriers" model was the most effective framework for comparing the planning teams' initial efforts and for understanding why certain teams' efforts may or not be successful at creating systems-level change.

Methods

The FRPN research team conducted four formal conference calls with the planning team members from each state grantee during January–August 2019. In the first call, participants discussed the state's goals and intended activities. In the next two check-in calls, planning team members provided information on their progress as well as the facilitators and barriers they were experiencing. The fourth call focused on debriefing about the project, summarizing accomplishments and discussing next steps.

Utilizing an open coding methodology, researchers developed categories of "facilitators" and "barriers" that the planning teams encountered in conducting state-level initiatives to include fathers in policies and programs dealing with families and children. Open coding involves comparing events, actions, and interactions across a data set for similarities and differences, and then developing conceptual labels for similar groupings to form categories and subcategories (Corbin & Strauss, 1990). For this study, a research assistant took detailed notes during each call with a state planning team, including direct quotes. After the first round of check-in calls, the lead researcher and the research assistant independently completed an open coding process in which call notes were analyzed for recurring themes and relevant examples were selected to highlight these themes. This process resulted in the development of subcategories of "facilitators" and "barriers" that were common across multiple state planning teams. Then, a third researcher compared the two lists of subcategories and identified where the subcategories overlapped. This process was repeated after the second round of check-in calls (the researchers were not restricted to the subcategories developed in the previous analysis). Finally, upon receipt of the planning teams' final reports, the categories were reviewed and amended.

Enablers

Planning teams mentioned the following items as helpful to their efforts to improve father inclusion.

Piggybacking on Existing Initiatives

Nearly every state planning team looked for ways to "piggyback" the father engagement issue with other scheduled events, conferences, and planning groups. As a member of the Colorado planning team put it, "Any time we can tap into something existing, it gives us a head start." Thus, the Rhode Island planning team was assembled from a planning committee convened for a strategic planning effort on fatherhood that it conducted two years ago. The Washington planning effort coalesced around a statewide summit on maternal and child health that had been planned a year earlier with the addition of new project-funded data-collection activities. North Carolina used the planning effort to augment an annual conference on fatherhood that it has held for the past seven years, with the addition of panels on child support and opportunities for fathers and child support agency personnel to interact. It also was successful in adding fatherhood resources to a broader multi-purpose resource network known as NCCARE360, which was developed under a grant by United Way and the Department of Human Services. As one North Carolina planning team member put it, "one advantage of piggybacking off of their network instead of starting from scratch is that the state is already committed to hosting and funding the NCCARE360 website, so we don't need to worry about those logistics." In a similar fashion, Connecticut worked with its United Way agency to introduce routine questioning of all callers for services about their parental status rather than exclusively focusing on their household status. As a member of the Connecticut planning team observed, "We need to be proactive about getting a larger picture about fathers and their needs no matter what they call about." Connecticut presented the findings of a data- collection effort conducted through the planning grant at a previously scheduled statewide conference conducted by its child welfare agency. And Colorado decided to wait a full year for a statewide convening in order to introduce a fatherhood track at a previously scheduled conference on families sponsored by the Department of Human Services' Early Childhood Education Division.

State planning teams also explored the feasibility of repurposing existing administrative entities to include fatherhood issues. For example, Rhode Island plans to feed the results of its planning efforts back to the Children's Cabinet, an influential, legislatively established body comprised of directors of different state agencies involved with children which reports to the Governor. Connecticut is exploring the feasibility of coordinating fatherhood work with the state's recently enacted two-generation (2Gen) legislation and reentry initiatives. Washington used the planning effort to grow an interagency Fatherhood Council comprised of agency and stakeholder representatives. Established a year ago after a statewide fatherhood conference, a planning team member characterized it as a "key voice in the planning process around family and early childhood programs and grants."

Procuring High-Level Champions

Virtually all state planning teams noted the importance of having a high-level champion and/or were actively engaged in attempting to secure one. For Michigan, the required support of the director of the state's Child Support Agency in the planning grant proposal, who was subsequently appointed by the Governor to be the State Director of Opportunity, means that the "conversation about the importance of fatherhood initiatives might be held at the highest level." Colorado planned to identify legislators who had supported a 2019 bill authorizing the use of TANF funds for employment programs for noncustodial parents and try to cultivate them to support the creation of a Fatherhood Commission. Connecticut reconnected with a newly elected state legislator who had supported fatherhood legislation in a different capacity 20 years ago. South Carolina convened a meeting of 23 representatives of key state agencies to build a "core group of fatherhood champions." As members of the South Carolina planning team noted, "If we build these internal ambassadors and champions, they will further fatherhood at staff meetings and trainings, and not just because of external pressure from fatherhood groups." The Washington planning team also contacted the legislative liaison for the state agency in which the planning effort was housed to identify potentially supportive legislators and to build a relationship with the Governor who is a strong proponent of poverty issues. As one member of the Washington planning team put it, "we hope to show him how fatherhood plays a role in that." Rhode Island hosted a policy breakfast for legislators and key agency representatives, including child support, corrections, labor and training, and child welfare. And the Pennsylvania team held a press conference featuring the CEO of a global business to deliver the message that fathers are important and followed up with obtaining legislators to sponsor and introduce a bill in the House and Senate to establish the Strong Families Coalition.

Building Relationships With Other Agencies

Virtually every site planning team credited the engagement of representatives of a variety of state human services agencies in a series of meetings on father inclusion with generating enthusiasm and moving the agenda forward. As a member of the Michigan planning team noted, "The planning meetings have been very exciting and invigorating, because there's so much passion about working with fathers, and the need for this work is so clear." For most sites, regular meetings are a "vehicle for networking and collaborating and identifying issues and policy hotspots that need attention."

Some planning teams were very mindful about the selection of agency participants. For example, South Carolina considered a list of 70 agencies and selected 20 to target that touched children, families, and fathers. Wyoming convened agency representatives to get an idea of what programs and planning activities were already in place as a prelude to conducting a two-day facilitated strategic-planning process. Regular meetings helped the North Carolina planning team learn about fatherhood activity around the state and gaps to address, including possible legislation on fatherhood by a State Senator and a newly formed 15-member Council on Child Wellbeing that lacked father representation.

Collecting Data on Fatherhood

Collecting data on the status of fathers in the state is also credited with moving the planning agenda forward. Minnesota and Connecticut both decided to conduct focus groups with fathers throughout the state to identify areas of unmet need and to build the qualitative evidence base for improving father engagement in a wide array of state and local agencies. While fathers are commonly associated with the child support agency, there is less recognition of the potential role of fathers in agencies that deal with child welfare, maternal and child health, and education. One purpose of conducting focus groups and interviews with fathers throughout the state is to highlight their less well-documented experiences with agencies other than child support as well as demonstrating the uneven geographical distribution of resources and understandings about fatherhood. Michigan and Washington opted to use online surveys to capture father experiences with various programs and agencies as well as unmet needs. All state planning teams were using local, county, and state agencies to distribute surveys and/or recruit fathers to participate in focus groups. Finally, some planning teams felt that surveys and focus groups with fathers can improve "accountability" with various state programs and agencies. As one Connecticut planning team member explained, "authentic father voices saying they feel left out enable us to ask, 'what are you doing about father engagement and what do you need to do a better job?'"

Another type of data that planning teams seek are baseline assessments of father engagement in various agencies that serve families and children. This could serve as a benchmark against which the results of future engagement initiatives might be compared. Rhode Island administered a revision of the Father Friendly Check-Up developed by the National Fatherhood Initiative (NFI) to gauge the use of father-friendly practices in state agencies (NFI, 2020). South Carolina was doing site visits to various agencies to get a sense of "on the ground realities" and creating its own survey to assess father engagement needs and barriers.

A useful form of data on fatherhood for funding purposes are Return on Investment (ROI) studies. The Colorado planning team reported that on the strength of an ROI study of a workforce program for fathers in the child support system conducted in 2011, the legislature had approved a three-year allocation of $1.8 million of TANF funds per year for NCP workforce programs. A similar legislative measure had failed to pass during two previous years because the argument was made with less persuasive, descriptive information. The South Carolina Center for Fathers and Families prepares an annual ROI report and featured it at a press conference it organized in February 2019, right after the agency lost a portion of its TANF funding.

Involving Fathers in the Planning Process

Some planning teams reported that father spokesmen were effective ambassadors for the planning effort. On the basis of the useful feedback that fatherhood program participants in Rhode Island provided to the planning team, they were subsequently invited to meet with child welfare agency administrators for additional "enlightening discussions" about father experiences with the agency and worker biases. South Carolina used an activity that highlighted how a single father is affected by multiple agencies to instruct agency partners on connectivity and shared caseload to make the case for the importance of collaboration. Washington includes ten fathers on its Fatherhood Council, including two in leadership positions. Wyoming was actively seeking father participants to help guide the work of its fatherhood advisory board and was struggling with ways of eliciting "authentic" father input as well as the participation of "unreachable families."

Participating in a Catalytic Initiative and Getting FRPN Funds and Technical Assistance

Despite the small size of the FRPN grant ($10,000) and the brevity of the project (nine months), the FRPN initiative was credited with being a catalyst for action. FRPN directors connected planning team members to national experts and to one another across state lines. FRPN funds were flexible and could be used for many things that are difficult to pay for with agency money: participant incentives, food costs for meetings, stipends for data collection, duplication costs for materials, and consulting fees for professional facilitators.

FRPN's Learning Community was also credited with helping planning teams make progress at the local level. Thus, Rhode Island found a webinar FRPN organized on how to engage state legislators particularly helpful and subsequently held a round table to educate legislators about fatherhood. Washington found the same webinar useful and contacted a presenter for additional resources and tips to guide their legislative outreach efforts. Peer learning was another plus for the planning effort. Rhode Island, which had pursued a strategic planning effort a few years ago with the assistance of NFI facilitators, supplied Kentucky with a copy of its strategic plan and discussed its planning experiences with Wyoming, which was about to retain NFI to conduct a similar planning effort. Kentucky tapped the head of the South Carolina planning team to be the keynote speaker at its statewide fatherhood summit.

FRPN's grant requirements and bi-monthly check-in calls were also valued. Michigan thought the kick-off logic models that FRPN prepared for each site clarified objectives and planned activities. The Wyoming and Minnesota planning teams felt as though the bi-monthly calls improved "accountability" and kept the teams on track. The required participation of the State IV-D directors and at least one other high-level state official led to the development of strong relationships between fatherhood and key state agencies. Thus, at the conclusion of the nine-month planning grant, Michigan had been invited to submit a proposal to its TANF director for funds to continue fatherhood planning activities, and the child support director in Pennsylvania decided to create a state-level advisory committee comprised of parents, grandparents, and advocates to help shape child support policy.

Getting Press Coverage

A few planning teams pursued press coverage and found that to be helpful. South Carolina held a press conference to release an impact report for the South Carolina Center for Fathers and Families. The planning team credited the well-publicized event with "energizing folks" and helping with the process of recruiting agency partners to participate in the planning process. Pennsylvania held a press conference to release a report on fatherhood and roll out its campaign to create a fatherhood commission. Held in the statehouse with a "rotunda full of people," the press conference is credited with "creating a sense of urgency about fatherhood...and an understanding that we can't drop the ball here." In Kentucky, a planning team member was a guest columnist for the state's newspaper in which he highlighted the importance of fatherhood work.

Barriers

Planning teams mentioned the following items as unhelpful to their efforts to improve father inclusion.

Scheduling Challenges and Competing Priorities

Just as the planning teams agreed about the enablers to the planning process, there was a good deal of consensus about the barriers. Chief among them was the difficulty of scheduling meetings with busy agency personnel and policy makers and the understandable rejection and delay due to competing priorities. The difficulty of finding a convenient time and place for statewide meetings was a theme echoed by planning teams in Michigan, Colorado, and Connecticut. Pennsylvania observed that other events such as shootings in Philadelphia over Father's Day took legislators' attention away from fatherhood work and caused several meetings to be rescheduled. Kentucky team members said that it both was challenging to get 10–15 professionals together who run major agencies and have limited time, and to get them to "attend to the homework in between meetings." Washington was worried about keeping state agency leaders at the table. As one planning team member put it, "They will be there on paper, but we want to keep them in the room and engaged." North Carolina and Wyoming found that they needed to give potential attendees more advance notice of meetings and do more active reminder calls and emails. And several sites were concerned about enthusiasm flagging if the planning process dragged on too long. As the Pennsylvania planning team observed, "The longer these things take, the more difficult they become. People lose interest, they become more involved with other things, life kicks in. How do you continue to keep the excitement alive over time?"

Difficulties Engaging Fathers or Utilizing Them in Effective Ways

As with fatherhood services and programs, it is often difficult to engage fathers in the planning process. Several planning teams that wanted to engage fathers in focus groups and/or to serve on advisory boards and be the "face" of fatherhood discussions, found it hard to get fathers to participate. And while some agency partners could identify father spokesmen and client representatives, it was much more challenging to find "unreachable families" and those who might have a more "authentic voice." Numbers of father respondents to online surveys and focus groups at some sites were lower than planning team members had hoped. For example, Connecticut had attempted to conduct focus groups with 64 fathers but was able to engage only 38, some of whom had to be interviewed one-on-one. Washington State, on the other hand, had the opposite problem, and project leaders struggled to accommodate all interested fathers in constructive ways.

Bureaucratic and Political Challenges

Frequent turnover in leadership in key state agencies often spells the loss of fatherhood champions, change in agency priorities, and delays in the planning process. Several states experienced new administrations at the start of the planning grant on January 1, 2019, which delayed the appointment of new agency and program heads and the onset of the planning process. Just a few weeks after conducting a state-wide fatherhood summit that the planning team had executed with the existing administration, Kentucky faced a gubernatorial election and the defeat of their hitherto supporter. Planning team members in South Carolina observed that the Department of Social Services had experienced four different directors over six years. As a result, the team had decided to target mid-level staff in their outreach about the importance of fatherhood since they often have longer tenure than top leadership. As one member observed,

> Our goal is to get to more of the permanent civil services staff who don't change around as much and have influence over incoming administrations.

It's a question of getting in touch with the right person who has enough influence and decision-making power to be effective but who isn't going to leave in the short term and cut short all our progress.

The Colorado planning team expressed similar frustrations about changes in administration and the loss of institutional knowledge engendered by frequent staff changes. While sympathetic to fatherhood issues, the new governor appears to want to reduce the number of governor-appointed commissions, which might make it harder to achieve a new fatherhood commission. The collapse of the Colorado fatherhood organization that received the planning grant and its transfer to a new entity also engendered some delay. Planning team members noted the need for more "cross-systems training" to improve connectivity across agencies and the preservation of fatherhood knowledge and resources when staff retire or move on. In a similar vein, the Michigan planning team mourned the existence of many "siloes in fatherhood work across the state," and the discomfort of not knowing what might be going on. As a team member put it, "It is good to stumble across things, but it makes you wonder what you are missing."

Fiscal Challenges

All states face inadequate and/or unstable funding for fatherhood. Although the federal government has been urging states to use surplus TANF funds for fatherhood, and many states do have unobligated TANF balances, others do not. North Carolina is one such state, and although the State TANF director has been present at planning meetings, there has been no discussion of the use of TANF funds for fatherhood. Other states have discovered that there are many competing demands for TANF funds. The SC Center for Fathers and Families, which had enjoyed TANF funding for over eight years for statewide operations, faced a sudden 40% funding cut when the state lost a lawsuit dealing with foster care and money was transferred from fatherhood to address the issues raised by the court order. As the planning team observed, "TANF funding is wonderful and horrible. It's so flexible, but it gets pulled toward so many things. They are using it to plug a different hole right now." Washington said that it isn't likely to obtain TANF funds for fatherhood services and programs because unobligated balances are being used for a home visiting program for new mothers as well as a statewide program on innovation. According to the Washington planning team, mothers tend to dominate in most funding discussions to address the needs of families and parents, and while there is "openness to including fathers, we need to be in the room."

State funding for fatherhood has also been erratic. In Connecticut, which is one of only four states in the nation with a fatherhood commission enshrined in state statute, funding for programming has waxed and waned over 20 years with the vagaries of federal grants and small state appropriations which have been made and withdrawn in the wake of other financial needs.

Lack of Data on Fatherhood

With the exception of child support measures like rates of paternity establishment and child support payment, there are few indicators of father inclusion, father absence, and/or child outcomes pertaining to fatherhood and father participation at the local, state, or federal level. As a result, there are few "baseline measures" against which a father inclusion initiative might be measured. More to the point, many planning teams feel that the failure to count fathers renders them "invisible." Rhode Island was trying to engage managers of various state agencies to generate information on father involvement from automated management information systems. Connecticut was urging state agencies and programs and United Way to ask men they served routinely whether they are fathers and if so, whether they lived with their children. Minnesota was hoping to augment a 2007 survey of 58 social service agencies and education programs to estimate the number providing services to fathers and the number of fathers served. Kentucky planning team members also mourned the lack of data on fathers' state of engagement. "There's not a lot of data available on fathers. The lack of measures now makes it difficult to get a baseline of where we are at, what our strengths and weaknesses are, and which laws, policies and procedures within different agencies need to be changed." Planning teams wished that there were more instruments on father engagement at the agency level. With the exception of NFI's Father Friendly Survey, site representatives were unaware of tools that would help state and local agencies and programs identify their strengths, needs, and barriers. Finally, several planning teams noted the absence of a comprehensive resource directory of fatherhood programs and services at the state level. Indeed, the compilation of such information is one objective of several of the FRPN's planning teams.

Changing the Societal View of Fathers and Fatherhood

Including fathers in programs and policies that affect children and families is a complex process that will not be easily accomplished. Virtually all the planning teams felt that it would require substantial change on multiple levels; several teams referred to the process of embracing fatherhood as requiring a "paradigm shift." As the Kentucky planning team observed:

> People are not used to looking at these issues through the lens of fatherhood or even considering fatherhood in a lot of programming. People that we've talked to have an interest in working on fatherhood issues, but when it comes to making a commitment of dollars or people power, people end up defaulting to what is comfortable or usual for them. Likewise, it can be difficult for administrators to get frontline staff to buy in to the importance of this work and implement the changes on the ground level. Even when leadership is on board, the systems have to catch up with that.

The Pennsylvania team noted the importance of language and framing. While talking about fathers "isn't in vogue," talking about fathers within families "is easier to swallow." Focus groups and interviews with fathers in several states have revealed that individual workers in agencies play a key role in father engagement and fathers' inclusion. The challenge becomes what to do about improving client interactions with individual workers. Thus, while the Connecticut planning team asserts that there is a need for a statewide plan for meaningful father engagement, part of the plan might need "to involve worker training and re-training to make programs more responsive." The North Carolina planning team also came to the conclusion that there might be a disconnect between "how sensitive we think our agencies are to fathers and how they operate in reality." As a result, they have decided that they must do more internal work as well as external work to change the perception of agency workers about fathers and fatherhood. "Staff have to hear more detail about father perceptions and to continue to build relationships between fatherhood organizations and local child support offices." Still another aspect of system change and paradigm shift involves changing the public image of fathers and broadening the view of policy makers about fatherhood. "When people think of father inclusion, they immediately think of child support. They're missing whole other areas of things fathers need to be involved in, like health, education and employment. There are a lot of other things programs need to address to really serve families and fathers." To help accomplish this, Washington was developing a fathers' speakers bureau, and South Carolina was developing videos to highlight the voices of fathers. Across all sites, the objective is to keep fatherhood relevant and visible despite changes in administration. Although every site is seeking legislative and administrative champions, none want to be merely a "pet project" for a particular politician. Fatherhood has to be framed to appeal to conservative as well as left-leaning folks. As one planning team member put it, "Optimally, if we can position ourselves such that the work and resources transcend any individual administration, that's ideal."

Discussion

FRPN researchers identified a common set of enablers and barriers to creating and/or augmenting state-level planning efforts to promote father engagement by coding four telephone conference calls conducted over nine months with planning teams in 11 states awarded FRPN planning grants of $10,000. Planning teams reported that their efforts were enhanced by piggybacking on existing initiatives, securing high-level champions by conducing informational sessions for legislators and engaging agency directors in the planning effort, and building relationships with other agencies to highlight the salience of father engagement for them and to identify father engagement resources and issues that require attention. Various data-collection activities were also enablers: gathering compelling evidence on father needs and experiences with a variety of state programs, developing baseline measures of father engagement against which future progress might be measured, and/or compiling return on investment data to make the financial case for investments in fatherhood. Some sites saw benefits in involving fathers in the planning process and making them spokesmen for the planning effort. Finally, planning teams credited several aspects of the FRPN planning grant initiative with the progress they made. This included hosting instructive webinars, holding bi-monthly telephone conferences with the planning team which "kept the pressure on," and requiring that the state child support director serve on the planning team.

Just as there was consensus on the enablers of father engagement planning efforts, there was agreement on the challenges. Progress was thwarted by the difficulty of scheduling with busy agency personnel and policy makers; changes in state government administration, new agency and program heads, and staff turnover; and the decentralized nature of fatherhood services. Even though states are now being encouraged to devote unobligated TANF balances to allowable father engagement activities, several states lack unobligated funds, and all face stiff competition for these resources. The lack of data on fatherhood at the state level makes it hard to track changes in father engagement, highlight what agencies should be doing, and monitor improvements over time. Some sites that tried to engage fathers in interviews and focus groups found it difficult to involve "hard-to-reach" populations; other sites struggled to channel father interest in engagement in productive ways. Finally, progress is thwarted by the complexity and scale of the father engagement process and the need to change the image of fathers and fatherhood in substantial ways.

Several of the factors we identified can be applied to legislative and policy efforts on a variety of issues. Piggybacking, securing high-level champions, and building relationships with other agencies are familiar ways to advance a policy agenda and achieve sustainability. By the same token, changes in political administrations, legislators, and executive-level administrators can radically affect political will and policy decisions, not to mention the timing of change. Cost, competing budget priorities, and other fiscal challenges are concerns prevalent in most legislative and administrative decision making. And the lack of indicators and data on an issue can cripple policy making. While involving the local media is a key ingredient to most successful policy initiatives (Dodson et al., 2009), it was not pursued at most planning sites, probably because the father engagement initiatives were so young.

Intermediaries like FRPN have long helped to stimulate social change by serving as "field catalysts" (Hussein et al., 2018). Like other field catalysts, FRPN focused on achieving "population-level change" rather than simply scaling up an intervention, influencing the direct actions of others rather than acting directly itself, and concentrating on getting things done rather than building consensus. Though operating at only a tiny fraction of the funding levels and time frame for fields where catalysts played a critical role (e.g., marriage equality, cutting teen smoking, reducing teen pregnancies), FRPN performed some of the same roles: earning the trust of multi-organizational planning teams, helping to define the mission and the road map for change that site participants could rally around, fulfilling the evolving and disparate needs of each site, providing supporting capability, and coordinating planning efforts across 11 sites to transform a highly fragmented field.

The chief study limitation is the short timeline of the FRPN planning initiative. Due to the expected end of FRPN funding on September 30, 2019 (subsequently extended to December 31, 2019), it was necessary to formally end the planning grants in September 2019, which allowed only nine months between grant award and termination. All sites were in the middle of their planning activities when the project officially ended, so the factors and barriers identified in this article and culled from the four telephone conference calls conducted with each site should be viewed as "early" barriers and limitations rather than ultimate ones.

Another limitation is the absence of any objective interim or final measures of outcome. The factors affecting progress that planning team members cited were subjective and perceptual, and in the absence of state-level indicators of father engagement across multiple programs and settings, it is difficult to assess progress that participating states might have experienced.

Conclusion

While individual fatherhood programs can be impactful for participants, making sustainable change in father engagement at the state level requires the identification and adoption of effective policies and programs and the buy-in of administrators of multiple agencies and programs. As with all systemic changes, this requires the adoption of effective legislative and regulatory actions; the appropriation of sufficient resources; strong implementation of critical programs; and measurement, monitoring, and evaluation to track changes over time and to identify the need for adjustment and additional change. The FRPN planning initiative is a first step in this process in the fatherhood arena.

References

Child and Family Research Partnership. (2018). *A framework for evidence-based systems-level change* (B.036.0718). https://childandfamilyresearch.utexas.edu/sites/default/files/CFRPBrief_B0360718_SystemsLevelChange.pdf.

Coffman, J. (2009). *Overview of current advocacy evaluation practice*. Center for Evaluation Innovation. https://nyshealthfoundation.org/wp-content/uploads/2019/02/overview_current_eval_practice.pdf.

Corbin, J. M., & Strauss, A. (1990). Grounded theory research: Procedures, canons, and evaluative criteria. *Qualitative Sociology, 13*(1), 3–21.

Cowan, C. P., & Cowan, P. A. (2018). Enhancing parenting effectiveness, fathers' involvement, couple relationship quality, and children's development: Breaking down silos in family policy making and service delivery. *Journal of Family Theory & Review, 11*(1), 92–111.

Dodson, E. A., Fleming, C., Boehmer, T. K., Haire-Joshu, D., Luke, D. A., & Brownson, R. C. (2009). Preventing childhood obesity through state policy: Qualitative assessment of enablers and barriers. *Journal of Public Health Policy, 30,* S161–S176.

Falk, G., & Landers, P. A. (2019). *The Temporary Assistance for Needy Families (TANF) block grant: Response to frequently asked questions* (RL32760). Congressional Research Service. https://crsreports.congress.gov/product/pdf/RL/RL32760.

Grall, T. (2016). *Custodial mothers and fathers and their child support: 2013* (Current Population Reports, P60-255). U.S. Census Bureau. https://www.census.gov/content/dam/Census/library/publications/2016/demo/P60-255.pdf.

Hussein, T., Plummer, M., & Breen, B. (2018). *How field catalysts galvanize social change.* Stanford Social Innovation Review. https://ssir.org/articles/entry/field_catalysts.

Jones, H. (2011). *A guide to monitoring and evaluating policy influence.* Overseas Development Institute. https://www.odi.org/sites/odi.org.uk/files/odi-assets/publications-opinion-files/6453.pdf.

Klempin, S., & Mincy, R. B. (2011–2012). *Tossed on a sea of change: A status update on the responsible fatherhood field.* Center for Research on Fathers, Children, and Family Well-Being. http://crfcfw.columbia.edu/files/2012/09/OSF-Fatherhood-Survey_Final-Report_9.25.12_SK_RM.pdf.

Library of Congress. (2018). Bipartisan Budget Act of 2018, H.R. 1892, 115th Cong. https://www.congress.gov/bill/115th-congress/house-bill/1892.

National Fatherhood Initiative. (2020). *Father Friendly Check-Up^{TM}.* https://www.fatherhood.org/ffcu.

Office of Child Support Enforcement. (2018). *Use of IV-D incentive funds for NCP work activities* (Information memorandum, IM-18-02). U.S. Department of Health and Human Services, Administration for Children and Families. https://www.acf.hhs.gov/css/resource/use-of-iv-d-incentive-funds-for-ncp-work-activities.

Office of Child Support Enforcement. (2019). *Availability of section 1115 waivers to fund NCP work activities* (Information memorandum, IM-19-04). U.S. Department of Health and Human Services, Administration for Children and Families. https://www.acf.hhs.gov/css/resource/availability-of-section-1115-waivers-to-fund-ncp-work-activities.

Office of Family Assistance. (2016). *Healthy marriage and responsible fatherhood grantees.* U.S. Department of Health and Human Services, Administration for Children and Families. https://www.acf.hhs.gov/ofa/programs/healthy-marriage.

Office of Family Assistance. (2018). *TANF and MOE spending and transfers by activity, FY 2016.* U.S. Department of Health and Human Services, Administration for Children and Families. https://www.acf.hhs.gov/ofa/resource/tanf-and-moe-spending-and-transfers-by-activity-fy-2016-contains-national-state-pie-charts.

Pearson, J. (2020). *FRPN research brief: Implementation and lessons learned from the FRPN state planning grant initiative.* Fatherhood Research and Practice Network. https://www.frpn.org/asset/frpn-research-brief-implementation-lessons-learned-the-frpn-state-planning-grant-initiative.

Pearson, J., & Fagan, J. (2019). State efforts to support the engagement of fathers in the lives of their children. *Families in Society, 100*(4), 392–408.

Tollestrup, J. (2018). *Fatherhood initiatives: Connecting fathers to their children* (RL31035). Congressional Research Service. https://fas.org/sgp/crs/misc/RL31025.pdf.

15
WHAT HAVE WE LEARNED AND WHERE DO WE GO FROM HERE?

Jessica Pearson and Jay Fagan

Introduction

This book assembles 13 studies that were funded by the Fatherhood Research and Practice Network (FRPN), an entity created and operated during 2013–2019 as a result of a $4.8 million cooperative agreement with Temple University and the Center for Policy Research in Denver, CO, from the U.S. Administration for Children and Families (ACF), Office of Planning, Research, and Evaluation (OPRE). Designed to generate and disseminate research evidence on effective approaches to improving the engagement of low-income, nonresident fathers in the social, emotional, and financial lives of their children, FRPN sponsored 20 evaluations of various aspects of fatherhood programs and practice as well as planning initiatives in 11 states aimed at promoting father inclusion in policies and programs for children and families. (See Appendix A for a full list of final reports based on FRPN subawards.)

In this chapter, we summarize the questions, approaches, and findings for the 13 FRPN studies that are highlighted. These studies speak to some of the key questions about fatherhood programs, using a variety of methodologies, including randomized control trials, reviews and analyses of the literature, quasi-experimental designs using pre- and post-program assessments, and qualitative approaches.

Based on the 13 studies that FRPN sponsored and featured, we distill a set of learnings about fatherhood programs and practice. The distillation aims to build the evidence base on fatherhood programs and promote the use of evidence-informed practice. It adds to the growing body of research on fatherhood programs that ACF has sponsored in recent years with the conduct and evaluation of Parents and Children Together (PACT), and the emerging research on the 39 responsible fatherhood programs funded in the 2015 Healthy Marriage and Responsible Fatherhood (HMRF) grants (Avellar, Stanczyk et al., 2020).

We suggest some of the issues that remain to be studied in the areas of investigation targeted by FRPN. Clearly, there are many fatherhood program issues that we did not address with FRPN grants, and research is sorely needed on those as well. They include but are not limited to strengthening fathering skills; improving outcomes dealing with employment, earnings, and child support payments; deepening father engagement in the language, literacy, and math development of their children; and tracking the unique experiences of various ethnic and racial subgroups with fatherhood programs.

Finally, we urge continuation of research–practitioner relationships and collaborations that were so diligently pursued, nurtured, and achieved in FRPN. Generating intervention research that addresses the real-world concerns of practitioners necessitates partnerships. In a similar vein, ensuring that research findings are incorporated in program practices and formats necessitates the development of relationships built on trust and communication between and among researchers and practitioners.

Key Findings

This section of the chapter summarizes key findings of the 13 studies included in this book.

Fatherhood Programs Generate Significant Outcomes

Fatherhood programs have significant positive outcomes in most areas of performance expected of them, although the effect sizes are small. The Holmes et al. systematic review of 47 independent studies revealed that fatherhood programs have positive outcomes in five areas of interest: father involvement, parenting, coparenting, employment/economic prospects, and child support payments (see Chapter 2). These findings are consistent with the results of an earlier meta-analysis study that the authors conducted for FRPN that focused on evaluations of 34 programs that used rigorous designs, including a randomized control group design or nontreatment comparison group. Taken together, the findings of positive outcomes with small effect sizes are based on a total of 77 studies contained in 62 reports.

Program Intensity Matters

The modest changes observed in the fatherhood field may reflect the fact that most programs lack the intensity or duration of services needed to create change among low-income populations with many barriers and challenges. The FRPN study conducted by Kim and his colleagues suggests that this may be the case (see Chapter 4). Kim's randomized control study of the TYRO Dads program, operated by The RIDGE Project, based in McClure, Ohio, illustrates that significant pre- and post-test improvements in parenting satisfaction, parenting efficacy, or the belief that they will be able to perform parenting tasks, and co-parenting relationships with the other parent, only occur among fathers who participate in at least eight two-hour sessions of this ten-session program, which is the minimum required by the program to graduate and acquire a new identity as a "responsible father." At lower levels of program participation, fathers in the treatment group looked statistically identical to their counterparts who wanted to attend TYRO Dads but were assigned to a nontreatment control group when both groups were surveyed four months after the first data-collection episode and assessed on key parenting outcomes.

Curriculum Matters

Another program feature that is associated with positive outcomes is having workshops with a structured curriculum (see Sarfo & Wallace, Chapter 3). This finding comes from a study that used a randomized experimental design to compare 89 fathers exposed to the *Developing All Dads for Manhood and Parenting (DAD MAP)* curriculum, which is used by the Baltimore Responsible Fatherhood Program (BRFP) at The Center for Urban Families (CFUF), with 75 fathers who participated in an unstructured, peer-led support group. The analysis revealed that while the peer-support component of the program was liked, when used in isolation, it was less apt to create change among low-income populations. Thus, at the three-month follow-up, fathers in the curriculum group scored significantly higher on parental support, nights spent with children in a typical week, and money spent on children in the last 30 days.

Explicit Training on Father Engagement Is Effective

Yet, another program feature associated with a positive outcome, albeit a modest one, is explicit staff training on how to engage fathers and overcome common challenges. In an evaluation of Dads Matter-HV, a father engagement intervention for perinatal home visiting programs (HV), Bellamy and her colleagues used a clustered randomized control trial (RCT) to test some of the differences in teams comprised of HV supervisors, workers, fathers, and mothers, who were exposed to standard service delivery as compared with teams that used standard services plus Dads Matter-HV (see Chapter 5). An analysis of results indicated that most HV visits did not include fathers in both groups, but home visitors who received focused training on father engagement techniques achieved significantly higher rates of father participation in home visiting sessions (33% vs. 20%). Workers trained in Dads Matter-HV used a larger variety of engagement strategies as compared with those who received standard service training only. While father engagement efforts did not jeopardize relationships that workers developed with mothers, the modest improvements in fathers' perceptions of their relationships with workers in the intervention group that were observed at the four-month post-baseline, were not maintained at the one-year follow-up.

Online and Text-Messaging Techniques for Parent Education Have Limited Effectiveness

Online programming formats for parent education were expected to be more accessible to low-income, unmarried parents, but garnered very low rates of usage and received mixed ratings. Although Tomlinson and her colleagues attempted to conduct a quantitative study of unmarried parents scheduled for an initial court hearing for child-related issues who were randomly sent an order by U.S. mail by a family court in Indiana that instructed them to access a court website to complete one of two online parenting programs designed to improve coparenting and child well-being, they needed to switch to a qualitative assessment due to low rates of parent compliance with the order (see Chapter 7). Interviews with 43 unmarried fathers and mothers referred by the court to participate in an online coparenting intervention revealed that while some found that the online format was convenient, most held negative views including not understanding the reasons for the order, not liking being notified by mail, feeling that the program was unnecessary, and/or lacking Internet access. Indeed, some were unaware of the fact that they had been even ordered by the court to do something. The small fraction of parents who participated in the program characterized it favorably, enjoying its interactive and engaging components like videos and quizzes, and cited its benefits in improving communication, parenting ability, and coparenting skills.

In a similar vein, Lewin-Bizan's study of fathers who participated in a program to improve father engagement with children using brief text messages about parenting and child development sent to fathers three times a week over a 12-week period of time, yielded mixed results (see Chapter 6). While quantitative data-collection efforts at baseline and 12-weeks later failed to find post-program changes in self-reported measures of father engagement and parental self-confidence (even among the highest dosage groups that read all of the texts that were sent), qualitative interviews with 17 fathers revealed substantial satisfaction with the text messaging intervention. Consistent with other program studies, however, text messages appear to lack the intensity or duration to produce measurable changes in parenting outcomes. Text messages may serve as a useful supplement to in-person interventions in fatherhood programs, but not a replacement.

Mandates to Include Fathers Can Be Effective When Backed Up With Strong Relationships and Appropriate Supports

Fathers were rapidly included as residents (along with their families) in nine of ten family homeless shelters in Philadelphia, Pennsylvania, following the adoption of a new policy requiring shelters to admit them. The qualitative analysis conducted by Eyrich-Garg and Hudson involved interviews with 13 staff members of the Philadelphia Office of Homeless Services (OHS), which mandated the change, three focus groups with 20 shelter staff, and ten focus groups with 94 mothers and fathers who resided in the ten Philadelphia emergency shelters (see Chapter 12). The study revealed different patterns of compliance. Three shelters that had private rooms for each family were the early adopters that permitted fathers to reside in their shelters prior to the OHS policy. Three other shelters that were classified as late adopters supported father inclusion but struggled with their heavier use of communal space. Laggard shelters struggled with architectural challenges and philosophical disagreement with the policy, with one shelter applying for a waiver/exception. The authors credit the rapid adoption process to the strong relationships between OHS and the shelters that were slower to adopt and the provision of resources to assist with the transition, including funding to hire male shelter staff. Another transition facilitator was peer support and the advice that early adopter shelters provided to late and laggard shelters about how to make father inclusion work. The study highlights the importance of mandates in system change as well as the role of communication, support, and resources.

A Comprehensive Approach to Addressing Domestic Violence Is Recommended

The recommendation to use a supportive but comprehensive approach to address domestic violence in fatherhood programs is the conclusion of an exploratory study by Thomas and Mederos (see Chapter 11). The study involved a review of widely used fatherhood curricula and in-depth interviews with 40 fatherhood leaders, fatherhood program facilitators, and domestic violence advocates. It concludes that educating fathers about domestic violence, processing their own experiences as victims of and/or users of violence, and preventing future domestic violence requires interventions of sufficient intensity and duration. The authors urge programs to commit the resources and staff training needed to accomplish these objectives at a program level, including building authentic collaborations with domestic violence programs.

Engaging Mothers in Coparenting Interventions Is Challenging But Effective in Reducing Disagreements With Fathers and Realizing Other Benefits

The support of the custodial coparent remains the most important factor in fathers' ability to participate in the lives of their children, especially for unmarried fathers who lack the legal rights to custody and/or visitation that are standard components of the divorce decree. Three FRPN studies in this volume deal with attempts to engage the coparent partners of fatherhood program participants in parallel, mother-only interventions on coparenting. One study by Sperber and Whitton of an attempt to initiate coparenting services that were expected to be more appealing to mothers at Talbert House's Fatherhood Project in Cincinnati, Ohio, is extremely cautionary (see Chapter 10). Interviews conducted with 16 mothers and 30 fathers following the abandonment of the coparenting intervention due to mothers' complete disinterest, revealed the usual logistical barriers (e.g., time, transportation, childcare), as well as those that reflected their lived experiences and perceptions. Thus, mothers expressed mistrust of the fatherhood program hosting the intervention, frustration with father behaviors, and safety concerns. In addition to recommending that the fatherhood program be more diligent in its outreach efforts, the authors recommend that programs that have historically served fathers only will need to overcome mother mistrust and a perception of bias.

To contrast, two other research projects described in this book reached different conclusions. Although outreach to mothers and their engagement in a parallel, mother-only coparenting interventions offered in conjunction with six fatherhood programs in six different states was challenging, requiring persistence and effort by female outreach workers, interest was strong, and mother engagement was successful. The study by Fagan and his colleagues found that mothers who participated in *Understanding Dads^{TM}* reported more confidence in their ability to coparent and reduced levels of disagreements with the father (see Chapter 8). Three months later, participating mothers still reported these improvements plus reductions in their perceptions of engaging in behaviors that could be viewed as undermining the father.

A coparenting study conducted by Perry and his colleagues at the *4 Your Child* fatherhood program in Kentucky using a rigorous random assignment design, reached similar conclusions (see Chapter 9). Following brief announcements about a new coparenting intervention for mothers at the fatherhood workshops, 153 of a possible 285 mothers who could be reached by staff (53.6%) agreed to participate and were randomly assigned to a treatment group that received a one-time, mother-only workshop that lasted two hours followed by a focus group. A control group received no services. A comparison of surveys administered at baseline, and three- and six-month post random assignment found that intervention mothers reported greater improvements in their perceptions of conflict resolution, fathers' involvement, and coparenting relationship than control group mothers, with statistically significant improvement in conflict resolution and coparenting relationship quality at the six-month follow-up, and progressively better quality ratings across the three data-collection waves.

Monetizing the Economic Return of Successful Fatherhood Program Participation and Conducting State-Level Mobilization Efforts Facilitated by an Intermediary May Be Effective Ways to Achieve Social Change

Federal support for fatherhood programs since 2005 has not translated into sustainability and long-term support. The last section of the book presents policy-oriented approaches to building capacity and sustainability in the fatherhood field. Chase illustrates how to make a financial case for fatherhood programs by monetizing the economic returns and avoided costs of outcomes associated with participation in fatherhood programs (see Chapter 13). Based on a return on investment study of the Goodwill/Easter Seals of Minnesota's FATHER program, the estimated per-father value of all potential earnings, payments, and savings that would accrue for each successful participant in a fatherhood program is about $177,000. Chase also suggests a novel two-generation approach to assessing benefits by estimating the potential monetary value of fatherhood program outcomes for children due to increased participation of fathers in their children's lives and of improved parenting skills.

The last chapter in the book describes how to build sustainability and long-term support by mobilizing states around fatherhood (see Chapter 14). It describes an initiative conducted by the FRPN to create and catalyze social change at the state level in order to achieve more lasting support and commitment to father inclusion. An analysis of early planning experiences in 11 states that received small planning grants awarded by FRPN, highlights the factors that propel community mobilization. In addition to the effective intermediary activities of FRPN, other factors included piggybacking on existing initiatives, securing influential champions, and collecting compelling evidence of father needs and experiences in a variety of state programs. The barriers planning teams encountered included changes in administration and staff turnover, competing fiscal and policy priorities at the state agency level, the lack of data on father engagement, and the scale of the changes that need to occur. The chapter highlights the important role that a field catalyst such as FRPN can play in galvanizing social change as well as the limits.

Key Learnings

The next section presents key learnings based on the 13 studies included in this volume.

Making a Change in Key Father Outcomes Is Hard and Takes Intense, Sustained Interventions

The importance of intensity and duration of fatherhood services to generate change is underscored in Kim's study as well as other studies of fatherhood programs highlighted in a recent FRPN review (Fagan & Pearson, 2020). Engaging fathers in programming and retaining them in a sustained intervention remains the core challenge for fatherhood programs. A Mathematica report on recruitment and service delivery among 85 Healthy Marriage and Responsible Fatherhood programs in the 2015 cohort confirms that most programs were short-term, with workshops lasting only five to six weeks for a total of 26 hours

(Avellar, Stanczyk et al., 2020). More to the point, client attendance was the most common implementation challenge, and programs struggled to keep fathers engaged. Although none of the chapters in this book explicitly address methods of engaging and retaining fathers in programs, Kim's full FRPN study (Kim & Jang, 2018), suggested that the use of real-world incentives such as hard skills job training with guaranteed work opportunities played an important role in keeping fathers who enrolled in programs engaged. Other promising incentives include reinstatement of drivers' licenses suspended for nonpayment of child support, make-up class opportunities, extensive reminder efforts, and building strong relationships with program facilitators and case managers (Fagan & Pearson, 2020). Recognizing the importance of program dosage, the Office of Family Assistance required that applicants for HMRF grant awards in 2020 commit to delivering a minimum of 24 hours of programming (Administration for Children and Families, 2020a). Given PACT evaluation findings showing that some of the strongest outcomes occurred at the one program site where participants received an average of 88 hours of programming (Avellar et al., 2018), the new ACF requirement may not go far enough to change key outcomes. It is relevant that a new major ACF initiative, Strengthening the Implementation of Responsible Fatherhood Programs (SIRF), will work with programs to overcome common implementation challenges (e.g., participant retention), and test possible real-world solutions (Administration for Children and Families, 2020b).

While Parents Appreciate the Flexibility of Asynchronous Internet and Text-Messaging Interventions, They Present Different Accessibility Challenges and Are Not Associated With Post-Intervention Changes in Parenting

Using the Internet and text messages to deliver parent training interventions can increase access to programs by facilitating delivery in remote geographic areas and eliminating the barriers of transportation and childcare that are endemic to in-person formats. They also allow parents to access content at a time and place of their choosing. Nevertheless, like in-person formats, new media approaches also suffer from low rates of participation and present different types of accessibility challenges. This includes the lack of smartphones, computers, and reliable Internet, and/or the lack of skill with new technology. Finally, at least some parents exposed to new media interventions would like more in-person interaction, peer support, and connection with a facilitator. As a stand-alone intervention, text messaging and asynchronous Internet interventions are not associated with post-program changes in parenting attitudes and behaviors. Some preliminary research suggests that hybrid approaches that blend smartphone-based mobile applications with interactive tools and/or in-person or live online interactions with staff and other participants might be more effective (Patnaik & Avellar, 2020).

Engaging Mothers Is Challenging But It May Be a Key to Realizing Improvements in Father Engagement and Coparenting Outcomes

Since nonresident and unmarried fathers typically lack legal access to their children through court-ordered parenting time plans, mother support is vital to their ability to be involved with their children. Although some evaluations of father-only interventions show improvements in fathers' reports of coparenting relationships, involving mothers is viewed as one way to improve fathers' access to their children and involvement in their lives. While many mothers refuse to engage in mother-only coparenting interventions because of poor parental relationships and/or they distrust the fatherhood program to represent their interests, engaging mothers is not impossible, with two studies showing that approximately half of targeted mothers are interested following persistent, respectful outreach by female facilitators. Once engaged, mothers find the program valuable and report significantly fewer disagreements with the father and increased confidence in their ability to coparent with the fathers. These improvements remain after three and six months, with the addition of other benefits such as decreased maternal undermining of fathers—a finding corroborated in interviews with some fathers. Qualitative interviews with mothers suggest that mother-only coparenting classes using the *Understanding Dads*^{TM} curriculum and a hybrid approach that combined elements of *24/7 Dad* and *Together We Can* curricula, do a good job of fostering empathy among mothers, more realistic expectations of father's behavior, and self-reflection. Although more research is needed to determine the best approach for engaging mothers whose child's father is enrolled in a fatherhood program and replicate outcomes, the studies in this volume lend support for conducting separate coparenting interventions for fathers and their coparenting partners, and the use of curricula that teach both behavioral strategies like communication and conflict resolution as well as skills in support, empathy, and acceptance.

Training Workers in Human Services Agencies and Programs on Father Engagement Strategies and Techniques Improves Father Participation But the High Rate of Worker Turnover in Such Agencies Presents Serious Practical Challenges

Many human services agency workers would like to do a better job of engaging fathers in interventions for children and families but lack the experience and skill. As the study by Bellamy and her colleagues shows, explicit training can help. The training should address the importance of father engagement as well as methods of outreach and engagement, adaptations to existing program curricula needed to address the needs of fathers, and relevant resources and sources of support for fathers. Worker training will be a vital component of expanding father inclusion in state and local programs that service children and families. One important challenge, however, is the high rate of staff turnover in human services agencies. For example, home visiting teams in the Bellamy study experienced worker turnover of 50% or greater during the 30-month study. At a minimum, this necessitates the development of continuous training strategies, and/or the incorporation of father engagement training in all new and continuing worker training initiatives.

Achieving Sustainability and Stability in the Fatherhood Field Will Require Evidence and Mobilization That Go Beyond the Individual Program Level

Despite federal expenditures of approximately $50-$75 million per year for fatherhood programs from 2005 to 2020, the fatherhood field remains fragmented and unstable, with a small number of programs (39 in 19 states during 2015–2020) receiving outsized federal awards as part of the HMRF grant program and the rest struggling to survive. The failure reflects the absence of effective mobilization around fatherhood at the state level, and the lack of credible research in some important areas. While the economic costs of childhood poverty (McLaughlin & Rank, 2018) and father absence have been estimated (Nock & Einolf, 2008), programs and evaluation researchers typically have failed to collect, analyze, and publicize the data that measures the financial benefits of fatherhood programs to families and the larger society. The few states that have invested money in workforce and fatherhood programs for low-income, nonresident fathers (e.g., Colorado, Ohio, Texas, South Carolina) (see Pearson & Fagan, 2019) have used studies of financial benefits (wages, taxes paid on wages, child support payments) and avoided costs (reduced payments of public benefits, incarceration costs), to justify the expenditure. Better information on economic benefits and avoided costs for fathers who participate in programs promise to strengthen support among policy makers and the general public for fatherhood programs. Even more powerful would be research on the benefits of father engagement in programs on child well-being, including documenting the long-term financial benefits and avoided costs for children of program participants as a result of the improved quality of parenting that their fathers acquire.

FRPN's efforts to catalyze father inclusion efforts in 11 states offers some clues on how to mobilize for collective impact and "move the needle" on father inclusion in state-level programs and policies. By convening multiple stakeholders in 11 states and augmenting their efforts with structure, resources, information, and supporting capability, FRPN catalyzed state planning teams to piggyback fatherhood with other relevant initiatives, procure high-level champions, build relationships across multiple agencies, collect data on gaps in fatherhood services, and procure authentic father input. Future efforts to achieve sustainable social change dealing with fatherhood should involve an effective and well-resourced catalyst to build momentum and fill capability gaps over a sustained period of time.

Finally, the FRPN study by Eyrich-Garg and Hudson of a system-wide policy change to include fathers (with their families) as residents in ten family homeless shelters in Philadelphia underscores the role that public agencies at the federal, state and local level can play in making policy change. While the authors note the role of a grass-roots movement of local leaders on fathers experiencing homelessness, the critical catalyst for father inclusion was a grant requirement by the U.S. Department of Housing and Urban Development to demonstrate non-discrimination across several protected classes, including sexual orientation and gender identity. Pursuant to this requirement, the Philadelphia Office of Homeless Services developed and adopted a Nondiscrimination Policy that required each family emergency shelter to admit fathers as residents. Although the shelters reacted differently and could be classified as early adopters, late adopters, and laggards, over a period of approximately 24 months, the number of family shelters admitting fathers moved from three to nine, with only one shelter applying for an exemption/waiver from the father-inclusion policy. Legal mandates are powerful instruments of social change in many arenas and should be pursued where feasible. However, they do not operate effectively in isolation. The authors credit the successful transition for late adopters to the strong relationships that the regulatory agency developed with shelters and the resources they provided to assist with the transition. Another important ingredient was the support that early adopter shelters provided to their peers on how to make things work.

Future Research

How to Teach Effective Parenting Behaviors

One important line of needed investigation and experimentation deals with how to increase the impact of fatherhood programs on the use of effective parenting behaviors by enrolled fathers. A recent brief (Patnaik & Avellar, 2020) identifies several promising approaches. These include a form of cognitive behavioral therapy known as behavioral parent training; video modeling in which trained people demonstrate desired parenting behavior and/or fathers record themselves interacting with their children and an instructor highlights and discusses specific behaviors the father demonstrates in the video; and web-based programs that involve video modeling, social connectivity and networking, and prompts sent by email and phone text messages. The Building Bridges and Bonds (B3) Study is testing a blended approach that combines skill-building videos, father–child play activities, and smartphone reminders and other interactive tools to strengthen father parenting skills (Manno et al., 2019). Still another possible approach is group-based visiting in a setting well stocked with toys and staff members who model positive play behavior and offer helpful suggestions about play activities in a nonthreatening manner (Pearson & Thoennes, 2000). In order to potentially improve child well-being, fatherhood practitioners should explore these and other ways to strengthen fathers' parenting engagement and skill. For their part, researchers should further explore the benefits and limitations of various approaches to parenting engagement as well as the child development outcomes they inspire.

How to Estimate the Monetary Value of Fatherhood Programs

Making the financial case for fatherhood programs will require larger and more rigorous studies of short and longer-term financial gains that participants exhibit as well as public costs that are avoided. Given the links between positive father engagement and children's socio-emotional and cognitive development (Adamson & Johnson, 2013), future studies should also seek to establish the monetary value of benefits that might accrue to children of more engaged and skilled fathers. For both generations, this would include monetizing increased lifetime earnings and the associated taxes paid, reduced rates of benefit program usage, and avoided costs associated reduced delinquency, juvenile detention, and arrest, and more favorable rates of foster care, teen pregnancy, and substance abuse. Ideally, such studies would involve use of a rigorous, experimental design that would permit comparison of financial outcomes and avoided costs in a treatment group with members of a control group. The studies on fathers would need to collect accurate pre- and post-program information on employment, earnings, child support payments, criminal justice activity, and use of various benefit programs. Researchers should undertake studies of the monetary value of fatherhood programs for both fathers and children, as well as conduct cost-benefit studies that compare the value of those benefits to the costs for the programs to produce those benefits.

How to Increase Father Engagement in Child Literacy

Parent participation in formal and informal home literacy activities such as home-book reading (Sénéchal, 2006) is positively correlated with increased reading and math achievement and social-emotional development for children (Baker, 2013; Suizzo et al., 2014). Importantly, fathers play a major role in the literacy development of their children with shared literacy activities also serving to strengthen the bonds between children and their fathers (Jarrett & Coba-Rodriguez, 2017; McWayne et al., 2013). A study sponsored by FRPN, but not featured in this book, examined *Real Dads Read*, a literacy program based in approximately 80 barbershops in African American neighborhoods conducted by Fathers Incorporated in Atlanta, Georgia, to help fathers support their children's academic success by getting them interested in and engaged in reading. Surveys with 81 fathers and interviews with 21 barbers in 35 barbershops revealed that both held positive views about the program but that there was need for more research on fathers' successes and challenges as well as how to promote stronger father engagement and use of effective book-reading strategies (Bingham, 2020). In light of recent research showing significant longitudinal associations between father engagement in early cognitive stimulation activities and children's school readiness, Cabrera and her colleagues (2020) urge childcare centers and other programs to include both mothers and fathers in their early education programs. Fatherhood programs should be involved with those efforts too. Future collaborative projects between researchers and practitioners are needed to develop and evaluate ways for fatherhood programs to help low-income, nonresident fathers become more interested in and adept at engaging in literacy activities with their children.

How to Increase Participation in Fatherhood Programs

Fatherhood programs are most effective when participants have substantial exposure to them (Fagan & Pearson, 2020). Higher program dosage has been shown to track with outcomes in father involvement, parenting, coparenting, employment/economic prospects, and child support payments. The rigorous study that Kim and his colleagues described in their chapter found that participants who failed to attend TYRO Dads at a certain level, looked no different than the nontreatment control group on post-program surveys. Attrition is a significant problem for most fatherhood programs, and many who enroll fail to attend most workshops and/or never "graduate" or achieve a level of participation considered to be vital to proficiency. More research is needed on how to improve participant retention. A recent brief (Avellar, Gordon et al., 2020) identifies the factors that appear to be associated with father engagement. They include relevant workshop content delivered in an interactive setting with dedicated staff with whom participants can identify and relate; flexible and adaptable structures that include opportunities for make-up sessions, home meetings, and the use of other convenient locations; managing expectations about what program participation can and cannot accomplish, including the prospect of rapid employment or changes in relationships with their coparent and children; including children in the program; and linking incentives to tangible employment opportunities, such as forklift certification. Drivers' license reinstatement that is keyed to program attendance is also associated with enhanced participation (Davis et al., 2014).

How to Improve Coparenting Relationships

Developing and maintaining positive coparenting relationships is critical to fathers' ability to access their children. While the study findings noted in the chapters by Perry et al. and Fagan et al. offer encouraging findings with respect to both the willingness of mothers to participate in a mother-only coparenting intervention and its effectiveness in improving reported relationships with the other parent, the research is preliminary. More definitive studies with larger samples and stronger designs are needed to gauge with confidence whether and how mother engagement is best achieved and the length, composition, and components of the most effective interventions to improve coparenting. Both projects utilized a facilitated mother-only workshop ranging from a single two-hour session to six two-hour sessions; neither brought mothers and fathers together singly or in a group. Nor do we know enough about how programs and their workshops can strengthen father outcomes dealing with communication, conflict resolution, relationship expectations, and other underpinnings of effective coparenting. We also need to explore whether and how formal parenting-time plans might be explained and generated to reduce the uncertainty and opportunity for conflict about how the child's time will be divided. Practitioners and evaluators should look to the literature on parent education programs for divorcing couples for some clues on effective curricula, formats, and outcomes; they should explore collaborations with Access and Visitation grant programs to explore methods of incorporating formal parenting time plans in activities pertaining to coparenting. Finally, as the chapter by Thomas and Mederos underscores, fatherhood programs must integrate domestic violence into core workshops and address the issue in a more holistic manner. Future research should assess whether such treatments of the issue succeed in addressing and preventing safety issues from arising in the course of establishing coparenting relationships and exercising access and visitation. Researchers should also examine whether more substantial treatments of domestic violence in programs affect the way in which participants and the mothers of their children handle conflict and disagreements.

How to Improve Fathers' Employability

Holmes et al.'s (2020) meta-analysis (funded by FRPN) found that programs had little to no effect on fathers' employment or child support payments. This finding stands in stark contrast to the outcomes for father involvement with children, parenting attitudes, and coparenting, which although small, were on the average positive and statistically significant. Although several evaluations of NCP employment programs reported more promising impacts (Lippold et al., 2011; Pearson et al., 2011; Schroeder & Doughty, 2009), the weak effects observed in the fatherhood field are consistent with findings observed for employment and training programs serving low-income populations other than fatherhood program participants (Sama-Miller et al., 2016) The very limited evidence available on effective approaches suggests that providing intensive and comprehensive work-related services with sufficient dosage might improve fathers' employment and economic stability (Baumgartner et al., 2020). Thus, at the one PACT site that generated participants with significantly better employment outcomes, most fathers participated in daily classes for six weeks and received an average of 47 hours of content dealing with economic stability issues as compared with 2–12 hours at the other three sites (Avellar et al., 2018). The fatherhood field would benefit from greater collaboration with public workforce programs that provide more intensive employment services for fatherhood program participants that meet eligibility requirements. This would include the dislocated workers programs available through the Workforce Innovation and Opportunity Act and the Supplemental Nutrition Assistance Program's Employment & Training Program. Fatherhood programs should also explore the feasibility of incorporating hard skills training opportunities, subsidized jobs, apprenticeships, and other alternative employment services. While evaluations of traditional employment services typically yield little or no impacts, transitional jobs programs produce more substantial effects (Landers, 2020), as might other alternative approaches that are currently under investigation (Fishman et al., 2020).

How to Use New Media Effectively

Fatherhood program participants and mothers and fathers targeted for parent education sessions value the convenience of text messages, online curricula, and other technology-based delivery modes. At the same time, they miss the human interaction that comes with in-person formats. Peer support and strong relationships with program staff have been the hallmarks and chief attractions of fatherhood programs since their inception in the 1990s, especially among racial minorities (Johnson et al., 1999; Pearson et al., 2003). Practitioners and researchers should continue to explore how to combine the convenience and flexibility of online delivery modes with the critical components of in-person formats: community and support from other participants, identification, and role-modeling with staff. This might take the form of hybrid models that utilize both types of formats and/or the development of more skillful online techniques for practitioners to use to create more opportunities for engagement, interaction, and emotional connection. Exploratory studies (i.e., qualitative research) are needed at this time to ascertain how to combine online and in-person so that maximum impact on fathers and families is achieved.

Conclusion

Created to generate research that addresses the issues that programs face and to communicate research findings to practitioners who are in a position to implement them in real-world settings, FRPN funded 20 evaluations of fatherhood programs that had the active engagement of researchers and practitioners. Practitioners, researchers, and policy makers were also active participants in the 11 fatherhood planning projects that FRPN funded and catalyzed. By building in the requirement to jointly engage practitioners in every funded project from its inception to its conclusion, all studies and action projects were informed by practitioner perspectives. Practitioner support was a prerequisite to project funding; following the funding award, researchers and the fatherhood program practitioner met with the

FRPN directors on a monthly basis to review implementation of the evaluation, data collection, problems, unanticipated developments, and needed changes to the research design and process. Project findings were vetted through a practitioner lens with additional analyses recommended by practitioners. And the required project products included both a final report suitable for a research audience as well as a summary report suitable for a practitioner audience. To further disseminate findings to the practitioner community, FRPN hosted 22 webinars in a six-year period of time that featured researchers and practitioners who discussed the various research studies, key findings, and their implications for future research and practice. As the authors of a recent research brief note (Avellar, Gordon et al., 2020), research and practice relationships do not happen organically, and funders, evaluators, and programs must carefully cultivate such relationships. During 2013–2019, FRPN fostered these relationships. Hopefully, its legacy will continue and serve as a model of future effective ways of furthering practice-informed research and evidence-informed practice.

References

Adamson, K., & Johnson, S. K. (2013). An updated and expanded meta-analysis of nonresident fathering and child well-being. *Journal of Family Psychology, 27*(4), 589–599.

Administration for Children and Families. (2020a). *Fatherhood—family-focused, interconnected, resilient, and essential (Fatherhood FIRE)* (HHS-2020-ACF-OFA-ZJ-1846). https://ami.grantsolutions.gov/files/HHS-2020-ACF-OFA-ZJ-1846_0.pdf.

Administration for Children and Families. (2020b). *Strengthening the implementation of responsible fatherhood programs (SIRF), 2019–2022*. https://www.acf.hhs.gov/opre/research/project/strengthening-the-implementation-of-responsible-fatherhood-programs-sirf.

Avellar, S., Covington, R., Moore, Q., Patnaik, A., & Wu, A. (2018). *Parents and children together: Effects of four responsible fatherhood programs for low-income fathers* (OPRE Report #2018-50). U.S. Department of Health and Human Services, Administration for Children and Families, Office of Planning, Research, and Evaluation. https://www.acf.hhs.gov/sites/default/files/opre/pact_rf_impacts_to_opre_508.pdf.

Avellar, S., Gordon, H., & Wood, R. G. (2020). *Highlights from the FRAMING research responsible fatherhood technical work group* (OPRE Report #2020-86). U.S. Department of Health and Human Services, Administration for Children and Families, Office of Planning, Research, and Evaluation. https://www.acf.hhs.gov/sites/default/files/opre/framing_rf_twg_brief_7220_508.pdf.

Avellar, S., Stanczyk, N. A., Aikens, N., Strange, M., & Roemer, G. (2020). *The 2015 cohort of Healthy Marriage and Responsible Fatherhood grantees: Interim report on grantee programs and clients* (OPRE Report #2020-67). U.S. Department of Health and Human Services, Administration for Children and Families, Office of Planning, Research, and Evaluation. https://www.acf.hhs.gov/sites/default/files/opre/interim_report_on_2015_hmrf_grantees_508.pdf.

Baker, C. E. (2013). Fathers' and mothers' home literacy involvement and children's cognitive and social emotional development: Implications for family literacy programs. *Applied Developmental Science, 17*, 184–197. https://doi.org/10.1080/10888691.2013.836034.

Baumgartner, S., Friend, D., Holcomb, P., Clary, E., Zaveri, H., & Overcash, A. (2020). *Pathways-to-outcomes: How responsible fatherhood program activities may lead to intended outcomes* (OPRE Report #2020-58). U.S. Department of Health and Human Services, Administration for Children and Families, Office of Planning, Research, and Evaluation. https://www.acf.hhs.gov/sites/default/files/opre/pact_responsible_fatherhood_060520.pdf.

Bingham, G. (2020). *Examining the Real Dads Read program: Barbers' and fathers' reflections and experiences*. Fatherhood Research and Practice Network. https://www.frpn.org/asset/frpn-grantee-report-examining-the-real-dads-read-program-barbers%E2%80%99-and-fathers%E2%80%99-reflections-and.

Cabrera, N.J., Moon, Uj, Fagan, J., West, J., & Aldoney, D. (2020). Cognitive stimulation at home and in childcare and children's preacademic skills in two-parent families. *Child Development, 91*(5), 1709–1717. https://doi.org/10.1111/cdev.13380.

Davis, L., Pearson, J., & Thoennes, N. (2014). *Building Assets for Fathers and Families in Tennessee: BAFF final report*. Center for Policy Research. https://centerforpolicyresearch.org/wp-content/uploads/TNBAFFF.pdf.

Fagan, J., & Pearson, J. (2020). Fathers' dosage in community-based programs for low-income fathers. *Family Process, 59*(1), 81–93.

Fishman, M., Bloom, D., & Elkin, S. (2020). *Employment and training programs serving low-income populations: Next steps for research*. (OPRE Report 2020-72). U.S. Department of Health and Human Services, Administration for Children and Families, Office of Planning, Research, and Evaluation. https://www.acf.hhs.gov/opre/resource/employment-and-training-programs-serving-low-income-populations-next-steps-for-research.

Holmes, E. K., Egginton, B. M., Hawkins, A. J., Robbins, N. L., & Shafer, K. (2020). Do responsible fatherhood programs work? A comprehensive meta-analytic study. *Family Relations, 69*(5), 967–982.

Jarrett, R. L., & Coba-Rodriguez, S. (2017). We keep the education goin' at home all the time: Family literacy in low-income African American families of preschoolers. *Journal of Education for Students Placed at Risk (JESPAR), 22*, 57–76.

Johnson, E.S., Levine, A., & Doolittle, F.C. (1999). *Fathers' Fair Share: Helping poor men manage child support and fatherhood*. Russell Sage Foundation.

Kim, Y.-I., & Jang, S. J. (2018). *Final evaluation report: A randomized controlled trial of the effectiveness of a responsible fatherhood program: The case of TYRO Dads*. Fatherhood Research and Practice Network. https://www.frpn.org/asset/frpn-grantee-report-randomized-controlled-trial-the-effectiveness-responsible-fatherhood.

Landers, P. A. (2020). *Child support enforcement-led employment services for noncustodial parents: In brief* (R46365). Congressional Research Service. https://www.everycrsreport.com/files/20200518_R46365_8f93f2572418775d34c8e41df655ca40430c997a.pdf.

Lippold, K., Nichols, A., & Sorensen, E. (2011). *Strengthening families through stronger fathers: Final impact report for the pilot employment programs*. Urban Institute. https://www.urban.org/research/publication/strengthening-families-through-stronger-fathers-final-impact-report-pilot-employment-programs/view/full_report.

Manno, M. S., Mancini, P., & O'Herron, C. (2019). *Implementing an innovative parenting program for fathers: Findings from the B3 study* (OPRE Report 2019-111). U.S. Department of Health and Human Services, Administration for Children and Families, Office of Planning, Research, and Evaluation. https://www.mdrc.org/sites/default/files/innovative_parenting_b3_findings_dec_2019_0.pdf.

McLaughlin, M., & Rank, M. R. (2018). Estimating the economic cost of childhood poverty in the United States. *Social Work Research, 42*(2), 73–83.

McWayne, C., Downer, J. T., Campos, R., & Harris, R. D. (2013). Father involvement during early childhood and its association with children's early *learning: A meta-analysis*. *Early Education and Development*, *24*, 898–922.

Nock, S. L., & Einolf, C. J. (2008). *The one billion dollar man: The annual public costs of father absence*. National Fatherhood Initiative. http://www.fatherhood.org/one-hundred-billion-dollar-man.

Patnaik, A., & Avellar, S. (2020). *Improving children's well-being through responsible fatherhood programs* (OPRE Report 2020-94). U.S. Department of Health and Human Services, Administration for Children and Families, Office of Planning, Research, and Evaluation. https://www.acf.hhs.gov/opre/research/project/strengthening-the-implementation-of-responsible-fatherhood-programs-sirf.

Pearson, J., Davis, L., & Thoennes, N. (2003). *OCSE responsible fatherhood programs: Client characteristics and program outcomes*. Center for Policy Research. https://www.frpn.org/asset/ocse-responsible-fatherhood-programs-client-characteristics-and-program-outcomes.

Pearson, J., Davis, L., & Venohr, J. (2011). *Parents to Work! Program outcomes and economic impact*. Center for Policy Research. https://www.frpn.org/asset/parents-work-program-outcomes-and-economic-impact.

Pearson, J., & Fagan, J. (2019). State efforts to support the engagement of nonresident fathers in the lives of their children. *Families in Society*, *199*(4), 392–408.

Pearson, J., & Thoennes, N. (2000). Supervised visitation: The families and their experiences. *Family and Conciliation Courts Review*, *38*(1), 123–142.

Sama-Miller, E., Maccarone, A., Mastri, A., & Borradaile, K. (2016). *Assessing the evidence base: Strategies that support employment for low-income adults* (OPRE Report #2016-58). U.S. Department of Health and Human Services, Administration for Children and Families, Office of Planning, Research, and Evaluation. https://www.acf.hhs.gov/sites/default/files/opre/eser_ib_summary_110116_508.pdf.

Schroeder, D., & Doughty, N. (2009). *Texas non-custodial parent choice: Program impact analysis*. Ray Marshall Center for the Study of Human Resources. http://raymarshallcenter.org/files/2005/07/NCP_Choices_Final_Sep_03_2009.pdf.

Sénéchal, M. (2006). Testing the home literacy model: Parent involvement in kindergarten is differentially related to grade 4 reading comprehension, fluency, spelling, and reading for pleasure. *Scientific Studies of Reading*, *10*(1), 59–87.

Suizzo, M., Pahlke, E., Yarnell, L., Chen, K. Y., & Romero, S. (2014). Home-based parental involvement in young children's learning across US ethnic groups: Cultural models of academic socialization. *Journal of Family Issues*, *35*, 254–287.

Appendix A

Studies funded by the Fatherhood Research and Practice Network (Reports available at www.frpn.org)

1. Armon R. Perry, The University of Louisville, Kent School of Social Work, and Aaron C. Rollins, Jr., The University of Louisville, Department of Urban and Public Affairs. "Fatherhood and coparenting."
2. Selva Lewin-Bizan, University of Hawaii. "A text-messaging intervention to deliver parenting ideas and support to low-income fathers" and David

"Kawika" Mattos & Edeluisa M. Baguio-Larena, Maui Family Support Services, Inc., Hawaii.
3. Erin K. Holmes, Alan J. Hawkins, and Kevin Shafer, Brigham Young University. "Do responsible fatherhood programs work? A comprehensive meta-analytic study."
4. Qiana R. Cryer-Coupet, North Carolina State University, Department of Social Work. "Understanding the experiences and needs of nonresident fathers in the context of kinship care."
5. Sarah Whitton, Kimberly Sperber, and Harold Howard (Talbert House, Cincinnati, Ohio). "Evaluating mother and nonresidential father engagement in coparenting services in a fatherhood program."
6. Francesca Adler-Baeder and Jessica Jackson (Alabama Department of Child Abuse and Neglect Prevention). "Considering contextual influences on fatherhood program participants' experiences in Alabama."
7. R. Anna Hayward and Romarie McCue (Retreat, Inc., Suffolk County Fatherhood Initiative, Suffolk County, New York). "An RCT to examine the impact of cell phone technology on engagement and retention of fathers in a fatherhood program."
8. Amy Holtzworth-Munroe, Amy G. Applegate, Judge Kimberly S. Dowling, and Judge Marianne Vorhees (Family Court, Delaware County, Indiana). "An RCT of two online parent education programs targeting paternity cases."
9. Lenna Nepomnyaschy, Allison Dwyer Emory, and Alexandra Haralampoudis, Rutgers University, New Jersey. "State policies and employment outcomes among fathers with criminal records."
10. Kristie Thomas and Fernando Mederos, Simmons University, Massachusetts. "Responsible Fatherhood groups and domestic violence education: An exploratory study of current practices, barriers, and opportunities."
11. Shawna Lee and Joyce Lee, University of Michigan. "Testing the feasibility of an interactive mentor-based text messaging program to increase father's engagement in home visitation."
12. Gary E. Bingham, Georgia State University, Urban Child Study Center, Georgia. "Real Dads Read evaluation study."
13. Solveig Spjeldnes and Jennifer Shadik, Ohio University, "Secondary analysis of data collected by the Ohio Commission on Fatherhood."
14. Jennifer Bellamy, University of Denver, Colorado. "Home visiting for fathers."
15. Paul Lanier, University of North Carolina. "Enhancing social support for low-income fathers."
16. Bright Sarfo (MEF Associates and Center for Urban Families, Maryland). "The DAD MAP Evaluation: A randomized controlled trial of a culturally tailored parenting and Responsible Fatherhood Program."

17. Young-Il Kim and Sung Joon Jang, Baylor University, Texas. "A randomized controlled trial of the effectiveness of a responsible fatherhood program: The Case of TYRO Dads."
18. Karin Garg and Karen Hudson, Temple University and Children's Hospital of Philadelphia. "Exploring systems change: Adoption, implementation, and consequences of the inclusion of fathers with their families in homeless shelters."
19. Julia Kobulsky and Rachel Wildfeuer, Temple University. "Child protective services-investigated maltreatment by fathers: Distinguishing characteristics and disparate outcomes."
20. Richard Chase (Wilder Foundation). "Potential monetary value of Responsible Fatherhood Program outcomes for fathers and children."

INDEX

Note: References to figures are in italics and to tables are in bold.

Administration for Children and Families 5, 12, 199
anger management skills, *DAD MAP* curriculum 39–40, 42
assessment tools, Dads Matter-HV interventions *61*, 62
attendance: challenges 223; *DAD MAP* program 35, 41; of parent programs 92; TYRO Dads program 51, 54

Baltimore Responsible Fatherhood Program (BRFP) 29–31, 39, 41
barriers to engagement of father 134–5
barriers to participation: Dads Matter-HV intervention 68; online parenting programs 96–9; of parent programs 92; perinatal home visiting programs 60; TYRO Dads program 54
barriers to state-level programs 208–12
batterer intervention programs 155

caregiving strategies, text-messaging interventions 80–1
Caring for My Family study 106
case manager support 40
cell phones, text-messaging interventions 7, 75–88, 223
Center for Urban Families (CFUF) 29–31, 41–2
child literacy, father engagement in 227–8
child support: *DAD MAP* program 34–5, 37, 39; demographics of noncustodial parents 2–3; effectiveness of fatherhood programs 22–3; monetary value of fatherhood programs 188–9; welfare reform law (1996) 3–4
Child Support Noncustodial Parent Employment Demonstration (CSPED) 2–3
Children in Between (online parenting curriculum) 92
coding of qualitative data: effectiveness of fatherhood programs study 15, 17; online parenting program interviews 95; Talbert House Fatherhood Project interviews 140; *Understanding Dads*™ focus groups and interviews 113
Colorado fatherhood programs project 200–1, 204–6, 208, 210
communication skills, *DAD MAP* curriculum 39–40, 42
community involvement, monetary value of fatherhood programs 189
conclusions: *DAD MAP* curriculum 38–43; Dads Matter-HV interventions 73; domestic violence, addressing 165–6; homeless shelters in Philadelphia 182–3; state-level programs 214; Talbert House Fatherhood Project 146–7; text-messaging interventions 87–8; *Understanding Dads*™ program 117–8
conflict resolution, *4 Your Child* outcomes **128**, 130
Connecticut fatherhood programs project 200–1, 204–6, 208–12
Coparent Court project 120
coparenting 13; *see also* Talbert House Fatherhood Project; *DAD MAP*

outcomes 34, 37; Dads Matter-HV intervention *61*, 62; effectiveness of fatherhood programs 20–1, 106–7; father involvement and 135; father-only interventions 106; *4 Your Child* outcomes **128**; future research 228–9; importance of 106, 119; literature 119–20; mothers, engagement in 107, 119–32, 136–47, 220–1, 224; mothers' reports of 123–4; studies 8; TYRO Dads program 49, 52; *Understanding Dads* effects 112–3 *Coparenting Relationship Scale* 34, 49

court-ordered online parenting programs 91–103

curricula: *Developing All Dads for Manhood and Parenting*; *see* DAD MAP curriculum; domestic violence, addressing in fatherhood groups 150, 154; positive outcomes 218; *Together We Can* 121

DAD MAP curriculum 6, 29–43; application 31; attendance 35, 41; baseline characteristics for participants 34–5, **36**–7; case manager support 40; child support outcomes 34; coparenting cooperation outcomes 34, 37; description 29–30; discussion and conclusion 38–43; employment outcomes 34; fatherhood pledge 32; implications for practice 41–3; incentives for attendance 41; involvement with children 35–7, **36**–7; limitations 40–1; measures 33–8; method 30–4; modules and sessions 31; mother engagement specialists 42–3; outcomes 33–4, 37–43, 218; parental support 35, 37, 39; participants 30–1; perceptions white employers may have about black men (handout) *33*; rationale for study 29; recruiting participants 31; research groups 31–3; results 34–8; support groups 31–3; surveys 31; time spent with children 39

Dads Matter-HV interventions 60–73; assessment tools *61*, 62; barriers to fathers' participation 68; baseline sample of participating families 64, **65**; conclusion 73; content 61–3; coparenting modules *61*, 62; data analysis 66; development of 61; discussion 70–3; engagement modules *61*, 62; father engagement strategies 68–9, **69**, 72, 224–5; father participation in 68; home visitor attitudes about working with fathers **67**, 67–8, 71; interviews 66–7; limitations 72–3; measures 64–6; method of study 63–7; modules flowchart *61*; parent-reported measures 65–6; parent-worker relationships 70–2; pilot test 61; qualitative methods 66–7; quantitative methods 64–6; randomized controlled trial 63; results 67–70; staff turnover 72–3; study flow chart *63*; training 62–3, 218–9

data analysis: Dads Matter-HV study 66; *see also* quantitative analysis; *4 Your Child* 124; homeless shelters in Philadelphia 173; text-messaging intervention focus group content 79

"deep work," addressing domestic violence 158–60

demographics: Dads Matter-HV families and home visitors 64–6, 70; online parenting program study participants 95; text-messaging intervention participants 79; TYRO Dads program participants 49–50; *Understanding Dads*^{TM} participants 110

design of study: Dads Matter-HV intervention 63–4; *4 Your Child* interventions 122; text-messaging intervention evaluations 78–9; TYRO Dads program 47

Developing All Dads for Manhood and Parenting; *see* DAD MAP curriculum

disciplining children 21–2, 80

discussions: addressing domestic violence 164–5; DAD MAP impact study 38–43; Dads Matter-HV intervention 70–3; *4 Your Child* study 129–30; monetary value of fatherhood programs 194–5; state-level programs 212; text-messaging interventions for fathers 85–7; TYRO Dads program 53; *Understanding Dads*^{TM} study 115–7

domestic violence (DV), addressing: balancing empathy and accountability 161; batterer intervention programs 155; cognitive learning 158; collaboration with DV programs 152–4; comprehensive approach 220; conclusion 165–6; curricula 150, 154; discussion 164–5; education 8, 149–66;

Index

emotional learning 158–60; engaging in "deep work" 158–60; facilitator strategies and practices 155–63; facilitator's reflective use of self 163; fatherhood groups and 149–50; focus on children's well-being 156–7; funding 150, 152; future research 229; goals for fatherhood programs 151–5; harness men's desire to be good father 156–7; incorporating DV content into core curricula 154; interviews of stakeholders 151; overview of current study 150; program-wide commitment to DV 152; research results 151–63; safe space for discussion and self-reflection 162; staying true to fatherhood program's purpose 154–5; study method 150–1; study rationale 149–50
dosage: *4 Your Child* interventions **128**–9, 131; improving fathers' employability 229–30; program intensity matters 217–8; text-messaging interventions 78, 85, 87; TYRO Dads program, effects 47, 51, 54; *Understanding Dads*™ intervention 111

economic stability of fathers 4, 22, **36**, 229
economic value of fatherhood programs; *see* monetary value of fatherhood programs
education: basics of child development, text-messaging 79–81; *DAD MAP* baseline characteristics **36**; monetary effects of early childhood education 191–3, 195; monetary value of fatherhood programs 188; online parenting programs 91–103
effectiveness of fatherhood programs study 12; child support assessments 22–3; coding elements 15, 17; coparenting outcome 20–1; elements of 6–7; employment and economic well-being outcomes 22; father involvement 12–3, 19–20; fathers' perceptions of 19–24; implications for practice 23–5; intense, sustained interventions 222–3; meta-analysis 13–5, 23–4; meta-synthesis study 15, 23–5; method 15–7; mothers, engagement of 224; outcomes 16–7, 19–25, 217; parenting outcome 21–2; positive effects 17–8; qualitative findings 18–22; recruiting and retaining participants 18; results 17–23; study characteristics 16; TYRO Dads program 45–55; variety of program options 23–4
emotional learning, addressing domestic violence 158–60
employment: *DAD MAP* outcomes 34; improving fathers' employability 229–30; outcomes, effectiveness of programs 22; women in the workforce 2
engagement of father: barriers to 134–5; in child literacy 227–8; *DAD MAP* curriculum 33–5, **37**, 38, **38**, 39; Dads Matter-HV intervention *61*, 62, 68–9, **69**, 72; *4 Your Child* outcomes 126–7, **128**–9, 130; parenting programs and 12–3; staff training 218–9; text-messaging interventions 81–3, 85–6; trends 2; TYRO Dads program 46, 48, 54–55

facilitator strategies and practices in addressing domestic violence 155–63
family life in the U.S 1–3
Father Engagement Scale 33–4
father involvement; *see* engagement of father
fatherhood pledge, *DAD MAP* curriculum *32*
Fatherhood Research and Practice Network (FRPN): awards 5–6; *Father Engagement Scale* 48; as field catalyst 213–4; meta-analysis of programs 14; *Parenting self-efficacy scale* 48; state planning grants 200–1; studies funded 233–5
father's satisfaction with parenting 46, 48
focus groups: homeless shelters in Philadelphia 171–2, 181; state-level programs, fatherhood data 206; text-messaging intervention evaluations 78–9; *Understanding Dads*™ study 113
4 Your Child interventions 7, 120–30, 221; control and intervention group mothers' reports of outcomes *126*; data analysis 124; description of 120–1; discussion 129–30; dosage 131; effectiveness of coparenting intervention 126–7; interviews with mothers 127; measures 123–4; mothers' reports of coparenting relationship 123–4; mothers' willingness and unwillingness to coparent 125–6; outcomes *126*, 126–7; parenting plan/mediation services 127–9; participation of never-married mothers 129–30;

procedures 122–3; qualitative analysis **128**–9; qualitative data 124; recommendations 130–1; recruiting mothers 124–6; recruitment, exclusion, and enrollment flow chart *123*; study limitations 130; study methods 122–4; study participants 122; workshops 120–1
FRPN; *see* Fatherhood Research and Practice Network
funding: ACF responsible fatherhood initiative 12; domestic violence, addressing 150, 152; FRPN funding 5–6, 200–1, 230–1; HMRE and HMRF grants 4, 199, 216, 222–3, 225; homeless shelters in Philadelphia 170, 173, 226; state-level programs 199–200, 210, 225
future research 226–230

Goodwill-Easter Seals FATHER program 185, 187, 222
grants; *see* funding

Hawaii, text-messaging interventions for fathers 75–88
Healthy Marriage and Relationship Education (HMRE) grants 4
Healthy Marriage and Responsible Fatherhood (HMRF) grants 4, 199, 216, 222–3, 225
home visiting programs 59–73; *see also* Dads Matter-HV interventions; perinatal home visiting programs
homeless shelters in Philadelphia 169–83, 219–20; benefits of change 176; commitment to system change 178; conclusions 182–3; context for study 170–1; data analysis 173; discussion 179–80; early adopter, late adopter and laggard shelters 172–3; family homelessness 169–70; family-oriented approach 180–1; father inclusion in 169–70; focus groups 171–2, 181; funding 170, 173, 226; future research 182–3; impacts on families 177–8; motivation for system change 173–4; nondiscrimination policy 170–1; objections to change 175–6, 179; perceptions of OHS staff 173–5, 177–8; preparation for system change 174–5; qualitative data 173; recommendations 180–2; research measures 172–3; research questions 171; results 173–8; short-term system change 175–6; staff advocacy and training 181–2; study 8; study methods 171–3; study recruitment and procedure 171; trauma-informed care 182; unintended consequences 176–7
hypotheses of TYRO Dads study 46–7, 50–53

implications for practice: *DAD MAP* impact study 41–3; effectiveness of fatherhood programs study 23–5; monetary value of fatherhood programs 194–5; Talbert House Fatherhood Project 144–6; TYRO Dads program 54–5
incarceration, reduction of recidivism 189
incentives for attendance 41, 223, 228
incentives for participation in studies 117
Internet parenting programs; *see* online parenting programs
interpersonal skills, *DAD MAP* curriculum 39–40, 42–3
interviews: Dads Matter-HV study 66–7; domestic violence, addressing in fatherhood groups 151; *4 Your Child* study 127; online parenting programs 94–5; Talbert House Fatherhood Project participants 138–40; *Understanding Dads*^{TM} study participants 113–4
involvement of fathers; *see* engagement of father

joint custody of children 2

Kentucky fatherhood programs project 200–1, 207–9, 211
Key to Kane, text-messaging interventions 75–88

limitations of studies: *DAD MAP* curriculum 40–1; Dads Matter-HV study 72–3; *4 Your Child* study 130; monetary value of fatherhood programs 186–7; state-level programs 214
low-income, nonresident fathers 2–4, 13–15

marriage rates in the U.S 1
Maternal, Infant, and Early Childhood Home Visiting Program (MIECHV) 59

maturity of participants 51
Maui Family Support Services, Inc. (MFSS) 77, 84
measures: *DAD MAP* impact study 33–8; Dads Matter-HV study 64–6; *4 Your Child* study 123–4; homeless shelter research 172–3; TYRO Dads program 48–9; Understanding Dads™ study 110–1
mediation services: *4 Your Child* parenting plans 127–9
meta-analysis of programs 13–5, 23–4
meta-synthesis study 15, 23–5
methods: *DAD MAP* impact study 30–4; domestic violence, addressing in fatherhood groups 150–1; effectiveness of fatherhood programs study 15–7; *4 Your Child* study 122–4; homeless shelter study 171–3; online parenting programs study 92–5; Understanding Dads™ study 108–9
Michigan fatherhood programs project 200–1, 205–6, 208, 210
Minnesota: fatherhood programs project 200–1, 206, 208, 211; monetary value of fatherhood programs data 187
moderation tests 111
Mom as Gateway 137
monetary value of fatherhood programs 8–9, 184–96, 221–2; child support payment increases 188–9; community involvement and leadership of fathers 189; discussion 194–5; educational attainment 188; effects of early childhood education 191–3, 195; fathering and parenting programs 193–4; framework for estimating 185; future research 227; impact parameters 186; implications for policies and programs 194–5; implications for researchers 195; introduction 184–5; lifetime earning increases 187–8; Minnesota data 187; model 185; monetary value outcomes for children 191–4, **192**; outcomes of fatherhood programs 186; per-child monetary values **192**; per-father estimate 187–94, **191**; recidivism reduced 189; sources of data 186; study limitations 186–7; taxpayer benefits 189–90; two-generation value of fatherhood programs and early childhood education 195; wage increases 188
mother engagement and coparenting 7–8, 106–7, 220–1, 224; *see also* Talbert House Fatherhood Project; Dads Matter-HV intervention 70; fatherhood program, recruitment into 136–47; paternal interventions, engagement in 119–32; services at Talbert House 137–44; specialists 42–3; Understanding Dads™ study 115–7
mothers-only program 106–116

NCCARE360 204
nonresident parents 1–2, 13–5; public policy 3–4; TYRO Dads intervention effects 46–7, 53, 55
North Carolina fatherhood programs project 200–1, 204, 206, 209, 212

Office of Homeless Services (OHS) (Philadelphia) 169–76, 178–9, 181–3, 220
On My Shoulders 137
online parenting programs 7, 91–103, 223; barriers to accessing court website 94–6; barriers to program participation 96–7; coding of interviews 95; convenience/inconvenience of programs 100–1; *4 Your Child* interventions **129**, 131; future research 230; hybrid approaches 223; introduction 91–2; limited effectiveness 219; participant eligibility criteria 93; positive and negative perceptions of program 97–9; qualitative interviews 94–5; recruitment 93–4; social support 99–100; study method 92–5; study participants 93–5; subsample sizes 94; technology associated with programs 100–2
OPRE catalog 5
outcomes: *DAD MAP* curriculum 30, 33–4, 37–43, 218; economic measures of 8–9; effectiveness of fatherhood programs study 16–7, 21–2, 24–5, 217; *4 Your Child* program *126*, 127; intense, sustained interventions 222–3; monetary value of 184–94; mothers, engagement of 224; text-messaging interventions 78, 85–8; TYRO Dads program *52*, 53; Understanding Dads™ coparenting study 116–117

parenting plans: *4 Your Child* mediation services 127–9

Parenting self-efficacy scale: TYRO Dads program 48
Parenting Together intervention 120
Parents and Children Together (PACT) study 5, 13, 106
participants: DAD MAP impact study 30–1; *4 Your Child* study 122, 129–30; online parenting programs study 93–5; recruiting; *see* recruiting participants; Talbert House Fatherhood Project coparenting services 138–44; text-messaging intervention evaluations 78–9; TYRO Dads program 47, 49–50; Understanding Dads^{TM} study 110, 113
participation of fathers: Dads Matter-HV intervention 68; future research 228; TYRO Dads program 47, 54
Pennsylvania fatherhood programs project 200–1, 205, 208–9, 212
perceptions of programs; *see* qualitative analysis
perinatal home visiting programs 59–60; *see also* Dads Matter-HV intervention; barriers to engagement of fathers 60; Dads Matter-HV intervention 60–73
Philadelphia, Pennsylvania homeless shelters 169–83
Philadelphia Office of Homeless Services (OHS) 169–76, 178–9, 181–3, 220
Potential monetary value of Responsible Fatherhood Program outcomes for fathers and children (2019) 184–5
press coverage of state-level programs 208
public policy: low-income, nonresident fathers and 3–4
public workforce programs 230

qualitative analysis: coding; *see* coding of qualitative data; Dads Matter-HV study 66–7; effectiveness of fatherhood programs study 18–22; *4 Your Child* study 124, **128**–9; homeless shelters in Philadelphia 173; online parenting program interviews 94–5; text-messaging interventions 78–87; Understanding Dads^{TM} study 108, 113–5
quantitative analysis: Dads Matter-HV study 64–6; text-messaging interventions 78; Understanding Dads study 108, 110–3
quotes from participants; *see generally* qualitative analysis

racial considerations: *DAD MAP* baseline characteristics **36**; domestic violence in context of structural oppression 149; homeless shelter focus group facilitators 171; homeless shelters in Philadelphia 173, 179; single-parent households 134
randomized controlled trials (RCTs): Dads Matter-HV study 63–4; online parenting programs 92–4
Real Dads Read program 227–8
recidivism reduction, monetary value of fatherhood programs 189
recommendations: *4 Your Child* interventions 130–1; homeless shelters in Philadelphia 180–2; online parenting programs 102–3; Talbert House Fatherhood Project coparenting services 143–4
recruitment: *DAD MAP* impact study 31; effectiveness of fatherhood programs study 18; *4 Your Child* study **123**, 124–6; online parenting programs study 93; Talbert House Fatherhood Project, recruitment of mothers 137; text-messaging interventions 77; Understanding Dads^{TM}, recruitment of mothers 108–9
Relational Health Index—Mentor Scale (RHI) 65, 70
responsible fatherhood (RF) 4
Responsible Fatherhood Network (RFN) 5
responsible fatherhood program (RFP) 4, 12
results: Dads Matter-HV study 67–70; of effectiveness of fatherhood programs study 17–23; homeless shelters study 173–8; online parenting program study 95; research on addressing domestic violence in fatherhood groups 151–63; text-messaging intervention evaluations 79–85
retaining participants 18
return on investment (ROI) studies 187, 206–7; Goodwill-Easter Seals FATHER program 185, 187, 222
The RIDGE Project 45–6, 54, 106, 217–8
Rhode Island fatherhood programs project 200–1, 204, 206–7, 211
roles of fathers: text-messaging interventions 83, 85–6; TYRO Dads objective 46, 49, *52*

shared custody of children 2
single-parent households 3, 134
social support, online or in-person 99–100
South Carolina fatherhood programs project 200–1, 205–9, 212
staff support and encouragement of participants 18
staff turnover 224–5; Dads Matter-HV intervention 72
state-level programs 9, 199–214, 222, 225; activities pursued by FRPN planning grant teams **201**; advocacy and policy initiatives 201–3; barriers 202–3, 208–12; bi-monthly check-in calls 207–8; bureaucratic challenges 209–10; catalytic initiative 207–8; challenges **202**; competing priorities 208–9; conclusion 214; data on fatherhood 206–7, 211; discussion 212–4; enablers/facilitators 202–8, 212–3; engaging fathers in planning process 209; fiscal challenges 210; FRPN as field catalyst 213–4; FRPN planning grants 200–1; funding 199–200; introduction 199–200; involving fathers in planning process 207; limitations 214; literature review 201–3; methods 203; nine-month planning processes 201; piggybacking on existing initiatives 204; political challenges 209–10; press coverage 208; procuring champions 205; relationships with other agencies 205–6; scheduling challenges 208–9; societal view of fathers and fatherhood 211–2; statewide fatherhood commissions 199; statewide team activities 200
status of research on fatherhood programs 6
studies *see* particular study, program
support groups: *DAD MAP* curriculum 31–3; Talbert House Fatherhood Project, for mothers 137
surveys: *DAD MAP* impact study 31; TYCO Dads program 51, *52*; *Understanding Dads*™ study 110
sustainability of policies and programs 8–9, 225–226

Talbert House Fatherhood Project 135; anger at father 143; barriers to participation in coparenting services 138–43, 146; coding of interviews 140; conclusions 146–7; coparenting services offered to mothers and fathers 136–7; engagement of fathers in coparenting services 138; evolution of coparenting services 136–7; frustration with father behaviors 142–3; interviews with participants 138–40; lessons learned 144–5; mistrust of fatherhood program 141–2, 144–5; mother engagement in coparenting services 137–44, 220–1; overview 136; perceived value of coparenting services 140; practical implications 144–6; recommendations 143–4; recruitment of mothers 137–8; support group for mothers 137
TANF funding 4; state-level programs 199–200, 206–720, 210
taxpayer benefits 189–90
technology associated with online parenting programs 100–2
text-messaging interventions 75–88, 223; basics of child development 79–81; caregiving strategies 80–1; conclusion 87–8; content and target audience 86; convenience of 83–4; delivery mode 86–7; discussion 85–7; dosage 85, 87; engaging with one's child 81–3, 85–6; future research 230; gaining confidence in fathering role 83, 85–6; hybrid approaches 223; the intervention 77; introduction 75; lack of human interaction 84–5; limited effectiveness 219; messages 77; outcomes 85–8; overview 76–7; parenting interventions 75–6; procedure and analysis of focus groups 79; qualitative evaluations 78–87; quantitative evaluation 78; recruitment 77; results 79–85; standalone vs enhancement to in-person interventions 86–7; study design and participants 78–9
Together We Can curriculum 121
training: Dads Matter-HV intervention 62–3; Dads Matter-HV workers 71; engagement of father, staff training 218–9, 224–5; future research 226–7; homeless shelter staff in Philadelphia 174–5, 181–2; improving fathers' employability 230; Talbert House Fatherhood Project staff 145; trauma-informed care 182
trauma-informed care 182
24/7 Dad A.M. 121

Two Families Now (online parenting program) 92
two-generation value of fatherhood programs and early childhood education 195
TYRO Dads program 6–7, 45–55, 106; analysis plan 49; attendance 54; attrition 47–8; barriers to participation 54; characteristics of participants 49–50; comparison of control and intervention group participants **50**; description of study 46–9; discussion 53; dosage effects 47, 54, 217–8; effectiveness 50–3; hypotheses 46–7, 50–3; implications for practice 54–5; measures 48–9; outcomes 53; rationale for study 45; research design 47; results 49–53; study participation 47; survey results 51, *52*; TYRO declaration 55

Understanding Dads™ 8, 119–20; conclusions 117–8; discussion 115–7; dosage 111; effects of intervention 112–3; eligibility of participants 108; focus groups 113; interviews 113–4; moderation tests 111; participant characteristics 110; preliminary analyses 111–2; purpose of 107; qualitative research component 108, 113–5; quantitative research component 108, 110–3; recruitment of mothers 108–9, 221; results 111–3; sessions 107–8; study 107; study measures 110–1; study method 108–9; surveys 110
unmarried parents 1, 3, 91–2
U.S. public policy 3–4

victims of crime funds: monetary value of fatherhood programs 189
visitation rights, unmarried, nonresident fathers 3
volunteerism and monetary value of fatherhood programs 189

wage increases, monetary value of fatherhood programs 187–8
Washington fatherhood programs project 200–1, 204–10, 212
welfare reform law (1996) 3–4
Wilder Research of Goodwill-Easter Seals FATHER 185, 187, 222
Within My Reach 137
worker relationships with parents 70–2
worker turnover 72, 224–5
Wyoming fatherhood programs project 200–1, 205–9